Triangular Pegs

By
Heyward R. Inabinett

Triangular Pegs

By
Heyward R. Inabinett

Copyright 1986
Revised 2005
Fiction: Based on true events

Heyward R. Inabinett
670 Seaside Road
St. Helena Island, SC 29920

HYPERLINK "mailto:habeshirl@comcast.net" habeshirl@comcast.net

(843) 838-2427

Copyright © 2007 Heyward R. Inabinett

All rights reserved.

ISBN: 1-4196-8350-0

ISBN-13: 9781419683503

Library of Congress Control Number: 2007909401

Visit www.booksurge.com to order additional copies.

This is a work of fiction. Names, characters, places and incidents either are the product of the author's imagination or are used fictitiously, and any resemblance to any actual persons, living or dead, events or locales is entirely coincidental.

About the Author

Heyward Reginald Inabinett is one of eight children born to John and Spencer Inabinett in 1938 in rural Colleton County, South Carolina. He grew up on the family farm until the death of his father in 1948.

In 1950, he moved with his family to a Gullah speaking community on St. Helena Island, South Carolina. Being black, and having a white complexion created problems of rejection for him from classmates and the Gullah community in general.

Inabinett spent six years in the army, three years as a white person and three as a black man. While in the army, he attended high school in Tacoma, Washington; attended diesel engine school in Germany, where under German instructors, he obtained marketable knowledge in diesel technology. Inabinett obtained additional educational background in diesel mechanical technology and metal fabrication fields. In 1968, he founded Heyward's Marine Diesel Service, which he owned and operated until his retirement in 2002.

Heyward has been married to Shirley Brown Inabinett for 49 years. They live on St Helena Island. They are the parents of four children and six grandchildren. He attends Deep Creek Baptist church in Islandton, South Carolina.

Inabinett's hobbies has included traveling, reading, building wrought iron pieces, flying his Cessna 172, growing scuppernong grapes and spending time with his grandchildren.

Acknowledgements

My wife Shirley: for her support and tolerance over the past twenty years, while I toyed with the idea of writing the book.

My children, Sharon, Gail, Beth and Heyward R. II "Reggie" for their encouragement and financial support in getting it published.

Darlene Dopson: Darlene convinced me that computers could become a productive tool if I "kept my grimy little paws off it" after she had straightened it out for the umpteenth time; also for her many hours of teaching me how to use and keep it running smooth.

My sister Mary Mack and Dr. Rachel Elahee for their editing.

Etta Mann, my eight-grade literature teacher and Vermell Mathews for their support in making it possible.

Lamar Inabinett: My cousin, buddy, friend and pal for his continuous effort in finding publishers and agents.

Newell and Andre Philbrick of Forsyth, Montana for the serenity of their ranch, where I often went to relax.

This book is dedicated to Shirley:
My shelter in times of storm

Table of Contents

Chapter 1	Rice Patch	1
Chapter 2	Janie And Jake	7
Chapter 3	Alfred Dubois	23
Chapter 4	Early Farming Year	27
Chapter 5	Incompatible	39
Chapter 6	Parallels	51
Chapter 7	The Move To Seaside	55
Chapter 8	Religion, or Segregation	61
Chapter 9	You Are In The Wrong School	75
Chapter 10	The Second Seat	83
Chapter 11	My Introduction To Passing	95
Chapter 12	My "White" Army Years	107
Chapter 13	The Summer Of 1956	125
Chapter 14	Seattle, Oh What A Town	141
Chapter 15	The Dreaded Return To The South	157
Chapter 16	Back To Square One	181
Chapter 17	My "Black" Army Time	189
Chapter 18	Germany	217
Chapter 19	Sister Maria And The Orphanage	239
Chapter 20	My Migration North	251
Chapter 21	Learning To Survive In The South	271
Chapter 22	Flying with Lester	315
Chapter 23	The Cadet Program	325
Chapter 24	Please Be Careful Doctor	345
Chapter 25	Renewal Of A Lasting Friendship	349

Chapter I

RICE PATCH

In the years leading up to and following the Civil War, a community in South Carolina known as "Rice Patch," had become a haven, a sanctuary, even a dumping ground for the children of slave masters, their families and their slaves. They were often well taken care of by their former white owners and parents. Many were given enough money and property to get started in life as farmers or tradesmen. The whites took every precaution they could and created laws to make sure these offspring that looked white would never pass into white society. One of our older statesmen once said, "It would breed mongrels;" and that has remained the mindset of many people. The people of Rice Patch would become a very independent group; they intermarried within the same "color line" to maintain the traits that their former owners and parents insisted they do if they were to continue to be recognized as "family." Though most had been rejected and sent away, they still considered themselves blood members of the white families that they were born into, as indeed they were. They usually kept the race a secret as well as their white counterparts did. For years it was all but impossible to get the older generation to openly talk about their family background.

As I grew older, I realized there were many reasons governing this rationale. Much of the secrecy was maintained out of fear of white reprisal. It would also be admitting that their ancestors committed adultery. To admit that someone in your family had committed the grave sin of adultery, in the strict religious community that I grew up in, would have been unthinkable. As the years went by and the white ancestors considered themselves forgiven for their, "sins of adultery," they never openly admitted that they were related to, or that they ever had a sexual relationship with a Black person. After slavery when the races became more divided because of segregation laws and customs, the Negro and White societies grew farther and farther apart. After a couple of generations had passed, you don't have to have much of an imagination to realize what would happen if a black child met the white cousin on the street in rural South Carolina, and told him he was his cousin. A lot of the secrecy on the part of Black parents was to keep their children within the law and hopefully out of harms way.

Most of the people of mixed race that came to Rice Patch were allowed to attend the white controlled Salkehatchie Church. They were required to sit in the rear and were never accepted as anything other than Negro. A few of the families, who were very white in color, simply lived as white people. Some were found out in later years and had to revert to being Negro. My paternal grandfather, William Kaiser, was a good example of this. William Kaiser and his brother Alex came to Rice Patch with their white father when they were in their early teens. Their mother was never discussed and as the boys grew older, they assumed that she had died. When they started going to the Salkehatchie Church they sat on the front seat with their father. They both had blue eyes and light brown straight hair; even they didn't know that they had Negro blood. Their father died when William was sixteen and Alex was fourteen. After the death of their father, their mother came to Rice Patch to find them. She had very light skin but was a Negro. William and Alex didn't have any problem accepting their mother but the people of the church made them move to the rear seats at the next Sunday service. Their mother remained in the house with them and they became another Mulatto family at Rice Patch. When the whites moved the Kaiser brothers to the rear of the church, they were brought to the rude awakening that because of their Negro ancestry, they were considered far from equal. The Negroes became tired of the practice of being in the rear of the church, and not being allowed to take part in the services, were prompted to build their own church. The move to the rear of the church created distrust within the Kaiser Brothers for the white society that would remain with them for the rest of their lives, and they would pass this distrust down to their children.

The whites and Negroes at Rice Patch for the most part got along quite well as compared to other parts of the state. They had a lot in common, they were all farmers, most of them attended the same church for a period of time and a lot of them were related. Even today in 2008, a lot of us still bury our families in the original cemetery, however, as we were required to sit in the rear seats of the church, we also buried our dead in the rear section of the cemetery. After slavery, a fence was erected to separate the two cemeteries. Our families had been buried there for generations, so we still use it as our family cemetery, even though for the most part, blacks and whites have different cemeteries in South Carolina. Segregation laws made it illegal for blacks and whites to bury in the same cemetery. I found this to be very evident when I was doing research. Whenever I asked directions to a certain cemetery the person practically always asked me if I was looking for a "colored or a white" cemetery, or they said, "It can't be down this road, there are only colored cemeteries down there."

In the Negro, or black society, for a long time it was the practice for Negroes of light skin to marry only other Negroes of light skin. Often it was a lot easier to get accepted as officers or homecoming queen at one of the traditionally black colleges if you had the "proper" skin color. The practice created a prejudicial system within black society that was as great or worse than the system that existed between the Negro and White races. Not only were Negroes divided by racial laws and prejudice from the whites, we also in a lot of instances, separated ourselves according to color within the Negro race.

The white relatives of the Negro contributed to the practice of color separation within the Negro race. Even though white parents sent their mixed Negro children away and sold them for a profit, they still didn't want them to become black in color; they wanted them to marry a mixed race spouse to maintain the color. They very often chose the spouse their offspring would marry, usually their only requirement was for the intended spouse to have the proper color.

According to oral history and family photographs, the practice of marrying to maintain color separation was practiced in my family. My DNA is certified as 49% European, 34% African and 17% Native American. My paternal and maternal families appeared to be white but were considered to be Negro or mulatto. No mixing with the "white race" has taken place in my family since slavery. I include my certified DNA in case someone challenges my having the required amount of Negro Blood to be considered "legally" Negro. In the past, according to South Carolina law, if a person had "one-eighth" or more African or Negro blood he or she would be classified as Negro. I include the European and Native American ancestry to show, in my opinion, how ridiculous the "one eight", or in other states, "one drop" rule was.

Some Negroes transitioned into the white society in one or two generations. Often when a member was born light enough to pass, they were sent away, or moved voluntarily and lived as members of the White race. A lot of it was out of necessity, as the birth certificate read Negro but his color said that he was white. In most cases you had to give up family members, which frequently brought on a lot of depression. I can recall at least four cousins that couldn't tolerate the pressure. They left the area never to be seen again, which left their family, including spouses and children, to suffer from depression.

It has been said Negroes of light skin had an advantage over the Negroes of darker skin when dealing with whites. This was never an advantage for the black man; in fact it only made matters worse because it drove a wedge, and created resentment between the darker person and me. A person who had a lighter skin color seemed less threatening to whites because he/she was seen as having, "white blood" and would be less threatening and easier to communicate with.

In my business, I repaired large off shore fishings vessels, and my clientele consisted of about a fifty-fifty black-white ratio of owner/captains. In most cases when I was in a group of black owners, and a white person approached and needed to know the tide schedule or when the next catch would be in, etc, they usually walked past every black person to ask me for the information. I didn't own a boat or had a tide chart. The only answer that I could give was to point to the black captains. The white person often became red-faced, intimidated or embarrassed when he realized the tradition that he was still influenced by and blamed me for "putting him on the spot." At the same time, if the black person didn't know me and I answered the question, they became upset with me. To a lot of people, black or white, it is mind boggling as to why the reaction from different races would be so different. From the white prospective, historically the white man had always been in charge and from learned behavior still practiced the tradition. He would therefore approach the person most like him. The black person who remembers how it used to be, preferred that I force the white person to communicate with, and recognize him as the owner, which I usually did, and the cycle continued.

Chapter 2

JANIE AND JAKE

It was near midnight, a very cold December night in 1850, with temperatures in the low twenties when Robert Montgomery and his sixteen year old son Jake, hitched the team of horses back to the wagon. They had taken them out to get on the ferry to cross the Savannah River for the thirty-mile trip home before morning. For most of the day, Robert drank coffee and haggled with old Mr. Drake over the price that he would have to pay for Nellie, the slave girl. She was asleep under the blankets and quilts in the bed of the wagon as it bounced along the bumpy road that led away from the river. She cost him a lot but he needed the new house servant to replace Nancy, who was now approaching seventy-five years of age. The pains in her legs and back were making it almost impossible to even get out of bed in the morning, let alone be of any help around the kitchen. Nancy had raised Robert and his sisters and brothers. She had seven children of her own and all had been sold away from the plantation. Robert would allow her to live out the rest of her life on the plantation without having to do anything. The ties that she had to the plantation and to the Montgomery family were far too great to have her work until she died. He would have Nancy train the new house servant to make the meals just the way he had been used to for the last fifty years.

The team kept up the steady pace for about two hours before they began to tire and slow down. The full moon had made it possible to keep them going at a full trot. Only the occasional live oak trees with Spanish moss hanging from their branches and cast long shadows over the road hampered the team. The team seemed eager to get home. Sixteen-year old Jake Montgomery, in spite of all of the clothes he was wearing, was chilled to the bone. It never seemed to bother Robert; he had grown accustomed to the chilling cold over the years.

He finally looked over at Jake and asked, "Are you cold?" He didn't have to wait for an answer because the young man was about to fall off the wagon from the chill that had overtaken him.

Robert asked him, "Do you want me to stop and build a fire?"

To prove to his father that he was about to become a man, he said, "I'll be all right," but Robert saw that he would have to do something about his young son or he would surely catch pneumonia.

It was two-thirty in the morning and they were still twenty miles away from the plantation. Jake had pneumonia last winter and the thought of him going through it again made Robert shudder. He yelled for the team to stop. "You better wrap in the blanket and lay close to Nellie and she will keep you warm." The boy hesitated but as the cold had gone completely through his body, it didn't take long for him to make his mind up. He wrapped in the two blankets that were left and Nellie was wrapped in three and had two on top of her. Jake eased the top blankets back and eased himself under the cover while trying not to touch the slave girl who had awakened from the commotion of stopping the wagon. To Jake, this young woman of eighteen smelled a lot different than Nancy. When Jake was a small boy, Nancy would cuddle him if he was upset or to keep him warm. Nellie had been given the sweetest soap to use and the pleasant smell was still there. Even with the blankets and being under the cover with Nellie, it took almost an hour for the young boy to stop shivering.

When Robert stopped the team at the entrance of the plantation, Jake and Nellie sat up to see how far they had traveled. They were surprised to find they had slept through the rest of the trip in spite of the constant bumping of the wagon through the holes and tree roots in the road. Jake could see Nellie for the first time now that it was daylight. He couldn't believe his eyes when he saw the beauty of the slave girl. Jake had been at his grandmother's house for most of the day while his father had gone to buy the girl. When Robert picked him up, it was already dark and Nellie was under the covers trying to stay warm and hold back the tears from having to leave her family. She always knew that she would be sold some day because she had watched as her older sister and brother were sold to different owners, never to see them again. Nellie tried to prepare for the day that she would be sold away from the farm and the family that she had known all of her life, but leaving was still very hard for her.

Nellie had a very smooth light tan complexion and black hair that hung down below her shoulders. She also had huge brown eyes and perfect teeth. She was a descendant of the Yemassee Indians that lived in the Savannah River area a century earlier. Nellie's Mother and father were a mixture of Negro and Indian.

When Nellie removed the covers from her face that morning in 1850, she managed to hold back the tears as she looked around and saw the huge house where she would be a slave. She also began to wonder what she would be required to do? Would she be raped, whipped, or put into a shed as breeding stock? Her new master had paid a lot of money for her, but why? Master Drake had tried to sell Robert two other girls but he insisted on buying Nellie as his personal house slave.

When the wagon came to a stop in front of the big house, Nancy came out to see the girl who would be her new helper and started training her right away.

"You better get yo'sef out of dat wagon, we got breakfast to fix."

Nellie took it in stride because she knew her duty for she had helped her mother prepare breakfast for the Drake family since she was a little girl. She looked forward to the day when she would have a family of her own to prepare breakfast for.

Nancy told her, "I don't care how long you been cooking, round here you have to learn to do it the Massa Montgomery's way. Massa Robert doesn't like lumpy grits and if you want you behind whipped, just drag around and not have it done when he comes home for dinner. If you break the yallah in the eggs just throw them out to the dog and cook mo 'cause Massa Robert won't eat dem if the yallah broke. When you go to get the chamber pot from under the bed, you better not wake Missie, if you do she will make a field hand out of you like she did them other yallah gals that Massa Robert had the first time. You mighty red, are you one of dem Yemassee's from that Savannah River bunch of funny looking people?"

Nellie didn't answer her and that proved to be the wrong thing to do.

"Lissen, you tink you better than the rest of us cause you come from that funny looking bunch from that Savannah River, but round here we all niggas so you just forget that Indians stuff. You sleep in Liza's bed; she won't be needin it anymo, she a field hand now. Her backside got too big for her britches and Missie Dell make her chop cotton, she now sleep in the shed with the rest of dem field gals."

In the months that followed, Nellie became a good house servant and proved to be worth the price that Robert paid for her. Even Nancy had reduced her criticism of her to an occasional scowl in the morning, just to let her know that she was still in charge of the Montgomery house; and the friction between the two women ceased. Adel Montgomery, Robert's wife, was enough of a problem for both of the house servants. They could focus their hatred toward her and not at each other. Adel did not like Nellie from the first day that Robert brought her to the plantation. She always held the threat over Nellie's head of making a field hand out of her. Her main reason for disliking her was that Jake spent a lot of time in the kitchen with her while she cleaned up after supper. She often told Robert that he would have to sell her or she would put her in the shed with the rest of the field hands.

Robert always told her, "I won't sell her. I paid five hundred dollars for her to replace Nancy and I also paid three hundred each for Liza and Pinkie and you didn't want to keep them either. Nellie is young and a very good servant and will be able to work for the next forty years without any problems if we keep her in the house. If you send her into the fields she will be worn out in twenty years."

Robert and Adel constantly argued about selling Nellie or at least sending her into the fields to chop or pick cotton. Robert always kept the upper hand when the argument came up. When he left the house and Nellie was alone with Adel she never let up and one day she sent Nellie out to pick cotton.

"You are going to have to learn to pick cotton with the rest of them niggas so you better start learning now."

Nellie went to the field and was glad for the time away from the house. Adel Montgomery went on a drinking spree as soon as Robert left the house. After the fourth day in the field, Nellie had gotten use to the routine and was eating dinner with Liza and Pinkie when Paul, the yard slave, came yelling that

"Missie Dell said that Nellie haves to come to the house right now."

When Nellie came to the house she found Nancy lying in a heap on the floor with blood coming from a laceration caused by the bone coming through her thigh. Adel was drunk and crying while she yelled and cursed Robert for not being there when she needed him. Paul hitched the team to the wagon and went into town to get the doctor. Nellie and the two other girls, who had also come in from the field, took Nancy and put her on the bed and waited for the doctor to come.

When Robert and Jake came home that night they found Nancy in bed with the lower half of her body in a cast. Pain showed on the old face that they both had known for so long, and they had to pause before asking Nellie what happened.

"She fell down the stairs and broke her leg," Nellie told them.

"Why didn't you go up the stairs for her!"

"I was out in the field picking cotton, Missie put me there when you left on Monday."

Robert went up to his wife's room and found her passed out from the bottle of bourbon she started drinking that morning.

Jake was very sad that night; Nancy had reared him from a baby, and she was often the only mother that he had. Jake sat at her bedside until after midnight. When Jake and Nellie left her they went to the kitchen and Nellie made a snack for the two of them. They sat and giggled like two little kids while they kept looking around to make sure there wasn't anyone watching. When Nellie went to bed that night, Jake went with her.

In the month following Nancy's accident, Nellie became the only servant in the Montgomery house. Her chores now included taking care of Nancy because Adel would never allow any of the other women back into the house. As the weeks passed, Nellie began to get sick in the morning when it was time to prepare breakfast. Once when she was in the room with Nancy, she grabbed the chamber pot and spewed vomit into it. The old woman knew right away what was wrong with her.

"What wrong wid you gal? You act like you pregnet."

Until that moment it had never occurred to Nellie that her sickness and dizzy spells were from the fact that she was probably pregnant and the baby's father would be Jake. The thought of it sent absolute fear through her, and Nancy saw the expression on her face.

"Is it for Massa Jake or one of the field hands when you were out their picking cotton?"

Nancy knew the answer to that before Nellie said, "Massa Jake." In the past month she heard the young boy slip into Nellie's room on more than one night.

"Gal you have gone and done it now, Missie Dell will sell you off this place as soon as she find out you been sleepin with Massa Jake. You better tell her it be for that yallah slave out in the field. With your color and Massa Jake's white skin the child will sho nuf be yallah. You better sneak out like you messin with that yallah field hand named Joseph. You better not make them tink that you try to run away. Massa Robert don't whip his slaves, but he sho will sell you to someone who will, and he don't care how much he pay for you either."

Nellie sat with Nancy for another ten minutes until she was totally overcome by fear.

She told Nancy, "I don't want to mess with that field hand Joseph."

"You don't have to, but you better make Missie think you do, just go out to the shed and sit with Liza for a few nights and I'll tell Missie that you done find a man and got yourself knocked up when she sent you in the field to pick cotton. It would make no never mind to Massa Robert but Missie would get you from here in a hurry, she don't like yallah slaves anyhow."

For the next few nights, Nellie put on a clean, starched and ironed dress and went out to the shed that Liza lived in. They sat and talked about how Missie used to get drunk and curse them out and how they would find her bottle and have a little drink for them-selves.

"Gal I use to have a good swig from that bottle and poe water in the place of the whiskey that I drink. When Missie got drunk she never know that it was mostly water that she was drinkin." Liza said, "I even brown sugar in the fry pan to make the water the color of the whiskey and she still don't know that we been in it. Massa Robert never touches the bottle because he is a Christian man and won't let anything like whiskey touch his mouth. That is why he don't whip us slaves and is always good to us."

"But he did whip that field hand Sam that killed the hog when it didn't go back in the fence," Nellie reminded her. "It ain't been much, he only lick him two chops."

When she talked about Sam she said, "Sam your man ain't he?" The smile widened as she rubbed her stomach and Nellie could see the little bulge that was beginning to grow in her stomach. Nellie rubbed her own stomach and smiled at Liza.

"You ain't never been wid any of the bucks here, how come you pregnet?" Liza's mouth flew open as to gasp for air as she thought of the answer to her question. "Massa Robert or Massa Jake?"

Nellie smiled and said, "Massa Jake." Nellie told Liza about the plan that she and Nancy had to make the Missie think that the baby was Joseph's.

"Gal you crazy, better not let Pinkie hear you say that you been to bed wid Joseph, it be better if Missie get your backside."

As the months passed, Nellie's stomach began to get bigger and Adel noticed but didn't say anything.

Nancy was able to get around the house on crutches and when she saw Adel looking at Nellie's stomach, she said, "You know, Nellie done got herself knocked up by that big yellah field hand Joseph."

Adel made no comment about Nellie's pregnancy, she just hoped that it would be a boy so the plantation would have a new field hand or they could sell it for a profit if they had a bad year with the cotton.

When a baby girl was born in the spring of 1852, she looked totally white and had a little crop of white hair on her head, but most of all, she had green eyes, a trait of the Montgomery family for generations. When Adel Montgomery saw the child for the first time she knew that it was either her husband Robert's or her son Jake's. The baby was a spitting image of the other Montgomery children who had been born since she married Robert thirty-seven years ago.

She told Nancy, "If anyone know a Montgomery child I do, and that there is one!"

Neither Robert nor Jake was home the morning the baby was born. They had gone to Augusta for supplies. When they got home, Adel had already passed out from having too much bourbon. When Adel awoke the next morning she started to raise hell again, only this time Robert was there to hear it.

"I told you to get rid of that wench the very first day that you brought her here, and now you have fathered a child of hers. If you don't get rid of her, I am going home to Atlanta."

Robert knew that Jake must be the father because he had often heard Jake slip into Nellie's room when Adel had gone to sleep or had passed out from too much whiskey. He had no choice but to tell his wife that the baby had to belong to Jake. Adel never slowed the cursing, only now she directed it all at Jake who had gone out into the field as soon as he saw the baby.

In the coming months, baby Janie began to crawl around the big house. Adel had stopped some of the yelling at her son and Jake began to take the child in his arms and play with her when he came out of the field.

After two years passed Adel never accepted the baby as anything except a little slave girl and kept Robert awake many nights trying to force him to sell Nellie and the baby. One night when Robert could take no more of Adel, he told her, "I couldn't sell her now even if I wanted to. She is the mother of my own flesh and blood and I could never bring myself to sell my own granddaughter into slavery."

"Your grand daughter!" yelled Adel. "Why that little wench could never be called my grandchild, and I am going to put Nellie in the field tomorrow and bring Liza back into the house!" She kept up the noise for another two hours.

Robert was up at four o'clock the next morning, and when daylight came, he saddled a horse and headed east. It was after midnight when he came back to the plantation, he unsaddled the horse and went inside where Nellie was warming his supper. Robert went over to his desk in the corner of the room, took out paper and pen and began to write. When he finished, he went to the table to eat, but first he called Nellie over and said to her, "I am going to take you away from the plantation on Wednesday. I have found a good home for you, and you can take Janie with you."

Nellie didn't want to be sold again but she was grateful to her master for selling her and the baby to the same owner. She said "Yassa Massa" and went back to the room where the baby had started to cry. When she got inside, she also started crying. Robert finished eating and went upstairs to tell Adel the news that she had been waiting two years to hear, he had sold Nellie.

When Robert woke Nellie the next morning it was still warm for November so she didn't have to build a fire. She dressed herself and wrapped the baby in a blanket. She took the few belongings she had and got into the wagon that Robert brought around. He shook the reins and the team headed east when it was still two hours before daylight.

They had traveled for four hours before Nellie dried her eyes and came from under the blankets to see where she was going. The sun had come up and was warming the blanket that she and the baby were under. She had tried to sleep but the bumping of the wagon and the thought of her being sold again kept her awake. Her mind began to wonder if she and her baby would be able to remain together, or would Janie be given to someone to keep while she worked in the fields. She began to blame herself for sleeping with Jake, was it all her fault? After all she was only a slave and for her to refuse his advances could have meant trouble for her, or would it have? She began to get angry with Jake. After all, he was the girls' father, or did he even care that it was his child? Nellie wondered about what kind of master she would have this time. Masters Drake and Robert had never whipped her but she felt that this time she would get a mean master and she started crying again.

Before going to bed the night before, Nellie packed a pan of biscuits, ham and sausage for their lunch. They crossed the Salkehatchie swamp around noon and Robert stopped the team to build a fire for warming the food. The team drank from the stream and grazed while Robert and Nellie made the fire. Robert was talking to her as he had never done before, not as a slave, but the way he talked to Jake or one of his daughters. When the food was warm, Nellie put it on the tailgate of the wagon. Robert said a grace and they began to eat. Robert took the papers from his coat pocket that he had been carrying around for the past two days and gave them to Nellie.

"These are your freedom papers," he told Nellie.

She took them and began to cry again. She had accepted slavery as a way of life and had never thought about what she would do if she were ever set free. As the tears ran down her face she asked, "But Massa Robert, where will I go? I have no place for me and Janie to stay."

Robert told her, "When I went away on Monday, I went to see Quarry, a man who was set free last year and is a furniture maker. Quarry lives near Rice Patch and he needs a woman to help him. His slave master father taught him well and gave him enough money and property to get him started and he has done well. He is a kind man and will make a good father for Janie."

After they finished eating, Nellie put the food that was left back into the wagon as Robert sat very still on the back of the wagon and stared into the distance.

"Some day all slaves will be free because in the eyes of the Lord it is the right thing to do but the time is not right. Freedom must be a gradual thing if it is to survive."

Nellie felt that she could talk freely with him now. "What about Pinkie and Joseph, they are both very hard workers and could make it on their own if you gave them a little piece of land to get them started, they could still work for you and pay for the land."

Robert snapped back, "That is the reason I didn't give you your freedom papers while we were still at the plantation! If we gave one slave freedom, all would want it and we wouldn't have anyone to work the fields!"

Nellie saw freedom differently than her master; she took the paper in her hand and wrinkled it as she gripped it harder and harder. Nellie knew that she would make it on her own and welcomed the thought of freedom. While she was at the stream washing the frying pan and coffee pot, Janie woke up and started crying. Nellie ran back to find Janie in the arms of Robert.

It was dark when they reached Quarry's house and they were both very tired. Quarry had added a new room to his neat little house for the coming of his new family. Nellie took her bag from the wagon and went inside and felt the warmness as she entered what was to be her room. Quarry had made a fire in the fireplace and he and Robert were sitting in front of it as they talked about furniture that Quarry was to make for the Montgomery family.

Nellie was tired from the ten-hour trip to Rice Patch and when she got Janie to sleep, she fell asleep across the bed.

The smell of cured ham and sausage woke her the next morning. She quickly got dressed and went into the kitchen because she considered breakfast her job and wanted to start by giving Quarry a good impression. When she got into the kitchen, she found that Robert had stayed for the night and she felt even more ashamed for not getting up and preparing breakfast for the two men.

As Robert had told Nellie, Quarry was a very kind man and she was eager to learn his furniture business. They became a perfect team. Quarry and Nellie were married December 23, 1861. They would have nine children in an assortment of colors from the English, Indian and Negro bloodlines of both Nellie and Quarry.

When Robert left the plantation that morning to take Nellie to Rice Patch, he didn't tell Jake where he was going or that Nellie had been sold. When Jake woke that morning his first thoughts were to go to the kitchen to see Janie. When he found Liza cooking breakfast and didn't see Nellie or the baby, he knew that his mother had finally won the argument of sending Nellie out to the shed as a field hand. Nancy was limping around on her crutches giving orders to Liza on how to prepare breakfast.

When Jake asked Nancy, "When did Missie send Nellie and Janie out to the shed?" Nancy held her head down and stared at the kitchen floor.

She finally said, "Massa Robert done sold dem. He went to take dem dis mornin." "Where?" asked Jake?

"I don't know, all I know is that Nellie was making bread for them to take on the trip. She didn't know either, all Massa tell her is that she been sold."

Nancy had seen a lot of slaves sold off the plantation, even her own children but this was different. He had sold his own granddaughter. Jake could not believe it either. His father had taught him to be a Christian. Even though Jake had a problem reconciling slavery and Christianity, he accepted it as a way of life but never would he be able to accept the selling of his own daughter.

When Adel Montgomery woke up that morning, she could hear her son yelling at Nancy and Liza.

"You know where he took them! He probably told you not to tell me, but if you don't tell me I'll send you both out to the cotton fields!"

Adel was pleased that he was angry and was yelling at the slaves. She had tried for years to get him to be hard and whip them but he never had the stomach for it. Adel also felt that she was getting even with her son for sleeping with Nellie. She finally came down stairs to join the conversation, and Jake was still trying to get an answer from the two women. Adel smiled at the thought of Jake finally being angry with the slaves, but what she was most pleased about was that he was also angry with his father. Adel considered this to be a good time to win him over. She had tried for years to get him to take her side in the family argument on whipping the slaves, but he had always taken sides with his father. When Adel came into the kitchen, she pretended that she hadn't heard the conversation between the two women. She was in a very good mood that morning.

She smiled at Jake and said, "Good morning Jake, your father finally sold that wench Nellie." Jake looked over to the corner where she sat enjoying her moment of glory and told her, "He also sold your granddaughter along with her!"

At that, Adel no longer cared for the affection of her son, "I told you that little brass ankle half-breed could never be my granddaughter! Just because you stooped low enough to go to bed with a slave wench, she is supposed to be my granddaughter!"

Jake could stand no more of the argument and ran out the door to the barn. He went up into the hayloft where he stayed for most of the morning and decided he would leave the Montgomery plantation.

On his last trip to Augusta with his father he had seen a lot of recruiting posters for the Confederacy. As he sat there in the hayloft, angry with his parents, he decided that he would go to Augusta and join up. After all, it was the proper thing to do, almost all of the other young men his age had already gone. Jake came down from the loft, saddled a horse and rode off to Augusta. He joined the Confederate Army in December of 1861 and served until he took a Yankee bullet through his chest in the spring of 1863. He woke to find himself in a church that had been converted into a hospital at Vicksburg, Mississippi. The female volunteers of the church nursed him back to life, but he was gravely ill for three months. Robert made several trips to Vicksburg to see his son and the conversation got around to Nellie and Janie. Robert told him that he had given them their freedom the same day they had left the plantation and that Nellie had married a free man who was a very good father to Janie. Robert took his son back to the Montgomery plantation where Nancy, now seventy-five years old, finished the job that the nurses at Vicksburg started.

While Jake was convalescing in Vicksburg, he had a lot of time to think. He promised the women of the church that he would serve the Lord for the rest of his life. He completely recovered from his chest wound and when the war was over, he went to the Baptist Seminary in Atlanta and became a minister. He later went to Law school and became a judge but he continued to preach the Gospel until his death in 1925.

Quarry Wilson was an excellent father, and as Janie grew older, he never tried to hide the fact that Jake Montgomery was her father. "Parson Jake," as the Wilson children knew him, came by often when he was in the Rice Patch area to preach at one of the churches. He always brought gifts for all of the children.

Quarry taught all of his children to read and write. He also taught them the furniture business. He taught the girls how to weave and the boys how to select the proper tree and carve it into legs and arms for furniture.

Janie graduated from the Rice Patch School in 1870. On the weekend before her graduation, "Parson Jake" came by and gave her a new dress as a graduation present. In the fall, Janie went to Orangeburg, where she enrolled in another school and became a teacher. Jake Montgomery paid for all of her education and was very supportive of her throughout his life.

Chapter 3

ALFRED DUBOIS

Alfred Dubois as a child would have been considered an absolute loser. He was born in 1854 along the lower Salkehatchie River and spent most of his early childhood there. He was described as a man of small stature who always wore bib overalls that were handmade but never completed. If one suspender held his pants up, he saw absolutely no reason to fasten the other one. He was a man of little conversation and always chose words that would end a conversation as quickly as possible. He was the only child of Pierre Dubois, a French Huguenot in the logging business who had settled along the swamp. His mother, Diana Arnaud, was said to be Negro and French. Alfred had curly black hair that was seldom cut and most of the time hung down over his face. He had very light skin that always seemed to be covered with the soot from the burned trees and mud from the swamp. The Dubois family built a bridge across the swamp by cutting a cypress tree that fell across the creek. For a long time, that bridge was Alfred's only gate to civilization. The bridge and the swamp in that area were referred to as the Dubois Bridge and the Dubois Ditch. His mother kept after him to go to school but he hid in the swamp for most of the day. Going to school was just too complicated for him. If the water in the swamp was too high to get across the bridge, he had to use the boat, which was usually full of water. On the days that he did make it to the other side and to school, he didn't fit into any group. He soon gave up the idea of going to school altogether.

When Alfred was fifteen he started going downstream on the log pile that his father floated to the rail trestle. He always longed to take the train to wherever it took the logs. One day when his father thought that he had already gone back upstream, Alfred got on the train with the logs and rode to Savannah. His parents thought that he had gotten lost or even drowned, and they spent most of the night looking for him. When the train came from Savannah the next day, Alfred was on it. His father tore his behind up with a rawhide whip but it never stopped him from taking the train to Savannah. That first trip introduced him to the freedom of travel. He rode the train whenever he could steal a ride, and the crew soon allowed him to ride on the steam engine with them as it huffed its way to Savannah. The logs were taken off the train at Savannah. Some went to the sawmill there while others were put on barges and shipped elsewhere. On one of his trips to Savannah, Alfred hired on with one of the barge crews going to Florida. He worked on barges until he decided he had enough. He got off in South Florida and lived there for a number of years. The last three years were spent with an Indian tribe, where he was comfortable and seemed to fit. Alfred logged with the tribe for the three years and decided to give it up in the summer of 1879.

When Alfred returned to Salkehatchie in 1879, it was to find that his mother had died a year earlier. His father was sick and no longer able to work in the logging business as he had done for most of his life. Alfred ran the logging operation until his father's death later that year. He sold all of the logging equipment and property. With the money he made from the sale, he moved to Rice Patch and away from the swamp that he had grown to hate.

When Alfred met Janie Montgomery, she was a teacher at the little Salkehatchie School. They started seeing each other and Janie soon had him going with her to the Salkehatchie Baptist church. The white people of the area had organized the church. A lot of Negroes, including Quarry Wilson and his family, went to the church. They all had to sit in the back and were never allowed to take part in the services. William Kaiser, my maternal grand father was a member, but he was allowed to sit among the white congregation for a while. He had light brown hair and piercing blue eyes. The Negroes soon grew tired of sitting on the back seats and not being allowed to worship, as they wanted to. In the spring of 1880, Quarry, Alfred, William and most of the Negroes withdrew from the white church.

They had very little money that they could put toward building a church. During the first year they bought land and built an arbor of vines and limbs to have services under when it wasn't raining. The arbor only provided shade from the sun. With Quarry's knowledge of carpentry and Alfred's knowledge of timber and lumber, they set out to build a church. Alfred cut the trees and brought them out of the swamp. He, Quarry, and the men of the church cut all of the sills and heavy beams with hand tools.

Alfred Dubois and Janie Montgomery were married in the new church in the fall of 1880. From the marriage of Alfred and Janie, ten children were born. My father, Joshua, was the seventh. Alfred purchased a hundred acres of land near Rice Patch and became a farmer. Janie continued to teach school for a few years. She later had to give it up to help with the farm. Teaching school and rearing ten children was more than she could handle.

Chapter 4

EARLY FARMING YEAR

Historians will tell you that the great depression ended in the 1930's or with the election of FDR as president. Ask anyone who grew up in the rural farm community of Rice Patch in Francis County, South Carolina and they will, without exceptions, tell you that it only ended in the late 1940's or later. I was born in Rice Patch in August 1938 and grew up on a two-horse farm. We grew everything that we ate and enough to trade for plows, harnesses and other necessities to maintain a bare existence and to bring up eight children.

My father was also born at Rice Patch. He left in 1915 to find work in New Jersey, and lived for the next fifteen years as a white person. In 1930 the family's land was divided and he was given a deed to his share. He saved his money and returned to Rice Patch to start his own farm. He bought a team of mules, and with the help of his brothers, got the land ready for planting in the spring of 1931. With the spring planting finished, the one thing left in my father's goal of becoming a rural South Carolina farmer, was to get married. At thirty-five, he had never married and in December of 1931 he married Mary Kaiser, the daughter of William Kaiser.

When my parents met, daddy was thirty-five and mother was seventeen, and the youngest of nine children. The only thing they had in common was their skin color. They had everything going against them from the very beginning. Daddy was eighteen years older than mother, had lived most of his life as a white person, was settled in life, and was a workaholic. Mother, at seventeen, having lived in the south all of her life, had no good thoughts of the white man or anything connected with him. She was also a Kaiser and had all of the traits that went with disliking white people. She was very conscious of her light complexion to the degree that she was ashamed of it. Mother always preferred to be with darker people. She had always been given her way and was unbelievably spoiled, a trait that remained with her until her death in 1995. I am still amazed that as incompatible as she and my father were, they managed to bring up eight children and each year produce a crop of tobacco, corn, cotton and enough food for the family to eat for the coming year.

I remember the farm as it was in the 1940's. It was all hand made. The corn, cotton, tobacco and smoke houses were all made from logs that were cut with a crosscut saw. The corners of the buildings had been formed with an ax; on the roofs were the very popular cypress shingles that were on most of the buildings in the rural part of the county. Even the fence that ran around the outer perimeter of the yard was made from hand split cypress, and all the pickets were the same thickness.

One of the very first chores that we were taught to do was to split shingles. Daddy always kept cypress blocks in the yard and the tools were always at hand. When we children were old enough to swing the hammer against the froe, we started making shingles. In the winter we had time to make more than we needed so we were only allowed to keep the perfect ones. We took a lot of pride in making them the same thickness and never had to be told to put any imperfect ones on the woodpile. As we grew older, we were allowed to go into the swamp with daddy to select a proper tree that would be easy to split. We cut it into blocks that we loaded on the wagon. We rode on top of the pile of blocks as the mules strained to bring the wagon out of the water and mud of the swamp. When the mules wanted to stop pulling, daddy cracked the rawhide whip above their behinds. He seldom had to actually strike them with the whip as over the years they had learned what it felt like and just the noise that it made was enough to persuade them to keep pulling. When we got home, we unloaded the blocks and waited in anticipation until they dried enough to start splitting and to see how well daddy had done in his tree selection. We often got one that was too twisted to make anything except firewood.

We got our water from a hand dug well. The "sweep," which was a long pole used to get water out of the well, was hand hewn, and the years of constant use made it as slick as glass. It seemed that we spent half of our lives at the well getting water for the animals, for cooking, bathing, washing clothes, and what seemed a million other reasons. Every drop of water we used was drawn from the well. It was often used as a refrigerator into which we lowered milk and other spoilable food so the cool water could keep it from spoiling as long as possible.

Each year our life continued with the same pattern. We used the turn plow to break the soil that seemed to get harder and harder with each passing year. We planted corn and spent most of the spring hoeing, and supposedly keeping the birds out by a method that I still question, which involved ringing cowbells that were supposed to frighten the birds away. I knew better than to ask my father to explain to me why the birds followed us as we walked through the freshly plowed fields and rang the bells. We were up before the first sign of daylight, or literally, before the birds. All of the neighbor children were still snuggled in their beds, thinking that we were foolish for doing such a thing. However, I also remember them having to replant a lot more than we did.

My siblings and I got more whippings for not ringing those bells than for anything else as we were growing up. The bells were the perfect tool for daddy to keep us working without being in the same field with us; they were like an automatic alarm. After being drug out of bed at five in the morning to walk through freshly plowed fields, we became tired and sat down and went to sleep. Of course if the bells stopped ringing, Daddy would be there in a flash to wake us up. We soon learned to take turns ringing the bells while the others slept. Just the thought of daddy coming out to settle an argument about whose morning it was to keep watch and warn the others when daddy was coming, made things go quite well among us. It was a relief in the fall when we put the bells back on the cows and we became the hunters to locate the cows and bring them in for the night.

When we finally got the corn planted and enough of a stand, that is enough plants had grown to a certain height that would justify leaving it and not plowing it up, we planted cotton. The birds didn't like baby cotton, so we never had to ring the cowbells over it. The cotton had ways of getting equal attention as the corn. As soon as the plants got above ground, we had to thin it, or as anyone who grew up on a cotton farm, knows the correct term was to "chop" the cotton. I remember it being a lot more than just a thinning process. We also had to replant where it had drowned from lack of drainage. Often it seemed the proper thing would have been to plow it up and start over again. We had to dig it out with a hoe, and by "chopping" time, the grass had grown a lot faster than the cotton. We hoped that the rain wouldn't come until we had an opportunity to dig drains for the water to run off, or until the plants had grown tall enough to survive. We had to constantly hoe the cotton until its roots were well established and Daddy could plow the alleys and add dirt to the plants. While plowing, some plants got covered.

Covering the cotton was no problem for daddy as we were all taken into the field to follow behind him and uncover plants that had dirt thrown on them. Sometimes a whole row would get covered. Daddy never stopped and we got behind and stayed behind for the rest of the day. Once we got the bright idea that if we skipped a row we could get through a lot earlier. He let us get home and ready for supper, then he told us about the row that we failed to uncover. He sent us back to the field with the kerosene lantern and our lips stuck out. We soon learned to get it right the first time. We also knew if daddy were to punish us the second time for the same thing it could be detrimental to our behinds. Daddy was a firm believer in the saying, "spare the rod and spoil the child." He never injured anyone but he kept us in line and made sure that we obeyed. I credit my siblings and my strong work ethic to our parents.

Once the corn got up and began to grow, very little was done to it, but the cotton always required attention. We had to constantly poison it to keep the weevils from destroying it. Chopping, hoeing, replanting and poisoning were all hectic jobs that had to be done in the cotton field, but nothing compared to picking it. I have done a lot of different things in my lifetime; some things that I'm proud of, some that I'm not proud of, and some that I would love to do over again. There were things that I wouldn't want to do over again, but if it came right down to making ends meet, I would. There is no reason on this earth why I would ever pick cotton again, not even if daddy returned from the grave with the rawhide whip. The rawhide whip used to frighten me more than anything that I later experienced in life.

I have never been a coal miner and I have a great fear of being trapped underground, but I would gladly give it a try if I had to choose between that and picking cotton. I have the greatest respect for coal miners, but I have a greater respect for the person who invented the automatic cotton picker. Once someone was doing a study of how the black man became unemployed in the south with the invention of the cotton picker. I say hallelujah; give that inventor the Nobel Prize. I can't remember any summer until I was twelve years old that I didn't have to pick cotton. Later in life I often looked back on cotton picking and thought about people having to do it all their lives from birth until death. I often think about my ancestors doing it as slaves. If some of my ideas sound exaggerated, then you have a very minute understanding of how I hated to pick cotton.

The temperature seemed to always approach one hundred degrees during cotton-picking season. The grass was always wet from dew the night before. Most people waited until the dew dried before they started, but Daddy had us pick it wet, spread it out and let it dry. I always seemed to have sores on my legs from the mosquito bites that I had scratched all night. They were raw and bleeding when I went into the field. There the gnats seemed to take pleasure in seeing the bleeding sores that they used as breakfast while the mosquitoes started a new crop.

I knew people who liked to pick cotton when I was a young boy growing up. My brother Mark actually loved to pick cotton and was very competitive. Of course this created a problem for me. I had to compete with him or become the victim of my father's frustrations at suppertime. This never really fazed me because I had no intention of competing with a younger brother for my father's attention by picking more cotton than he did. I always figured there just had to be a better way to make a living. I developed a mental block and a natural hate for the cotton field at a very young age and it has never left me to this day.

In 1978 my family and I were traveling through California's San Joaquin Valley. I had driven for miles through cultivated fields of green vegetation and kept wandering what it was. I stopped at a rest stop and walked to the outer perimeter of the area. As I neared the field, the smell of cotton entered my nostrils, and yuck, it brought back a lot of bad memories. If I had to say anything good about the cotton season, it would be to express my feelings when I saw Daddy take the turn plow to the field and turn it all underground at the end of the season. I also remember the trips to the gin on top of the wagon, piled so high with cotton that we all thought the two mules would never be able to move it. I also fondly remember the end of season graham cracker and pepsi cola treats at the gin.

As much as I hated to work in the cotton field, I realized that it was very necessary for our financial survival. Without it we wouldn't have clothes, shoes, school supplies or even food, and if we hadn't done it for ourselves we would have had to do it for someone else as sharecroppers. Daddy always said he didn't ever want to have to sharecrop, and this drove him as hard as he drove us to remain out of debt, and independent.

We started planting tobacco in 1943, which gave us some relief financially, but again, doubled our workload. The second year that we planted tobacco, daddy decided the hassle of having to wait for an available barn was more than he wanted to deal with. He told us, "If we are going to plant tobacco, we have to cure our own or get out of the business of planting it altogether."

Being tobacco farmers required a barn so we built one. Daddy, his brother and my two older brothers were in the swamps for most of the winter cutting trees. They cut the logs and had the mule team drag them out where they removed the bark. The logs were left to dry for a couple of month before they started putting the barn together. They were cut into the proper length for each side with the saw, and the corners were fitted with an ax. I still remember the sound of the ax as Daddy and the neighbors worked late into the night to complete the barn before planting time in the spring. When the sides were in place, they cut, peeled and let dry smaller poles for the rafters. Daddy ordered tin from the mail-order catalogue for the roof.

By the first of the year they had the main structure of the barn completed. All that remained to be done was to build the furnace and fill the cracks between the logs. Daddy dug a hole in the earth down to the clay. We mixed the clay with pine straw by tramping the straw into the clay with our bare feet. We put the mixture in the cracks between the logs and in a few weeks it became as hard as bricks. The whole operation took all winter, but we had our own barn before tobacco harvesting time the next season. We then returned to the woods to get wood to fire the furnace.

Someone always had to watch the temperature in the barn to keep it from getting too high and destroying the quality of the leaf. The barn would become a tinderbox as the leaves began to dry. Someone had to watch the temperature at all times because going to sleep could be disastrous. Daddy came up with this great idea for an alarm clock. He nailed two cans above the bunk, one above the other. The larger top can had a very small hole in its bottom. We filled the top can with water, and it dripped until it filled the bottom can, which in turn dripped on the sleeping person and woke him up. I don't ever remember anyone not waking up. This was a crude system to say the least, but one that I assure you worked. The fear of Daddy coming out and finding that we had slept somewhere other than under the dripping can, kept the system honest.

My brother Ron was always the one to try to beat the system that Daddy set up on the farm. Ron probably got more whippings from our parents than any of us. Ron was more like Alfred Dubois than any of the other Grandchildren. He believed that if a rule was made, it just had to be tried or it didn't count. He paid dearly for his defiant ways. He was the first to find a more comfortable spot to sleep than under that dripping can daddy called an alarm clock. Daddy's sixth sense woke him up one night to find the temperature about to blow the top of the barn off and Ron snoozing over in the cotton shed on a neat little pile of feed sacks. Even Daddy thought it was funny and let him off with just a few hits with his belt as he woke him up. One can always find humor even in the most trying times. It was however, enough to deter him or any of us from trying the same trick again.

Daddy usually hired extra help or we would swap work with the neighbors or other relatives. I remember this middle-age woman to whom you couldn't tell anything. She was the biggest know-it-all I had ever seen. The tobacco barn had different levels of timbers that the men would stack the strung tobacco sticks on. The men had to stand on the timbers below the ones that they were working on. The timbers were three feet apart and they had to spread their legs to stand on them.

One morning our uncle Sonny came from the barn with a shocked expression on his face and whispered, "You better tell Sarah to come down". Miss Know-it-all had insisted that she be allowed to stack the barn.

Daddy told Uncle Sonny, "If she want to, let her do it."

Our uncle thought that he had whispered low enough, but we heard him say, "But she don't have any drawers on." Then all of the men wanted to take a peek.

"You better tell her to come down," Daddy finally told him.

Uncle Sonny reluctantly went back in the barn and said, "You better come down Sarah."

After telling her over and over again, she kept insisting that she could do it. He finally gave up and she continued working without her panties and all of the older boys went to take a peek

We never had a moment of free time and were always up before sunrise. We fed the hogs and chickens, milked the cows, and put them out to pasture. We then harnessed the team of mules and went in the fields. The two older brothers helped daddy plow. Mother and the younger children chopped cotton, hoed corn, rang the bells to keep the birds out of the cornfields, or worked the tobacco beds. We all met at the house for the noon meal. We always had plenty to eat as long as my father was alive. I don't ever remember not having enough to eat. We canned vegetables, cured our own meat, and made sausage that would make any provision company proud.

When fruit was in season, mother took time out from the fields to can it. She saved most of the apples and peaches for the winter months to make pies and desserts that she often had hot for us when we came home from school. We always had more milk than we needed and we poured the fresh cream over these treats and ate until our hearts were content.

Daddy even tried to produce our flour one year. I don't think he was too happy with the results. When we got it back from the mill, mother made the biscuits that he demanded at every meal, and he wasn't very pleased with the results. He mixed the remainder of the flour with the hog feed and stuck to buying store bought flour after that.

On Sunday we were often given a choice of blueberry, pear, apple, or peach deserts. I now realize it was one of the few pleasures in life that Mother must have had when she prepared Sunday dinner for us. There were days that I thought we would never get off the bacon, grits, corn bread and biscuit diet. The quickly prepared meals were the only way to go when we only had a short time for lunch.

When we came home from school we ate and changed into work clothes and went into the fields until dark. If it was raining, we were sent in the corn house to shell corn for the chickens or to be ground into grits. Corn was shelled by hand until around 1945 when Daddy brought home a corn sheller, which also had to be turned by hand. We were really proud of it and that first night we stayed up well past midnight shelling corn. Daddy had to come out to the corn house and tell us to quit for the night.

Looking back now that I'm older, Daddy was the most independent person that I have ever known. There have been times that I felt, as I'm sure my sisters and brothers have, that his methods were crude, sometimes even cruel. As I look back, having lived through the segregated south in the 1930's 1940s and 50s, for him to remain independent was not an easy task. We never had to sharecrop and were always out of debt. He came back to South Carolina against all odds and the advice of others, and set his goals. He went to work along with all of the other hard working and independent people of the area. When I visited the area in the 1970s and 80s I saw some of the same people my father's age, still farming, still independent and still working hard.

Mother was also born in Rice, Patch and in spite of her sheltered upbringing became a very hard worker. She was always up before anyone else, had breakfast ready, fed us and got us off to school. When we were all out of the house, she went out to the barn to milk the cows and put them out to pasture. She then came back in to put the milk away and wash the dishes before going out to the fields to hoe corn or cotton; usually pregnant and carrying another baby on her back or in her arms. She carried a quilt with her to spread at the end of the field for the younger children to play on while she worked in the fields. Often she was in the fields before nine and had to leave in time to have lunch at noon. Lunch was prepared on a wood stove.

The temperature always seemed to stay above ninety degrees when it was time to hoe and pick cotton. I remember those being the days that we got our butts whipped at the drop of a hat so we stayed out of mother's way as much as possible. Once when Mother came back to the house to prepare lunch, she found that my two older brothers had taken the eyes that covered the holes out of the wood stove. They put the smutty eyes on the bed to play house with, and of course, they took the flour, milk and corn meal along to make bread. She later told me that was the day that she decided to take the quilt to the field for them to play on.

We worked until we had just enough light to get back to the house, and to feed the animals and milk the cows. It was always a game with us to separate the calf from the mother cow. The mother cow never wanted to be separated, and every night we went through the same process. It was fun for us to dare each other to get into the lot with the mother cow while she pretended to tear us apart with her horns. I believed that the she had as much fun as we did as she chased us around the lot. When she had enough playing, she helped us get the calf into the shed. She knew that once they were separated we would feed them.

As I grew old enough to understand what Mother had to do around the farm, I began to realize why she never seemed happy. She would whip us for what I considered trivial things. I remember one morning when the lot was frozen solid and the wind must have been blowing at least twenty miles per hour, Mother went out to the lot, washed the cow's udder and milked her with hands that were cracked and swollen while she was pregnant with my younger sister. When she got back inside the house, the younger children were screaming their heads off for breakfast. Mother took a strap to them and I thought she would never stop whipping them. When she stopped I saw that she was crying. I then realized that Mother suffered as we did.

Chapter 5

INCOMPATIBLE

There was a lot of distance between my parents. It is hard to see how they managed to have eight children. It didn't seem that they had that much time together or were that close physically. For all practical purposes Daddy was white or neutral and Mother was black. They were both Negro by law but Daddy was white inside, and Mother always let it be known that she was definitely not white. She might not have known what "mulatto" meant on her birth certificate but to her it sure as hell didn't mean white. Daddy even tried to teach us to think white while we went to black schools and churches. It became awfully confusing when we had to walk to school while the white children rode by in their new yellow buses and spat out the windows and called us niggers. In the beginning I used to think, "Surely they can't be talking to me," but some days I would be the only one on the road, and they still called me a nigger. It just didn't add up until I got older and began to realize that in spite of what my father led me to believe, in the eyes of the whites I was black anyway. I never had any cold sweats or bad dreams, but for a while it did confuse me.

Mother never talked to us about race or color, but it was understood from her that we were black all the way. Daddy never completely accepted the black or white culture. He grew up as Black and had lived as a white person, but he practiced whatever got him what he wanted or needed at any given time. He often called blacks "darkies." I don't ever recall him calling a white person anything except "Cracker," He often told us "as soon as you get old enough, get the hell out of the south and forget that you are Negro," or "colored" as he put it.

Whenever Daddy went to the bank, Mother either stayed at home or in the car while he went inside to transact business. It wasn't that he didn't want to be seen with her, but in earlier years men transacted most business. When she went to the bank after his death she had to work very hard to prove that she was his wife.

Once an insurance salesman sold Daddy some life insurance for the family, and Mother mailed the premiums in for about a year. Finally the salesman came out to the house and saw us. He soon figured out that we were something, "less than Lily white." The only mistake the salesman made was to tell Mother to her face that he would have to raise the premium because he sold daddy the policy thinking that we were white. He had the audacity to tell Mother that the premium was higher for blacks than whites. He should have written her a letter to explain that one to her. The things that Mother told him on that hot August day will remain in his mind for the rest of his life. I still remember it very well. The guy probably got completely out of the insurance business or he at least checked birth certificates after that. Mother was standing between him and his car and she cursed him for some of the worst things that I had ever heard a person called. Finally she told him what to do with the policy. My children now have a lot of trouble believing that their sweet old grandmother could have said anything like that; oh, but my mother could raise hell!

Mother did not like white people, and she often got into conflict with them. Once while out getting firewood, we caught some men hunting on our place. They were shooting birds that were flying in our direction. After being hit by birdshot we yelled to the men, telling them that we were being hit by their shots.

They laughed and shot in our direction again and shouted, "How do you like that niggers?"

We ran home to Mother; Daddy wasn't at home. She took the double barreled-shotgun and went down to the woods and shot in their direction with a barrage of shotgun fire and curses that made them crawl out of the woods toward their car. Mother had earlier spotted it and cut two tires with an ax. I remember her telling them, for starters, "You white son's-of-bitches will crawl up a buzzard's ass to shoot a bird!"

The one thing that my parents had in common was, if you bothered their children there was hell to pay. They also believed that we should be educated, and hard work was the best deterrent to getting into trouble. Daddy used his white side to get what he wanted or needed. He could go to another town and it would never be known that he wasn't white. Mother was light enough; she could have pressed her hair and passed for white as easily, if not easier than daddy, but being a Kaiser, she never would have considered it. It angered her when daddy did it.

In 1944 Mother had her seventh child and the law of genetic averages began to catch up with them. The baby was somewhat darker than most of us. Even though we ranged in an assortment of colors we all had straight hair and Daddy could live with that. The brother that was just born had less than perfectly straight hair. Daddy started telling the rest of us that he wasn't our brother because his hair wasn't as straight as that of the rest of us. Even though he had all of daddy's other features he kept telling the rest of us "he is not my child or your brother" and tried very hard to convince us and to turn us against him, but it had no effect on any of us. I hated daddy when he started this conversation. I also knew better than to disagree with him. He never abused or mistreated him because down inside he knew that he was his child, but just didn't want to accept the idea that he could father a black child or at least one that couldn't pass. He often picked at one of us and told us that we weren't his children. He even told me that a couple of times when I didn't get things done as fast as he thought I should, even though I'm the perfect image of him, including the color that he thought was so important.

My parents' marriage began to deteriorate even more after the last child was born. It deteriorated to a state that they stopped talking to each other altogether except for an occasional cursing spree and then back to the long periods or silence. Daddy always talked to us children but very little was said to Mother. He only gave her instructions about what had to be done, and the relationship became a mere existence.

In 1946, our younger sister was born even darker than the last baby. Daddy brought the midwife and waited until the child was born. He came out of the house in a rage, not saying anything, and we all knew that something was wrong with him. He went out into the field and worked almost straight through for the next three days. The law of genetic averages, or whatever, had caught up with him again. He tried even harder to turn us against the baby, but it never worked.

Daddy went into deep depression that continued for a long time. Finally he seemed to be coming out of it. He bought a lot of new equipment, rented more farmland and we also had another car now to replace the old one that we had all my life. Our hard work was beginning to pay off. We had a lot of hogs, cows, and chickens that we turned into cash. The tobacco and cotton were really doing well during and after World War II. In 1947 we were in a sound financial condition, but Daddy was never one to let up with the work that he had for us to do. When we had nothing else to do, we were sent into the fields at night to burn corn stalks. This was fun at times, especially around Christmas, we took corn stalks from the fire and threw them spinning into the air and watched hundred of sparks fly in all directions. I remember the cool fall nights while standing near the fire and enjoying the warm feeling. I often stared into the huge blaze and let my imagination run wild, and thought about far away places that I had read about in magazines and wished that I could be somewhere else. We also made cigars from the corn stalks when our parents weren't around. In 1946, Daddy brought home a stalk cutter, which meant the end of our Christmas sparklers and cigars, but there was always pea vine hay leaves for cigars.

We lived through the depression years and World War II with our family growing larger and my parents constantly fighting and cursing each other. The constant work and the pressure of long hours and constant fighting began to take its toll in the late 1940s. I can't give a date and time when it all started to fall apart, but Mother and Daddy stopped arguing and cursing each other. They even stopped talking to each other for what seemed like months at a time. Mother left home a couple of times and came back, but it just wasn't working.

In September of 1947, in the weeks leading up to our church revival, our parents were having some of their better days. We were anticipating the arrival of our "Big Meeting." Even in the leaner years, Daddy always came up with money for Mother to buy clothing for us for that special day in our uneventful lives. Mother would spend all day Saturday and most of the night, dressing chickens and soaking the salt from the smoked ham that was saved for the special occasion. Mother always baked a lot of pies and cakes that we children looked forward to most.

Big Meeting time at Rice Patch was a lot more than just a church service, it was homecoming, camp meeting and a carnival all rolled into one. It was a time when all of the people who had gone north returned in their long beautiful cars and fancy clothing to show the rest of us who remained in the south, that things were better up north. There was always a little booth where you could get your picture taken for a dime or if you really wanted to squander, you could get three for a quarter.

I always fell madly in love at big meeting time with some cute little girl who ran around with frills and braids with ribbon tied on the ends. Each year my newfound romance always looked like the one the year before did; to stay within my father's teachings, she would have light skin. Each year I had heart throbs for the weeks that followed.

There were ice cream cones, balloons, and little windmills that you had to run at a breakneck pace through the crowds to make turn. A person could walk a few paces off the church grounds and find the proper group behind a large oak tree and buy moonshine whisky by the half-pint. It almost seemed permissible to dare God at big meeting time. A lot of men carried their pistols to church. They always managed to get their coattails hooked over the butts of the pistols to make sure that everyone saw them. New Buicks were parked beside new wagons and the mules were taken out and tied to trees away from the crowd mischievous young boys picked at them to try to make them break loose. Picking on the mules came to a sudden halt when one of the owners tipped out of the bushes with a gallberry switch and tore the boys' behinds up.

My brother Ron had the fear of God scared into him one day as he sat beside our uncle Bill Kaiser. Uncle Bill was one of the people who considered it permissible to dare God on Big Meeting Sunday. The minister was wailing away on a roof-raising sermon, and Uncle Bill was clapping away and feeling real good from the moonshine that he drank before coming into the Church. He kept the feeling going by occasionally bending over behind the seat and taking another sip from the bottle that he kept in his coat pocket. Ron always made it a point to sit beside Uncle Bill until that day. The preacher was pounding the pulpit and the crowd had begun to get on its feet when Uncle Bill looked over at Ron and said, "I'll be god damned if that son of a bitch ain't preaching the gospel." Ron instantly got up from beside him and ran out of the church. He later told me that he just knew that lightning would strike the spot where he and Uncle Bill sat.

When we got home that evening, Daddy was drunk; I had never seen him drunk before. His younger brother was there and he was drunk as usual, and we all believe that he fostered the confusion that followed. Daddy had his pistol out and was waving it around while cursing and swearing to kill everyone around him. He fired the pistol dangerously close to us kids. One of the bullets ricocheted off a fence post and came whining only inches from my head. He reached into his pocket for another magazine and reloaded the war surplus German semi-automatic pistol. He turned around and fired at mother two times. Fortunately he was drunk and such a bad shot that he never hit anyone.

The sound of gunfire, the cows and mules yelling while trying to break out of the lot, and the chickens yelling and running in circles, has always remained in my memory. The hogs had broken out and the dogs were trying to put them back in which added to the confusion. Henry and Ronald, my two older brothers, tried to stop him. He shot at them again but miraculously missed both of them. He finally got mother on the ground as she fought tooth and nail to get us out of his reach. As she lay on the ground Daddy tried to fire at point-blank range into Mother's chest, but the gun refused to fire. Mother somehow managed to get from under him and ran out of sight. As mother ran around the corner of the building, daddy fired two more shots and this time the pistol fired perfectly both times. Until that moment, we really didn't think that our father could shoot us.

While shots were being fired, we ran into the cornfield and stayed there until after dark. Mother also had a chance to get away. We were out in the field in clothes that we had worn to church and were getting cold. We eased back to the yard to see what had happened to mother. It was quiet, and we became more daring and went into the house. I eased into the house expecting to find our mother's body in a pool of blood on the floor, and was relieved when I didn't. We looked around and didn't see anything. We then heard the noise over at Uncle Dan's house. Daddy had somehow made it over there and started the whole thing over with Uncle Dan but he didn't have the pistol. Aunt Ester said he started a fight with uncle Dan and dragged him around the yard and mopped up all of the chicken crap from the yard with Uncle's pants seat. I wasn't afraid of my father that night. I had been afraid of him before, and even after, but at that time I really didn't think he would shoot Mother or us. I also knew that there was something very wrong with him. As I grew older, I knew he could have very easily shot all of us that night, including himself.

The next day it all seemed like a nightmare. Daddy got up as usual and started working but was gravely sick from the liquor the night before. The depression and the uncertainty of the future were far greater pains than the hangover. I had never seen my father drunk or even take a drink until that time. After that night I began to see a man who was broken and confused. I still had the greatest respect for him but began to see him as a person and not a machine. I also began to see him as being vulnerable. Before that time I saw my father as being indestructible.

This all happened in September 1947 and for the next four months we saw our whole life fall apart. Mother had moved away to Savannah and we never heard from her, only the things that Daddy would come up with from his imagination. He was not the same person that we had known, but we managed to put our lives back together as best we could. My older sister took over most of mother's functions at home as well as working in the fields. She had a lot of growing up to do at eleven years old.

Daddy started doing all sorts of strange things; he became very paranoid, thinking that someone was out to get him. He tied strings across the road that led to our house. He would be up at five in the morning to see if anyone had broken the string while sneaking into the yard to get him. He started seeing root doctors and faith healers. He gave them a lot of the money that we had worked so hard for. It seemed as though he had just given up all hope. He never trusted anyone again. He started seeing medical doctors, and they finished taking him for most of the money that the root doctors left. He became very religious and would kneel and pray for what seemed like hours. One night when he started praying out loud in a voice that we had never heard before, I realized that he was crying. We were all sitting around the fireplace staying real quite and when it finally stopped, we all went off to bed without saying anything to each other. He dug holes in the yard looking for anything that anyone had put there to trap him or to cast a spell on him. All of this was going on at a time when most of the harvesting had been done. All we could to do was sit and stare at each other and watch our once strong daddy deteriorate before our eyes. When we did go to bed, we would lie and wonder what was happening to our lives.

I was nine years old; our eleven-year-old sister did the clothes and cooked for daddy and the eight siblings. We went to school everyday with heavy heart, acting as though nothing was happening, but word was out that our mother was "working in a whore house and our father was going crazy." I think back now, if someone would have listened to the imagination of the kids at school, as they believed that we were a case for the nut house and very dysfunctional, maybe someone could have helped. When we came from school, Daddy would usually be sitting on the porch, or under one of the large pecan trees in our front yard. Sometimes he would sit and stare for hours.

On one of his trips to the doctor, the doctor suggested that he go into the hospital for some tests. He kept complaining about a nervous feeling in his stomach. He went to the Veterans Administration hospital in Columbia where he was put in the mental ward. I didn't know that he was in the mental ward until sometime later. Our relatives didn't want us to know that he was mentally ill. We stayed with our uncles and aunts because mother was in Savannah. The separation of our family and mother not being there added to the confusion.

After spending a week in the hospital, Daddy wanted to get out. He constantly told the doctors there wasn't anything wrong with him. He convinced them that he needed to go home to take care of some urgent farm business. The doctors finally allowed him a weekend pass to leave the hospital. Uncle Dan was there when they let him out and brought him home. He stayed at home with our two older brothers and two cousins. They sat and talked for a while, mostly about next year's crop and how much we were going to plant, and they all went to bed.

When they awoke the next morning, they couldn't find Daddy and his bed hadn't been slept in. We weren't too concerned at first because we thought he might have gone to see mother. After making phone calls to her in Savannah and we still didn't locate him, we began to look around the area. Uncle Dan found his boot track that led away from the house and out of the dirt road to the pavement, where they lost the track. After looking and asking questions around the area and not finding him they organized a search party. They looked where they thought he might have been, but to no avail. They started the search early the next morning with the Sheriff's department joining in. They looked all that day and still didn't find him. In the meantime my siblings and I were staying with different relatives. The waiting and uncertainty was even greater because we didn't have the support of each other that we so desperately needed. My brother Mark and I stayed at Aunt Ester's house. We managed to get through the first two days without realizing what had happened or what could be the worst possible outcome. The older relatives kept it from us as long as they could. On the second night I overheard Uncle Dan say, "If we don't soon find the body it will be very bad." That is when I realized that Daddy was probably dead. I thought he had walked away in the woods and died from the sickness that he had been in the hospital with.

Our Uncle Paul came down from Maine to take care of our so-called financial needs. Daddy had drawn all of our hard earned money out of the bank. When my brother Henry visited him at the hospital, he told him where he had hidden the money. He also told Uncle Paul that he was to get it from Henry and to take care of us with it. But money does strange things to people. Uncle Paul paid his way, with our money, from Maine two times. He stayed only a couple of days in Rice Patch during the search and went back to Maine.

After three days of waiting, wondering, and crying, we were at Aunt Ester's house when someone told us that our father had been found and that he had killed himself. Hearing that he had been found and what happened relieved some of the pain of his death.

Daddy had told Uncle Paul to take us back to Maine with him. When mother heard of daddy's death, she came home from Savannah and would not allow the breaking up of the family. I am grateful to her for that today because it would have meant the permanent separation of our family. Uncle Paul's wife, Aunt Thelma, had all the money that daddy left and wouldn't give it to Mother. Aunt Thelma chooses the most expensive casket that was available She even chose the clothes that we would wear to the funeral, including Mother's. It was all done to spite Mother but all eight of us children later did without a lot of food and clothing for her deceitful ways. My Mother forgave her before she died in 1995.

Aunt Thelma often volunteered the information that she didn't cheat us out of anything, but it was never mentioned to her by any of us. I was surprised in 1962 when Uncle Paul brought the whole thing up to me. That was the first time that I had ever heard all the details. Most of us had forgotten about it by then, but I talked to Henry some years ago and found that it was still a sore spot with him. He still gets angry when he thinks about it. He was afraid to give the money to Uncle Paul and kept stalling but later decided if he didn't give it to him, Daddy would be angry. Not knowing that Daddy was already dead, he gave the three thousand dollars to him, which left us with very little cash to live on.

Chapter 6

PARALLELS

At the age of 53 my father had totally destroyed himself mentally and physically. Between the years of 1950 and around 1970 I learned some of the contributing factors that led to his suicide. In the driving of himself, he taught all of us to give life all that you can for as long as you can. The most important thing that I learned from his death was that I wanted to live as long as God intended for me to. That thought has kept me going when life sometimes seemed impossible in the years following his death. I have had days when I wanted to take that shotgun that ended his life and take it to the head of the cop who seemed to make it his private war to keep me in the "right" groove in this segregated society. I often thought of ways to get even with the schoolteacher who didn't think I should be in his or her class just because I looked different. I wanted to take it to the head of the station attendant who wouldn't sell gas to Negroes, or that minimum wage clerk who wouldn't cash a check for my wife but smiled and called me mister and cashed it right away for me. I also knew that death can come in many forms and I had no desire to go to prison and rot just because the local town cop thought I should. My father's suicide has been a great strength to me at times, for no matter how tough life might get, I still have life itself.

I don't want to give the impression that Daddy hated his black side or that he loved the white side. He often referred to blacks as "darkies" but he also called the whites, "crackers" or "dirty sons-of-bitches". When he used "their" bathroom or bought a sandwich in "their" restaurant, he always laughed about it and felt that he had beaten the system. I soon realized that my father had very little love for anyone, including his wife and children, or at least he never learned to express it.

I don't feel that he was born with the ability to hate as he did nor was he just the deceitful person I felt he was as I grew up under his strict hand. As a young son I was only able to see the outside of him. When I grew older and lived through the segregation era and his death, I learned what he must have had inside. In the late 1950's I was able to forgive him and get closure for his leaving us in the predicament we were in. After I found closure, I wanted to live a long life for the life he cut short.

I'm sure Daddy and I had a lot of parallels. I have had stages when I hated all black people. I have had stages in which I hated all white people and stages in which I hated everyone. As I looked back and saw what hatred did to my father and what it was about to do to me, I soon realized that hatred was not the answer. There were also times when I even hated myself, a feeling I never had until I went through the sixth grade at a strange school, and was introduced to the hard facts of discrimination.

I don't believe passing for white was any easier for my father than it was for me. I'm sure he hated every moment of it as I did. He, just as I did, eventually came back to where we began, so it leaves me with the impression that the cost of passing was too high for him as it later turned out to be for me. He was never able to set himself free from hating the system that said he was different or didn't fit in. He drove himself at an unbearable pace to stay independent and away from the system as much as possible, and it finally destroyed him. I know that it is totally impossible for anyone to live alone in this complicated society; we must depend on each other if we are to survive. In my earlier years I often wanted to be absolutely independent, or just to be left alone would be a better way to phrase it.

I have often wanted to fight back, but taking my own life was never an option I considered. I always wanted to hang around and be a thorn in the side of society for its obsession with race segregation. If I hadn't become curious I never would have experienced some of the harder facts of racial prejudices. If I, like some of my other sisters and brothers did, chose to remain in one small town and never allowed myself to venture out, life probably would have been a lot simpler. Even as a small boy, I was always curious and had the desire to explore.

After daddy's death in January 1948, Mother moved back to Rice Patch with us. We all tried to heal our wounds and get on with our lives as best we could. With very little money left, and without Daddy's leadership, we somehow had to get the crop in. After paying for the funeral and buying new clothes for us, what Uncle Paul left of the money Daddy had given him to keep, wasn't much to live on. Mother sold off the cows, hogs, and one mule. We also sold the car, which we didn't need anymore, and we finally had enough money to buy fertilizer for the next crop.

Mother bought the fertilizer and stored it at Uncle Sid's place that we were renting to plant corn. We worked twelve-hour days to get the ground plowed because we were already late. At the end of March we got it all plowed. In our haste to get the plowing done, no one took the time to make sure that the fertilizer was still where we stored it. When we went to get it that late March morning it was gone. At first Uncle Sid said that he never knew what happened to it. After an hour of oral abuse from Mother, he finally admitted that he had used it for planting his own crop. He promised that he would replace it by the end of that week. Time for planting was getting late, and the following Monday Uncle Sid hadn't gotten the fertilizer. Mother constantly pressured him, and by the first week in April, she got mad. Around midnight she started a cursing spree that we all thought would never end. After not letting up for a couple of hours, she sent Henry to a neighbor's house to get someone to take her to uncle Sid's place to have it out with him. She got her pistol and started to get into the car, still not slowing the cursing.

The neighbor quickly decided that he didn't want to get involved in a fight between mother and her brother. He had one of the earlier model Fords in which the starter would turn without the ignition being on. He sat in the yard and ran the battery down to keep from taking her. After an hour he finally got mother calmed down and asked her to let him go and have a talk with Uncle Sid. He left our house around two o'clock that morning and went straight to Uncle Sid's house and woke him up. When the fertilizer distributor opened that morning, Uncle Sid was his first customer. By the time we finally got the fertilizer in the ground and the corn planted, it was the middle of April, which was almost too late. In addition, Uncle Sid only brought back about half of the fertilizer; not only were we late with the crop, we now would have about half of what we planned in the beginning. Mother finally dropped the feud with her brother to keep peace in the family. They again became brother and sister, but I'm sure it was a learning experience for mother.

Chapter 7

THE MOVE TO SEASIDE

My older brother Henry, and Mother, never got along in the years following daddy's death. Mother started seeing different men and would have them over at our house and not caring about our feelings or respecting us as we thought she should. I'm sure at our age we didn't think anyone should take our father's place, and the neighbors made the worst of it. Frictions between mother and the rest of daddy's family, unending gossip from the neighbors, in addition to two crop failures were more than we could tolerate of Rice Patch.

We started visiting one of mother's brothers who lived on Seaside Island, in Stockton County. Mother enrolled Henry in school at Seaside High school. After the crop of 1949 was harvested and it was as bad as the year before, we decided that we would leave the farm and move to Seaside. At first I thought that it would be nice to move to a new area. Later I thought about family and friends that I would be leaving and having to sell all of our animals. It just didn't seem right. We had two new calves and a lot of small pigs. It was the only life that we knew and the thought of giving it up to start over again somehow didn't sit too well with me. Uncle Bennie, who lived at Seaside, told us of a white farmer who wanted us to live on his place and farm for him. That didn't sound too bad so mother and Uncle Bennie convinced us that we would "just love it there." So we all agreed to go.

One day as we were getting out of school at Rice Patch, Henry rode up on his bicycle and told us that he had ridden all the way from Seaside. At first we didn't believe he had ridden the seventy miles that day. It didn't take long for him to convince us that he had. Henry said that he was never going to school at Seaside again. He said that everyone called him a white boy, and he constantly had to fight. He told us that some of the teachers didn't help; they thought that it was all very funny. As we walked along with Henry from school that afternoon, we began to have a lot of second thoughts about going to Seaside. The wheels had already been set in motion for us to move and for our introduction to sharecropping. Henry was working part time for the farmer on weekends and after school. Even though he didn't have a driver's license, and barely knew how to drive, he was allowed to use the truck to move us to Seaside. Henry brought the truck to Rice Patch around noon on Saturday and it sat there as if it didn't exist. I believe at that stage even mother was having second thoughts about leaving Rice Patch. I didn't sleep much that night. We had already sold all of the animals that we weren't taking with us and quietness seemed to hang over the farm that night. As I lay in bed at three o'clock in the morning, I thought about the uncertainty that lay ahead for us, I got the feeling that Daddy would have whipped us for doing what we were about to do. Mother woke us up early that morning. She seemed happy and probably stayed awake as I had the night before, only she had decided that it was best that we get on with getting the truck loaded. After all she wouldn't have to go to school at Seaside.

We started loading the truck around eight on Sunday morning. We loaded everything except the cook stove and what we would need to prepare breakfast. We were allowed to have as many eggs as we wanted. Mother made pancakes for us after we had eaten the usual diet of grits, eggs, and bacon. It later made me think of a condemned man eating his last meal before being led off to the gallows.

As we left Rice Patch on that cold January day, to keep warm, we huddled in one corner of the open truck. I occasionally held my head up to take what I considered a last look at what we were leaving behind. As we pulled out of the road that I had taken to school all my life, a lump came up in my throat that wouldn't go away. I held back the tears and told myself that eleven-year-old boys weren't supposed to cry. When we got to an area that wasn't as familiar, the lump remained in the same spot. I saw one of the calves that we sold to a man who lived in that area. I turned my back on the huddle and let the tears flow freely for the first time since daddy's suicide. No matter how hard and unforgiving the farm at Rice Patch had been, it was home, and all the life that we had ever known. Again our lives seemed to be falling apart. It was hard for me to grasp at the age of eleven, and I again wondered when it would all end and we could settle down and live a normal life again.

The seventy-mile trip to Seaside took all afternoon and it was getting dark when we finally got to the place where we would call home for the next six months. We made a fire in the yard and began unloading the truck. When we got to the pot bellied stove we put it together and made a fire inside the house. Most of the smaller children had long since gone to sleep. Around midnight we finally got the beds and cook stove set up. Mother made a quick meal of grits and bacon, and we ate and went to bed. I thought that I would freeze before morning. The military barracks that was our house had no electricity, was only half put back together, and was impossible to heat and we hadn't unpacked all of the quilts. The next morning we got up early and again made a fire in the yard that was a lot more efficient than trying to heat the house.

Bill Smith was probably as misplaced as we were at Seaside. He had lived all of his life in the state of Maine. At the age of fifty-five he inherited his parents' holdings, and sold them all at once, moved to South Carolina and bought an old plantation. It probably took most of the money to buy the place because he took a job in town and never did anything to maintain it. My Uncle Bennie came to the Island about the same time that Bill Smith did. They got to know each other when Uncle Bennie moved into a house next to the plantation. Bill tried constantly to get him to work for him on weekends, but Uncle Bennie's Civil Service job kept him as busy as he needed to be and provided enough income to support his family, and his alcoholic habit. Uncle Bennie had no desire to give up his weekends of hunting, fishing and drinking to take on an extra job. To get Bill off his back, he led him to believe that if he turned the plantation into a farm it would become an overnight gold mine, with our help.

After all the years of Daddy stressing independence, in January of 1950 we went into the truck farm business as sharecroppers. In the past we had grown corn, cotton and tobacco. At Seaside we were to grow tomatoes, cucumbers, turkeys and pecans. Bill Smith knew less than we did about farming, and he and Henry started getting into it from the very beginning. Mother got a Civil Service job and could no longer do the maid's work that Bill insisted that she had to do if we stayed on his place. Threatening mother proved to be the wrong thing for him to do. Mother even refused to go in on weekends to do the laundry that she continued to do, even after she got the job at the military base. After Bill told her that she had to do it, she never went in anymore. Bill's wife Lydia came over to the house one Saturday morning and made the mistake of getting into a cursing match with mother. No one had ever told her that Mother was the champ at cursing contests. She left crying and almost flipped the car over as she left the house. Henry and Ron came in from the fields about an hour later and told us that Bill had given us thirty days to get off his place. About halfway through the crop that probably wasn't going to make anything, our short lesson in sharecropping came to an end. The morning after Mother's spat with Lydia Smith, Bill came over to the house and tried to smooth things over with Mother. She agreed to stay on to finish the crop.

Even though she agreed to stay, she also started making plans to give Bill Smith that house at the end of the thirty-day period.

Mother's job at the base and Daddy's VA pension, gave her enough income to qualify for a home loan. The property that we still owned at Rice Patch, gave us the extra buying power. It didn't take us the full thirty days before we were able to move into our unfinished house. We were getting ready to move when Bill caught us in the act. He insisted that we stay and finish harvesting the crop. Mother told him to kiss her behind and that no white son of a bitch was going to tell her what she had to do, and of course, they got into it again. He tried to match mother with words and told her that he should have known better than to trust half-breed niggers in the first place, and he wanted real niggers next time. The things that Mother told him that morning wouldn't do for family reading. He didn't really mean it when he gave us the thirty-day notice and was totally shocked by how independent we could be.

Chapter 8

RELIGION OR SEGREGATION

We moved to Seaside Island in January, and school was still out for the Christmas Holidays. We had a chance to get accustomed to the area before starting school in a strange environment. Ron had moved down before Christmas to help prepare for our coming. He went to school for a few days but decided to wait for the rest of us to come down before he would try it again. Going to Seaside Elementary school alone was just more than he had expected or could deal with.

At Rice Patch, our religious education was minimal. Very little emphasis was put on religion. We got a new teacher when I was in the fifth grade and she started teaching us hymns and had a devotional service once a week. She even tried to teach me to sing. I did a solo in class once and it really surprised me that I had the guts to do it. It didn't sound too bad even if I say so myself. After doing the solo I was no longer afraid to, at least sing along with the group. Before Mrs. Brown came to the school at Rice Patch, religion and education, for the most part were kept separate. We went to school for "teaching" and to church for "preaching." I remember Mrs. Brown making us feel bad for not having devotional services in the morning before class started. In order to remove the curse that we had created on ourselves for not having devotional services, we soon joined in. Mrs. Brown got married the next year and moved away. When we began the sixth grade at Rice Patch, our new teacher started the morning class without the religious service.

When I started school at Seaside, religion was always a part of the beginning of the school day and we all had to say a Bible verse. The first day that it came around to me, I had no idea what was going on. I suppose I knew a Bible verse but I just didn't know what or which one to say and after about thirty seconds I got a complete memory block. The class waited patiently for me to come up with a Bible verse. Finally the boy behind me whispered to me, "Jesus wept." After a few seconds I finally heard "Jesus wept" come out of my mouth and the rotation continued. I later learned that was the only verse that the boy knew and he very quickly wanted me to learn another one and leave "Jesus wept" for him. Later when we became friends he told me that was the shortest one in the Bible and he had no trouble remembering that one.

Religion was a very big part of the lives of the people at Seaside and it is just as strong today as it was when I moved to the Island in 1950. I joined in most of the practices and beliefs of the Island. It was almost all Baptist and I had grown up in the Baptist church, and I knew what was expected of me. We had Sunday school at the school and almost everyone attended. I didn't want to be different or left out so I went also. That time in my life played a big part in my getting some form of religious education.

In the early fifties, in order to become a member of most churches on the Island, you had to "seek" or "pray," as it was commonly referred to. The girls would cover their heads with a white cloth; the boys were allowed to leave their heads uncovered. You weren't supposed to have any oral conversation with anyone. You were to go out into the woods to pray and seek a leader or someone to teach you the ways of Christ. You weren't supposed to harm even the smallest bug or mosquito, if you were bitten, you were to fan it away. It seemed that there was always some playful dog that wanted to play but you had to get rid of him without losing your temper or "turning back" as it was called when someone started to seek and didn't complete the ritual. Visions were supposed to come to you in your dreams. It got to the point where everyone my age had already prayed or "seeked" and I was still considered to be a sinner, or someone who didn't belong to a church. We were encouraged to attend the praise services that were held on each section of the Island by the older church members. If you weren't attending one of the praise services, you were considered to be a sinner or at least different. Lord knows I was different enough as it was. I started going to the praise house along with the rest of the boys my age. To use an Island phrase, I "follow fashion." I hadn't prayed or joined the church yet so I had to sit on the back seat along with the rest of the seekers, as we were now called after we started attending the services. To stop or turn back now, as the Church saw it, would be equivalent to getting busted for a small crime in today's society.

I started to seek on Monday morning after a roof-raising sermon by one of the local ministers on, "If you don't seek you will surely go to hell." I started the silent stage, not killing mosquitoes, gnats or kicking dogs that wanted to play with muddy feet and doggie breath, while breeding gnats by the millions. Later that week I started going into the woods at three o'clock in the morning and sitting on my favorite stump and meditating. As the days went by and the trips to the woods got more frequent, I began to at least discover peace of mind and the desire to seek a superior being. I also began to pray, something that I had done very little of before.

After the third day, I went to bed early and dreamed about an old man who lived down the road from us. He was a leader in our praise house. I went to him early the next morning and told him the dream I had the night before. He listened very patiently and when I finished, he told me he would be my teacher and that I should visit him every morning and tell him what I dreamed the night before. He would interpret my dream according to scripture and tell me the good or bad points. Finally on the fifth night I dreamed I was being chased by a pack of dogs. After what seemed a mile, I was able to go inside the house and slam the door before they could get in. I dreamed that I waited for a long time for them to go away but they were determined to wait until I came outside. I dreamed that I looked around the house and found some food for them. I threw the food out the back door and as they ran to the back I ran out the front door and made my escape. The leader told me I had never tried to harm the dogs. He said I probably had guns in the house and could have used them, but I didn't; I only wanted to get away and not to harm any of God's creatures. He told me I was clean and had finished seeking and now I could join the church.

Even though I didn't join the church on the Island and seeking wasn't required at Rice Patch where I did join, mostly because it had been a family tradition for four generations. I had at least discovered solitude, how to take a long walk in the woods and think things over, and most of all, not to shoot dogs if they can be bought off with food.

I don't want to belittle the seeking or say that it was wrong, as a lot of the new ministers who later came along believed. It is no longer practiced on the Island. Some believe that it was a deterrent to young people joining the church. I also believe that the church of today can better reach people without it, but the practice never harmed me in any way. I was able to go back to my times in the woods while seeking to solve my inner problems. Just to be able to discipline oneself for that time without talking to anyone, engaging in play or killing mosquitoes is an accomplishment all of its own. Seaside is known for its mosquitoes and sand gnats, and I can honestly say that I never cheated. Seeking for me was a rite of passage.

Some teachers that weren't from the Island or didn't understand Island culture thought that seeking was some sort of African hocus-pocus ritual that was a waste of time. The teachers who respected the culture didn't call upon those who were seeking to participate verbally in class. Once I heard a teacher praying to the Lord to "Remove from the minds of these ignorant people the idea that they have to go out in the woods with a rag tied around their heads to find Jesus." Some of us who had recently been through the seeking process got upset about what he said. One boy even went up to him after devotion and asked him about it. He told the student to shut up and get his behind in class. In the years since then, I have seen a lot of things in our major religious denominations that looked and sounded just as ridiculous to a person of a different denomination. It is difficult for some people to accept that different, simply means different, not better than, or less than.

I still remember most of the class gathering around during the devotional services to see if I could sing. The students always told me that I wasn't saying anything. "We want to hear how white people sound. I bet you can sing hillbilly." I had never been able to carry a tune in a bucket and for sure I wouldn't have been able to sing with all of the pressure at Seaside school. Even if I could have somehow sounded like one of the famous quartet groups, I am sure I would have never met their expectations.

In the 1950s I was learning the rules and customs of the Island and how they were different from what I learned at Rice Patch. A lot of the ideas didn't make sense to me. One custom in particular that comes to mind was, if you asked directions to another's house, unless the person asked knew you, you would never be told. I used to wonder, "Why didn't he just go ahead and tell the asker that the person being looked for lived right next door." If the asker was white, he might as well leave the Island and try another source of information because whites could never get information from blacks. I made the mistake of telling an insurance salesman where someone lived, and the boys who were with me wanted to kick my butt. I was still too naive to realize what I had done was wrong. I asked the old deacon who had been my leader, and he enlightened me. He told me that the white man and his law could never be trusted on the Island for anything. I asked him, "What if someone killed another person?" He told me that if the person was guilty, the church would find out about it and the person would then be turned over to the law. That probably would have been a rare case for the church to handle.

For a long-time I heard a lot of negative remarks about Island culture and customs from white people but it was a system that had developed out of necessity. The system in town often waited for any little excuse to send someone to prison for a long time. Often the person involved would be given maximum punishment for the smallest offense, just to get even with the person for something that he might have said to a white man, or worst, a white woman a long time ago. I have also seen cases where a person might even be protected by family members from the law and sent north from the Island for an offense for which the penalty would have been more than he or she really deserved. I also can see where the system probably contributed to the black on black crimes that we are faced with today. For the most part, when the judicial system began to change in the 1960s, the system on the Island slowly began to disappear.

The very few whites that were let in on the system of self-protection by the Islanders almost always abused it. They found out the names of people and where they lived and became a source of information for other whites that wanted to gain control over the daily lives of the Islanders. For a long time, older whites bragged about the fact that they had betrayed the people that they had gained the knowledge from. Some even considered themselves unique and used it as a conversation piece that they were trusted by the blacks on the Island and had deceived them. The conversation often comes up when they know that I grew up on the Island but they don't recognize me as being black, or, "One of them"

The church has always played a role in the plight of the black man, and I think that it should. For one thing, it has been one of the few organizations in which the majority of blacks are on one accord. Secondly, we consider the church sacred and will abide by its rules. We belong to different denominations but for the most part it has been our strong belief in a superior being that has held us together as a group. Even with all of its good points for the black man, the church is also his most vulnerable point. I am not going to say that we shouldn't have it by any imagination, however, for a long time in the earlier years it could have been used as the load of bricks that could break our backs. It didn't take the opposition to integration long to figure out that if they used our strong religious beliefs they could manipulate us through our strong belief in a superior being.

It has always been the practice of the white politicians to gain access to the black churches when they were running for office. You could tell when it was election time by the number of white faces that showed up in church over a given period of time. I always resented it. For one thing, they always gave me the old stares and wondered what I was doing there and what I was running for. It would have been unheard of for a black person to enter the sacred meeting place of the whites to campaign for public office. Southern politicians learned that if they wanted to get the majority of the local black population in one spot and at their most vulnerable time, get to them while they were in church. It was, and I am sure that it is still a practice in the southern Baptist church, that the only person allowed in the pulpit was an ordained minister. The local white candidate would step into the pulpit, call the pastor by his first name and have his say. I became as angry with the minister as I was with the politicians for allowing them to do it. You never saw them again until they came in droves next election time. This would all be going on at a time when I had set through all of the other services and was as hungry as a bear and ready to go home.

As I grew older, I always made it a point to get up and leave when the politician got up to speak. I am sure most of the congregation resented it as I did, but this was the segregated south and to run him out could get you fired from your job or whatever they might dream up for you. A lot of it was allowed out of respect for anyone who came to church. The practice is being discontinued today. It has been a number of years since I have seen a politician in church.

On the comical side of the politicians in church issue, I was almost always taken for a politician whenever I showed up at a strange black church. After I had been in the army, lived away in New York and returned, I decided to start attending one of the churches on the Island. I knew the minister, who was "Old school," and I thought that he knew me. He lived less than a mile down the road from me. I sat through what turned out to be a very good sermon and when it was time for announcements, he looked in my direction and I started to slip down into the seat because I knew what was coming.

Just as I feared, he said, "I see we have one of our white friends here today. If there is anything that he would like to talk about he can come right up front and we are here to listen."

Most of the congregation knew me and at this time they were all slipping down in their seats also. My biggest concern was not to embarrass the minister so I stood up and made a very quick remark about how I had enjoyed the services, then sat down a little lower than I had been before. I liked his services and I decided to go to another church that he also pastored. I also hoped that someone had straightened him out, but they hadn't. He did the same thing again. In about three weeks I went to another church with my father in law, and guest who the guest speaker was. This time my father-in-law was there and I suppose he didn't want his son-in-law called a white man anymore. Being a deacon, Papa was sitting near the front; he stood up and in his best Gullah accent, sternly told Rev that I was his son-in-law and "He ain't no whaite man." Papa put him on the spot, but he remembered me from then on.

My wife Linda and I often visited Clyde and Jane Johnson; our old friends who lived in Florida and we usually went to church with them. Clyde was the Pastor. One Sunday while we were all standing outside waiting for Clyde to finish shaking everyone's hand, this well-dressed gentleman came up to me, grabbed my hand, gave it a firm grip and said, "I hope you win." It even went over my head that time but I soon put it all together and was smiling as we were getting into the car. Of course I had to explain it to everyone in the car. Jane almost wrecked the car from laughing at me. Before Clyde died a few years later, as he lay on his deathbed, he struggled to raise his hand, looked at me, smiled and said, "I hope you win, kid."

Politicians no longer have to come to church to divide us. They have gone high tech now. The game now is to get one of the TV evangelists to do it for them, "all in the name of the Lord." Often people get the idea that if they turn the radio or television off when someone is "preaching," thunder and lightning will strike them. I often visited my mother and would find the radio on a gospel station that had long since stopped playing the gospel music she initially turned it on for. In its place would be a "Moral Majority" preacher raising hell about one of his right-wing ideas. Even though she knew that he was full of bologna, she wouldn't turn it off because every other word is "Praise the Lord," and to her, he was preaching the Gospel and if she were to turn it off it would be "flying up in the face of the Lord." I didn't find her to be any different than a lot of other people. I am not saying that one shouldn't listen to the TV or radio ministers; but one should be aware of context and be knowledgeable enough about what the guy stands for before writing him a check and unknowingly help to elect some right-wing segregationist politician to office. I know a lot of little old ladies and men that will do without food in their homes and are just barely getting by on their social security, retirement or welfare check, but every month a part of that same measly check is set aside to send to some TV preacher that has a goal to elect a politician that will do his damnedest to have that check turned off. I often hear it said, "I don't care what happens to it once it's been given to the church." Well, I suppose I'm one of those sinful tightwads who wants to know what happens to mine once its been given, to keep everyone honest.

One very popular issue today is abortion. I have never talked to any women who think an abortion would be a pleasant experience or that it is something they would want to do. Most of us know that abortions have been performed in the local "Butcher shop" or in the back bedroom of someone's home under the most horrible conditions imaginable. No, I don't think that an abortion is the answer to all unwanted pregnancies, but the thought of being controlled by any religious group that believes we should govern by praying and their beliefs are the only one that matters, frightens me. The belief that separation of church and state should be done away with, and that all schools should be allowed to segregate by religious beliefs while the Federal Government pays the bill also frightens me.

If you study the moral majority, a lot of their ideas are to get conservative government elected. The best way to go about it is by using "Abortion" as a vehicle, they have something that even most of the black population will agree on. School prayer is another good one. Again, most blacks don't mind some form of devotional service in school, but with the mixture of toady's society, I question whose ideas will be used. Again, school prayer is another issue used for getting conservative candidates elected, so I am automatically forced to oppose it. After living in the south for most of my life,

Religion Or Segregation   71

I have found that "Conservative government" means the same thing that the segregation signs in the 1940s and 50s did, separation by ideals. Members of the right wing constantly complain about too much federal intervention when the goal is to give freedom but they constantly want new laws from the Federal government that will allow them to discriminate. It is because of Conservative" that the Federal Government had to get involved in education. A lot of states did like South Carolina; they screwed it up by not providing equal access.

I get to hear a lot of negative things pertaining to integration when I'm in a strange conservative group. I usually learn a lot more by just listening. It seems that everything negative that has happened to them in the last forty years was brought on by integration. I say to them, "Mister, it is the results of segregation that are making you miserable," and to the TV evangelist, "You are reaping what you have sewn".

In the early and mid 1960s, a number of private schools were being built throughout the South. At first, it was openly admitted that they were for the purpose of whites keeping their children from having to go to school with black children, or worse, having them taught by black teachers. Then the reasoning shifted to "We don't want them fighting, or they won't have a chance to play sports, or the public school is too big," and a hundred other petty reasons. For a while in the seventies it was, "They will get a better education." I have seen the products of numerous private schools, and I highly dispute that one. In the eighties and with all of the reasons given being without foundation it was an accepted practice to say, "I send them there to keep them from having to go to school with the blacks."

I am sure that most of the country is aware of the fact that South Carolina is at or near the very bottom in terms of quality education. The reasons vary with whom you talk to, but the bottom sentence in the last paragraph spells segregation. The white reason is "We only got there when we integrated." I say we got there because of segregation. We failed to educate the mass of the people, and like it or not, we are all now judged as South Carolinians. It is senseless to hope that some form of segregation will return and set us free. It will never be tolerated as we have seen it. Any form of segregation will only help to destroy us as a nation. I sat in a PTA meeting once where a group was trying to restrict the taking of the SAT to students with a certain grade point average, or as they put it, "Who had potential." This was one of the remedies that were supposed to make us look better on the National Education roster. If we would only stop fighting the problem of supporting public education, our standing would increase. It will take a few years, but we can get to the very top. It took an awfully long time and a lot of trying to get us to the bottom of the predicament that we are in.

I know the following is a sinister view to take of the private religious schools, and my minister friends will probably have me tied, gagged, and nailed to the pews the very next time I enter the church. The religious schools are proving to be the biggest contributing factor to segregation that we now have. A lot of die-hard segregationists are finally realizing they can't bring racial separation back. Even most whites disagree with them. Now they are trying to separate by religion. One must remember that we only had two races to keep away from each other in the old race games, but this time it will be a new ball game and it will all be done in "The name of the Lord." The most disheartening thing about it is that blacks will help bring it about: first, by sending those hard earned dollars to the TV ministers who will use them to get right wing Supreme Court Justices appointed, and secondly, by separating ourselves into all sorts of little groups and many times helping elect a segregationist politician who would have been highly opposed to the voting rights acts but said "Praise the Lord" in one of his campaign speeches. Now he is taken for a Christian or a man of good will, but beware of the bearer of good news. We also have the scenario that the first time little Johnnie gets an "A," he is considered smarter than the rest of us and needs to be segregated.

I have seen discrimination come from a lot of different directions and I have seen it in a lot of different forms that are often called something else, but no matter from whence it came, I have grown to hate it with a passion.

I have lived as a white person, I have lived as a black person and I have lived for fifty years in what appeared to be an interracial marriage. A lot of people tell me that all I had to do to solve a lot of my problems was to become an all-American white man. Usually these people don't know a lot about self, or racial laws that I grew up under. Later when the racial laws were relaxed, I had already seen what discrimination could do and I have a grave fear of it being forced back into the American society. It might come in a different form, or be called something else; even if it is supposedly done in the name of "Morality" it will still have the same effect. A lot of people still think that it is immoral to have blacks and whites congregate. To them it will breed mixed marriages. I listen to daily conversations to that effect from good church going Americans. That same group is working very hard to bring some form of sanctioned segregation back. It is now called "Prayer in schools", "conservative government" and my favorite, "morality." These are all good virtues, and almost anyone would want all of the above for his or her family, and indeed most of us have always advocated them and will continue to do so.

We cannot create a set of government rules for religion, even if the mighty TV ministers with their hourly preaching succeed in brain washing the majority of the people. It will only be a matter of time until we start thinking as individuals on how the law is affecting us. The most frightening aspect of the whole idea is what will be attached to the law. No one needs to tell any God-fearing man or woman when to pray. I don't recall who but some senator or congressman said it all in a nutshell when he said, "as long as we have math tests, there will always be prayer in school." To a lot of people, that sounds like a joke. I really do think it is a joke when we expect to mix government and religion in our public schools; but I keep forgetting, it's only called "Prayer in school" while in reality it is "The great American school separation" that we are talking about. We even want to make it tax-deductible. Segregation must be kept expensive, it must be a luxury that none of us should be able to afford.

Chapter 9

"YOU'RE IN THE WRONG SCHOOL"

I started school at Seaside in the second half of the sixth grade, and my first day confirmed what Henry and Ron told us. I came into the classroom and all noise immediately stopped and didn't start again that day. I became the center of attraction. My straight brown hair, green eyes, and white complexion just didn't fit into the group. The morning class never really got going in spite of the constant pushing from the teacher. Everyone just sat and stared at me as if they were in a trance. Mr. Hartman, the teacher, had to be out of the class for most of the afternoon and we were left alone and fights constantly broke out. I was relieved when they were kept away from me. I was horrified at being in a strange place and being so different from the other students. For the first time in my life, I wished that I could change to the color of charcoal. It probably would have made my days at the Seaside Elementary School easier to bear. Because of limited access and isolation, miscegenation had been very limited on most of the barrier Islands. The Islanders were proud of that fact, and it made me stand out even more.

Mr. Hartman was a very hard but fair teacher, although some might disagree with that statement. He carried around an auto fan belt as a "peace-keeper." The sixth grade at Seaside Elementary would have been a lot worse if it hadn't been for his fair ways and the peacekeeper.

On the second day, and for the rest of the week, the students began to loosen up, but there were still a lot of negatives. The ones that I heard most were, "You are at the wrong school. Why are your eyes green? Your school is in town, this is not your school, are you related to the Smith family?" The physical stuff would come later. I often had to fight my way home in the afternoon. We had a few boys who were about fifteen years old and I was no match for these bigger boys. They always told me that "White boys can't fight," and set out to prove it. I often had to defend the reputation of every white boy in the world, without much luck I'm afraid.

My brother Ron has dyslexia and was a very poor reader. When he was called upon to read, it was always laughing time for most of the class. I was the opposite of Ron, and was an excellent reader. I had read a lot of books and magazines before coming to Seaside. When it came my time to read, I flattened the whole class and scored one for Ron also. At least white boys could read, but I paid dearly for it at recess time, "You tink you smat" (a Gullah saying that was often used for, you think that you're smart) became the phrase for the day, and the arguments never let up until I decided to stumble over the words like the poorest reader of the class. One of the most disgusting and antagonizing things that happened was when this one boy started pinching me to see if my flesh would turn red. That was supposed to be a sign of me being white. It didn't stop with just that one boy. It became a way to have fun at recess time, pinch me and watch me turn red. I finally started leaving school at noon and returning after everyone was already in class. Years later, Mr. Hartman told me that he understood the situation and never said anything to me about coming into class late.

To make matters worse at the school, having grown up on a farm and never having any time of my own, I never learned most of the things that the other boys knew how to do. The baseball games totally amazed me. They were like professionals in spite of the constant arguing over whose time it was to bat or if someone was out or safe. Sometimes I stayed through the noon recess to watch the game, usually from a safe distance. At Rice Patch I had never learned to shoot marbles, swim, or even catch a ball. When the game wasn't serious, everyone wanted to see me bat. Some of the older boys who lived in the section of the Island that I did, taught me to bat as a joke on the rest of the school. After I learned "Basic batting" nobody would allow me to play on his or her team. If I ever lucked out and caught a ball and put another player out, I had to listen to a lot of verbal abuse. Seaside schoolboys always dared me to proposition one of the older, more experienced girls; one that they knew would beat the hell out of me. I also never had any of the wild stories about having sex with girls that they constantly lied about.

After the first three weeks, only about ten percent of the students were really a problem. Most of the students had average or above grades. I had very good grades in the sixth grade, so most of the average and above students accepted me after the first month. It was an acceptance as a white boy going to their school. I really didn't care how, because it took some of the pressure off. I began to lose interest in studying and never wanted to take part in any of the class activities. I just wanted the day to be over with.

I went to the Seaside school for only five months, but it seemed like years. In May 1950 I graduated from Seaside Elementary School, which has been one of my greatest life achievements thus far. I was the center of attraction at the graduation exercise because now all of the parents got a chance to see that "white boy" who everyone had been talking about.

That summer my brothers and I worked on the local farms; we picked tomatoes, cucumbers and worked in the packinghouse. I worked with a lot of other children from school and began to make friends. Now that the pressure of school wasn't on me, I could compete on even grounds. I enjoyed working on the farm that summer, and we made enough money to buy our own clothes for the next school year. We even got to choose what we wanted to buy.

In earlier years Seaside Island had a lot of little three and four-room schools located around the Island that taught up to the sixth grade. For high school, we went to Seaside High School. In 1948 the County took over the buildings and the schools became county public schools for blacks. When I started there in September of 1950, I rode the bus. The first time I got on the bus my mind went back to Rice Patch where only white children rode buses. I learned that the buses were relativity new when I went there. Most of the classmates that I had in the sixth grade went to the high school also, but they sometimes avoided me as if something might rub off me onto them. Again I met a new ten percent of hard cases. I also found another group of bullies determined to prove that white boys couldn't fight.

There were three teachers who were worse than any student. At first they just totally ignored me, which was fine with me because I had begun to appreciate being left alone. When they found out that I breathed, walked, and wore underwear like everyone else, they started singling me out for the class jokes. I had a shop teacher whose skin was very dark, he hated my guts and made no bones about letting me know it. Once when I couldn't get the use of a square, I used the old method of measuring from two square points and used a straight edge. He watched me do the whole thing and got a perfectly squared board. He called the whole class over for what I thought was a compliment until he started a long session of oral abuse. He wanted me to explain to the class what I had done. With his attitude, I briefly hesitated and he began to yell, which was strange for him because he seldom spoke above a whisper. I tried to explain to him that someone else was using the only square that we had and the measurement came out the same anyway. He talked about using the right tool for the right job for the rest of the period. Most of the class seemed to agree with me but he kept belittling me for the rest of the period. I cut his class for the next two days but finally had to go back to keep from failing. Two days later when I entered his classroom he started it all over again. I learned at Seaside Elementary that the best way to get people off your back was to just play dumb.

I finished my class project and left it along with the others. Even though it was as good as most, it was never put on display. When some of the other students asked him about it, he mumbled and told them to shut up. One day he made a paddle for the principal that he said he was going to use on me. At that point, I was fed up and I began to let him know it. I told him that if he ever laid a finger on me there would be trouble. I told him, "My mother will get the sheriff out here, and she doesn't allow anyone else to whip her children." Getting involved with my mother, that white sheriff, and me was more than he really wanted to deal with. Later in life I realized what might have been his reason for having prejudices against me. He was the darkest man that I had ever seen. When I first saw him I was impressed with his color, but he sure wasn't with mine. I'm sure in his college life he received a lot of heckling from other people, and most of them were probably of light skin. I don't think that he ever realized that he had the same prejudice that they did. The students that he often used to belittle me, called him "black boy" or "darkey," but never when he could hear them. I harbor no hatred for him; I just wish that he had found some other way to vent his frustrations.

I had an English teacher the next year that was as bad if not worse than the shop teacher. He often called me red head or white boy, and it always got a laugh from the rest of the class. After a few weeks I would never answer him and it angered him. For a while, he stopped calling on me to answer questions. My sister Rose was having an argument in his class with a girl who called her a "White bitch." Rose, not being someone to easily back down, called the girl a "Black bitch" in return. He got really upset about that and gave her a long lecture in front of the class. "Just because you are light skinned you didn't have to think that you are better than anyone else and have the right to call them names." Rose tried to explain that the other girl had called her the same name first. The next period when I came into his class, even though I didn't know what he was talking about, he started the whole thing over with me. I, along with the rest of the class had to listen to the whole speech. I had to spend three years in his class, and each year it got worse. One day in the middle of the tenth grade, he slammed the door in my face before the bell rang and wouldn't let me in class. I sat on the floor in the hall to do my work. The principal came up and started getting on me for not being in class. I explained to him what had happened but he told me to come down to the office. He sent someone to get the teacher. The teacher told him that I hadn't been in his class all morning. They decided to use the paddle on me. The way it was usually done was for the student to bend over and touch his toes while they paddled his behind a given number of times. Every time you moved they added another time with the paddle. I knew that the teacher had it in for me so I told him, "No way." It was either the paddle or be sent home for two weeks. I decided to take the two weeks home. The teacher wanted to paddle me and then send me home for two weeks. They both thought that was a real good idea and told me to bend over and touch my toes. They were laughing and saying that they were going to paddle my behind until it turned red. I told them to kiss my behind and that no one was going to touch me. I ran out of the office before they had a chance to catch me. I never went back to the building for my books, and that ended my stay at Seaside High, and also my education in South Carolina.

The school has a very long history that goes back to Reconstruction. It was a very good school but it didn't work for me. The majority of the teachers and students were very dedicated and the majority of students were interested in getting an education. This is evident by the number of well-educated professional people who graduated from the school. The buildings remain there today and I support its programs. It is not used as a school now. This book is not to be taken as a negative gesture against the school. I just happened to be there at the wrong time in history. I have the greatest respect for what the school did in the past and what it continued to do after I left. The state and society had written the rules and didn't include me. Had it not been for the school, blacks would have had very little chance for education on the islands.

Chapter 10

THE SECOND SEAT

Life for me got to be quite confusing while living in Stockton County in the years between 1950 and 1954. I finally became accustomed to going to school, or at least I learned to live with it, but going into town was something else.

There was a small bus service that took passengers to and from the Island and into the town of Stockton. All of the busses had white drivers. The first time I got on the bus, I sat beside a girl who I knew from school. After the bus driver had taken off, he looked in the mirror, jammed the brake on and yelled back to me "You can't sit back there boy!" I had never been on the bus before and didn't know why he wanted me to move. I was sitting beside a girl so I moved over and sat next to an older man. The driver finally got up from his seat and came back to where I was seated and told me that I would have to sit on the front seat. I didn't know why, so I moved to the front seat and rode into town. The girl I originally sat beside was upset with me, and when we got off the bus, she wouldn't talk to, or walk with me. I thought that she just didn't want to be seen with me, and I got upset with her. I came home and told mother and some of the neighbors about it. Mother sat down with me and told me about the law that required blacks to ride in the back of the bus. I felt like the world's biggest hick. I had never learned about riding the bus at Rice Patch and decided to go back to town and get the whole thing straightened out the next day.

When I got on the bus the next morning, I went to the very last seat as though I didn't remember the day before. I told myself that I didn't know what the problem was. The driver again stopped the bus and came back to me. Fortunately, this time there weren't many people on the bus and he realized that I didn't know about the segregation law. As he was explaining the law to me, several little old black ladies from the Island who knew I wasn't white, nodded their heads in approval as the driver spoke to me. I heard them out and told them I was "Colored." After studying me for about five minutes while he waited for other passengers to get on the bus, he shrugged his shoulders and sat down behind the steering wheel. Almost every black person who got on the bus gave me a strange look, and no matter how crowded the bus became, no one sat beside me.

As I began to get off, the driver asked me to stay on until everyone left. He told me I would have to ride in the front of the bus or stay off it. I told him, "I don't want to ride in the front of the bus, but I don't have any other way to get to work and I need the summer job to buy clothes for school." He decided to compromise. The driver meant well but I just presented a problem for him. He told me that it was illegal for me to sit in the rear of the bus. He told me to sit in the seat just behind the front seat and he would try that for a while, and if no one said anything about it, I could always use that second seat. Riding in that second seat made enemies out of the children from school. Their attitude was, "I thought you said that you aren't white." I finally found someone who lived near us to ride back and forth into town with. The bus driver was probably very happy about that.

Occasionally I had to ride the bus into town. It was always with a lot of hesitation that I got on, especially if there was a different driver. No white people rode the bus so the front seat of each row sat there with seat covers still like new. No matter how crowded the bus became, or no matter how many people had to stand in the Isle, those seats stayed empty as the bus traveled across the shaky bridge that crossed the river to the Islands. In the evenings I usually stood near the front of the seated area and the drivers seemed to accept that without any problems. I did the old second seat trick with the regular driver. I heard about my riding the front of the bus at school all the next term. Once the ICC police boarded the bus as it started across the bridge. Their first action was to point to me. This time I was in the third seat and the driver had to explain me to them. I think the ageing bus driver retired after that summer.

Facilities at that time were totally segregated in the South. To use the restroom in town was quite a feat for me. None of the laws about restrooms fit me, and you'd better believe the laws were enforced. The blacks enforced the laws with their children out of fear of the police. If a young black child would daringly go into the white restroom, he usually got his butt torn up on the spot. The parents did it to make sure that their children stayed out of trouble. Whites, and younger black people, often tell me that they never would have stood for this kind of segregation.

A lot of people my age were born into segregation so it is all most of us knew. It wasn't something that was just immoral; it was illegal to use the wrong restroom, sit on the wrong seat on the bus or drink from the wrong water fountain. Usually there was only one water fountain and the sign said, "White Only." The laws were enforced just as rigidly as any other law today, including murder or rape. It was easy enough for someone to tell me then and now that all I had to do was use the restroom that I wanted to. Usually I couldn't use either of them unless all parties standing around knew me and would vouch for me.

The theater in Stockton would admit blacks but we had to use the back door to get in. The first of time I went there, they wouldn't let me go in either place after I told them I wasn't white. The attendant got the manager and I tried to explain to him that I wasn't white. The manager was a punk looking kid who hadn't started shaving yet. He had some blond peach fuzz on his upper lip where he was hoping to someday have a mustache. I still remember the look on his face as he looked at me and expressed his superior status. For a lot of years, his was the face I saw when I got angry enough to have the urge to kill. He was the epitome of Jim Crow. I had the urge to put a red-hot poker in both of his eyes. I'm sure they would have done the same thing to me if I had punched him in the face. He told me if I wasn't white, I damned sure wasn't going downstairs. There were about five boys standing in line that knew me. They were giggling like hell and it made the manager really smear it on. I walked back to the bus stop at the foot of the bridge, caught the bus, sat on the second seat and came home. I had no intention of ever going into town again. On Monday morning I was back at my job as usual.

I worked in a clothing store, opening boxes, storing goods and helping in general. Mr. Cohen, the owner, didn't approve of the segregation laws. He knew about the problems I was having and if I worked late, he would take me home. He also knew about the situation with my trying to catch a ride out to the island after dark. We had talked about me going to the movies the week before. On Monday he asked me, "How was the movie?" At first I told him I decided not to go. He must have detected something in my voice or had figured it out and asked me, "I saw you in the line, what happened?" I tried to tell him but was so angry I started to cry and couldn't. Later we sat down and talked for a long time. He called the owner of the theater and told him what happened. Later that day the theater owner came to the store and they started arguing and pointing at me. Mr. Cohen was getting real angry, and later he told me I wouldn't have any more trouble going in the colored section of the theater. I never tried to go again. I didn't want to go through the humiliation. Mister Cohen also asked me, "How old are you?" I told him I was fifteen. He said, "You have to leave Stockton soon, but you are not old enough yet." I learned that is what he and the theater owner were discussing. He was to try to get me a job up north as soon as I got old enough. He said he thought I was at least seventeen. Years later I learned in one of my conversations with him that I was to be sent north and out of Stockton. They were to give me bus fare and a month's wages that some of the "other merchants" would pay.

I always managed to stay out of the way of the police until the summer I worked at the clothing store. The store always closed at noon on Wednesday and my ride didn't come through until five o'clock, and I had the afternoon to walk around town. One day I had a sandwich left from lunch and I left it outside of the store around back where I had discarded some boxes. About three o'clock, I decided to go and get it. As I was getting the sandwich, an old man came by. He stopped and stared for a few seconds and continued to walk. In about ten minutes the police found me sitting on a bench near other black people while I waited for my ride. They asked me what I had stolen from behind the store, I told them, "Nothing." They took me aside and told me to empty my pockets and started asking me for my parents' phone number, and where I lived. I told them we didn't have a phone at home, so they couldn't call anyone.

One of the unusual things about Seaside is that it had so few white families, and everyone knew all of their names, and my name didn't fit into any of them. When I told them I lived at Seaside, it just didn't make sense or sound right to him. I finally had to go back to the same old phrase, "I am colored." After I missed my ride and it was getting dark, he decided to let me go home until he had a chance to talk to my boss the next morning.

The next morning I was at the store before it opened, and was afraid I would be locked up. I didn't tell anybody about the incident with the night before and didn't sleep either. After waiting for about thirty minutes, two policemen and the old man came to the store. Mr. Cohen came up about the same time and asked me "Did you take anything from behind the store?" I told him, "Yes, my sandwich." Mr. Cohen told the police "He always brings sandwiches and saves one for the afternoon break when my wife makes coffee for us." The police believed him, but one of them took me out behind the store and gave me a long lecture about lying. He told me "The old man would never tell a lie" and if I ever got into trouble again, he would "lock me up and throw away the key."

I was depressed all that morning; I asked for the afternoon off and didn't come into town for two days. I had a sick and depressed feeling in my stomach, I wasn't making it in school or in town. I began to see everyone as my enemy. Two days later when I came back to work, my job was still there. I was relieved to find that no one had taken the boxes out or cleaned the storeroom. That one incident introduced me to the police. They knew me after that incident and just waited for me to use the wrong restroom or drink from the water fountain. There was a service station where I always used the only restroom they had. I stopped by a week later and the police saw me coming out of the restroom. The next day the owner was waiting for me when I got there. Before I asked for the keys he told me, "We don't have a bathroom for colored people." I quickly turned around and walked away. I had learned long ago you didn't argue about segregated facilities. I looked across the street and the cop was sitting in the patrol car with a smile on his face. I'm sure he was hoping I would have given the attendant an argument.

To make matters worse, I wasn't the worst looking fifteen-year-old boy in town and the young white girls started to notice. They often gave me little cute smiles and wanted to have conversation. It horrified me when they did it, often they were beautiful girls and meant well, I didn't want to be rude, so I always pretended to be shy and kept moving. If the police could have read my mind, they would have sent me to the gallows. In the minds of the police, the question always lingered on what I would do if they weren't keeping tabs on me.

The year I left school, I needed a full time job because Mother had been laid off at the navy base. It was in the month of November and the farms on our island weren't doing anything. I took one of the farm buses that went beyond town to work. I knew most of the people who rode the bus. Most were middle-aged and older women who were harvesting beets, radishes and cabbage. We worked out a system in which I would carry for them while they picked or pulled up the vegetables. The women always brought extra food for me, which always made my day. They always teased, joked and kept busy and time passed very well. This one little old lady always brought a shot of moonshine whiskey. She told me it would warm me up and keep me from getting a cold.

The system worked well for about a week. One day the foreman called me over and asked me if I wanted to work with him. I told him I would rather work in the field.

The next day he came back again and said, "Boy, if you want to work here at all you will work with me." The women in the field motioned for me to go with him.

As soon as I got into the truck the usual questions started. "Why would you rather work in the field with those old nigger women?"

To get it over with as quickly as possible I told him "I'm not white." His face turned very red and he began having a lot of problems looking me in the face, or even in my direction.

"To hell you say! Mr. John said for me to get your ass out of that field with them nigger women. The best thing that you can do is to work with me and keep your mouth shut."

At the same time, he tried to make me his pet. He always left me outside when they all went up to the "Big house" to eat. Because of the pesticides in the pickup, the Foreman always told me to leave my lunch on the bus, and I couldn't get to it until he was ready for me to have it. He always wanted to see what I had for lunch.

"What's in that bag boy? Smells like chitlins to me, I don't see how ya'll can eat them nasty, shitty hog guts."

Every time the foremen got together, one of them always brought up the conversation about me "Frigging one of them old nigger women." I got so sick of hearing them and all of their filth that I often tried to sneak away before lunchtime. They always managed to keep the upper hand and would "Have me over for lunch" to be the butt of their jokes.

At that stage in our lives we had become very poor. When I left school I knew that Mother could no longer afford to send us. In the beginning I could never accept being as poor as we had become. At Rice Patch we weren't rich by anyone's imagination, but we always had food and clothing.

The morning that I got in the pickup with the foreman I had on pants with a lot of patches. The soles had come off of my shoes, and I had wired them back on in about a half dozen places. I didn't look a whole lot different than the other boys working on the farm, or even some of the women and men. We were all poor; why else would we be pulling up beets and radishes in the middle of winter for twenty-five cents per box to make a living. When I came back to work on the second day, I had on the same pants and the shoes with the wire on the soles. The foreman looked at me as though I was going to contaminate his truck with some strange disease. "Don't you have some better looking clothes you can put on"? You look like the rest of them niggers out there." After an hour of telling me how ragged and how I looked liked, "The rest of them niggers" we came to what I assumed was his house. It was near the "Big house" of the farm. He jammed the brakes on, went inside and stayed for about an hour.

When he came out he was finishing off a biscuit that was the last of a late breakfast, and had a folded pair of pants draped across his arm. He came around to my side of the truck, jerked the door open and threw the pants at me and yelled, "Here, put these on before your nuts fall out." The pants looked awfully big, and I really didn't want them in spite of the way mine looked. I let them lie on the seat where he had thrown them. He pointed over to the fertilizer shed and yelled, "Get your ass over there and put them on NOW!" I walked back to the pickup while trying to get my belt tight enough to hold the pants up that turned out to be about two sizes bigger than mine. The guy thought that was the funniest thing that he had ever seen. "Leave them ragged son-of-a bitches over there, don't bring them back in here, Boy you look like bozo the Clown in dem big britches." I was as mad as hell with him and wanted my old ones back, but he had already driven away. I knew for sure to tell him I didn't want his oversized and worn out pants would mean I would be out of a job. I would have to find a ride back home, or worse, he would beat the hell out of me. I was totally afraid of him.

After a few more days of riding around with the foreman I finally found the nerve to tell him that I wanted to go back to the field. He again started the lecture of "Me and Mr. John trying to help you rise above them niggers in that field and you just didn't appreciate it." He looked almost desperate when he told me, "Mr. John said it just don't look good for you to be working in the field with them niggers when people come around. It's also illegal for you to be working out there with them colored women." He finally got around to looking me square in the face and said "But if that is what you want, get your ass out of my pickup." I instantly let myself out of his truck and went to my old group in the radish rows. The foreman never spoke to me again that day, and at the end of the day he told the bus driver not to pick me up anymore.

It wasn't that I didn't need or appreciate the easier job of riding around with the foreman, but his and the other foremen's rules were just more than I could play by. To make matters worst, when I got back to the radish rows I was met with a deep chill by the elderly women that I had so much respect and love for. In spite of me desperately needing to work, it was almost a relief on Monday morning when the bus driver told me I couldn't go anymore. As the bus pulled away from me that Monday morning carrying the other people that I had gotten on the bus with for the past week, I somehow felt left out. I hesitantly headed back to the house with a feeling of, "Why go back there." I ate my lunch on the way back home. I had the feeling that without a job there was no need for a lunch.

Around noon I caught a ride into town to look for another job. I found a job on the north end of town and had to walk about a mile through town, morning and afternoon. I had a lot of time to kill before the store opened in the morning and before my ride came by in the evenings. If the weather was good, I usually enjoyed the walk. One day while walking along one of the streets in town, a white girl came out and ran into me with her bicycle. When I stood up I had a limp from a pain in my right ankle. I wasn't really hurt, just frightened. Her mother came out and wanted to call the doctor, but I told her not to. She invited me into the house and gave me some milk and a piece of cake. I tried to leave but she kept insisting that I stay. I sat down and talked with she and her daughter for about twenty minutes. The mother kept asking me "Where do you live?" I told her I was new in town and lived at Riverview with my uncle. I lied about my name to keep from being asked the usual questions. I finally got away without them driving me home. I got downtown just in time to catch my ride to the Island. For the next week, every evening the girl would be outside waiting for me. She would walk along and talk with me for a couple of blocks. At first I enjoyed the walk with her; she was sixteen, cute, shapely, fully developed and she excited me. After a couple days passed, little ideas began to form in my head. After the third evening, she said she wanted to go to the movies and I was sure she wanted me to take her. The fear of her walking with me for the block every afternoon was enough, but now she was talking about going to the movies. I just didn't have the heart to say no, but I walked an extra five blocks for the next week.

One day she spotted me while out riding her bike and came over. She asked, "Where have you been?" I told her that my mother was sick in Savannah and I had to go home for a week. I started walking by her house again and all the time hoping to see her. I was disappointed when I didn't, but every time I saw her it frightened me more than before to have her walk with me or just stand and talk.

One day she said she wanted me to come to a party at her house, but I shouldn't tell her mother I wasn't going to school. She told me, "Mama don't like for me to talk to boys that aren't in school." I told her she shouldn't invite me if I wasn't going to school because all of her friends knew I wasn't in school and they might tell. I did promise to come by on Sunday afternoon and we would walk down to the cemetery.

I got to her house just before dark. She hesitated, but to my disappointment she decided to go anyway. Her mother was out until about nine and we walked and talked for about an hour. As we walked and looked at her family's headstones she started getting closer, and we soon joined hands. Suddenly out of the blue she pulled me to her and gave me an open mouth kiss. She frightened and excited me at the same time. I was so afraid for most of the time of someone recognizing me, and was glad when the walk was over. We were just getting back to the house when the police drove by, but I didn't think they recognized me. I gave her a good night kiss and she pushed her body to me and didn't want to let go. I was walking on cloud nine when I left.

When I had walked a couple of blocks, the cops came around again, this time from another direction and recognized me. They stopped the car and asked, "What are you doing around here boy?" I told them I was walking from where I worked. I lied; telling them I had locked up that afternoon and needed to make sure the back door was locked. Out of necessity I had gotten to the point where I could very quickly come up with a lie for every situation. His partner asked him something and he turned to me again and asked, "Weren't you walking with someone when we came around before?" I said no, and he began to get loud as usual. The girl's mother came up and wanted to know what was wrong. She told them that she knew me, and told them all about her daughter running into me with the bicycle. The police dropped it and insisted they give me a ride down town.

All the way there one of them gave me the same old lecture about staying out of trouble. I knew it was just a matter of time until he got around to telling the woman about "My little secret," and then she telling her daughter. The cop made it his personal obligation to let the whole town know about my little secret. I avoided the neighborhood for the next two days, but I constantly wondered if she had found out. I was quite naïve, and wandered how would she feel about me after that. On the third day I gathered enough nerve to take the street that went by her house. I was disappointed when I didn't see her. I knew for sure she had been told when I saw her bicycle. I saw her come to the window and wave ever so lightly. I knew then that it was over and I was relieved, but I really missed talking with her in the evenings. I always took another street after that and the police always seemed to be there to make sure that I didn't "Get into trouble." I also realized there were certain things that weren't available to me in Stockton, at least not at that time.

Chapter 11

MY INTRODUCTION TO PASSING

One evening I was waiting for my ride when Mr. Cohen stopped and asked if I wanted to go for a ride. He said he would take me home if I missed the bus. We drove around for about thirty minutes without saying anything, just driving and staring straight ahead. It worried me at first because he had never talked down to me and was always open in his conversation. I thought I had gotten into trouble without knowing it. Finally, after getting away from town, he started talking.

He asked me, "Were you talking to a white girl down on Green Street some time ago?" It frightened me when he asked me about it, especially after having driven out of town and away from the Island.

I said, "I don't ever talk to white girls it would be trouble for me."

He raised his voice and said, "You don't have to lie to me because I don't care who you talk to."

I agreed with him and remained quiet as he continued to talk. In a few minutes he again became silent. He drove for a while and then started talking again.

"Between the police, you talking to white girls, and the people around town, I don't know who will get you in trouble first. You are going to have to leave Stockton."

He asked me about any relatives that I might have up north that I could live with until I found a job.

He told me, "There are people around town who will pay your way and help you find a job in New York. They know people who will put you to work as soon as you get there.

At that stage in my life I really wanted to get away from Stockton but I also had developed a grave mistrust of everyone. I told him I would have to take time to work it out with my relatives in New York. On the way to the Island, our conversation got back to when I was working at the store for him and I relaxed and started talking. I told him I really didn't want to go to New York. The only relative I could think of at the time was one of mother's uncles that I didn't know.

Again he got uneasy and said, "You are going to have to go somewhere, because you can't stay in Stockton. If you do, you are going to get in trouble."

I got angry with him and said, "All I hear about is the trouble I'm supposed to be getting into."

We got into an argument and after a couple of minutes we got quiet again. I could always disagree with Mr. Cohen without him telling me to shut up. He would never tell me that I was getting "out of order" as was the rule for some of the other whites. Mr. Cohen had become a mentor to me so I usually took his advice. At least I trusted him.

Finally he asked me how would I like to go into the army.

I said, "Fine, but I'm not old enough, and I'm sure my mother wouldn't sign for me, even if I was seventeen."

"You won't have any trouble getting in, we can take care of that. Now that the Korean War is over, the army should be a good place for you, and you won't have to go to New York."

All at once the thought of getting out of Stockton didn't sound too bad.

He asked me "When do you want to leave?"

I was excited and told him "Right away."

He told me I would have to wait because the recruiter was only in town on Wednesdays. He said it would take them that long to get the paper work together to get my age put up to eighteen. On

Monday morning Mr. Cohen met me at the foot of the bridge on my way to work. He asked me to come into the store for a while.

"I need you to sign some papers, and I need to talk to you about getting along in the army."

He was very quiet that morning and I got the feeling that he was uncomfortable with what he was about to do. We both had coffee and donuts upstairs in their kitchen for the first time. When we were through with our coffee, he showed me the papers that he wanted me to sign. It was a form from the draft board saying that I was eighteen years old and had registered for the draft. He also gave me my draft card. I looked at it as if it was a ticket to my future. It also said in a few days I would be nineteen. I had gone from fifteen to almost nineteen in less than thirty minutes, and was old enough to volunteer for the army. I was so excited I didn't even bother to go in to work that day.

On Wednesday morning I was the first person there when the recruiter opened the door. He sat behind his desk and gave me some papers to fill out. I was about half way down the form when the police, Mr. Cohen and the old man who accused me of stealing from the store, came in and saw the form. They looked it over and where it said race, I had written "Negro." The policeman told me to change Negro to Caucasian. That was the first time I had heard or seen the word Caucasian, but I knew it had to do with race. Hesitantly I asked them what it meant, more or less just to see what race they were going to put me in. The policeman continued to look at the form while they all made the grand decision. The old man and Mr. Cohen both looked at the police. It was up to him to tell me what Caucasian meant. It seemed as though he couldn't find the words to tell me, and for a while I didn't think he knew what it meant. Finally he yelled "Never mind what it means, just put it down there and get the hell out of here!" By now I was leaving Stockton and wasn't really afraid of him, so I pressed him to tell me what Caucasian meant. He began to get angry and was shifting his feet around. He looked at Mr. Cohen for some support but found none. Mr. Cohen put on a stiff face and said, "Tell him Joe." I began to think that it was something dirty and insisted that they tell me.

The recruiter was in another room with some other people at the time and wasn't in the conversation. When they would whisper and look in his direction I got the feeling they were trying to put something over on the recruiter and me.

I got up from the desk and went into the other room and asked him, "What does Caucasian mean?"

He told me, "It's the same as white," and went back to his paper work.

I thought to myself, "Hell, what was so hard about that.

Mr. Cohen took me out into the hall and began to tell me what I would have to do while in the army.

He told me "You will have to go into the army as "white" or "Caucasian" as they are the same."

I somehow felt that he was supposed to have told me this while we drank coffee at his house the Monday before. He said that he hoped I wasn't offended by it, but that would be the only way that I would be able to get along, and the best thing for me to do was never again tell anyone that I was Negro. He also told me I should put in for overseas duty as soon as I could and see the rest of the world and how other people lived.

Mr. Cohen was sincere and I'm sure he meant well, he had explained the hard facts of life to me as neutral as he could without saying the wrong thing to the policeman or me. I began to get it all together and by that time I was convinced that I had to leave Stockton, and it didn't take much persuasion. I filled out the rest of the form and gave it to the recruiter without any questions. He looked it over, found it to be complete and gave me the test to take. I took it in record time because I wanted to get out of there. The recruiter told me to meet him there on Monday morning and he would take me to Jasper to pick up some other people. "At Jasper, you, along with other recruits, will be put on the bus to Fort Jackson."

I came home that day and didn't tell anyone I had joined up, not even Mother. I was afraid she would object and tell them I was only fifteen and they wouldn't let me go. That weekend I sat home and didn't go anywhere. My total thoughts were about what my life was going to be like as a white person. I never gave much thought about what it would be like in the army. My only thoughts were, I wouldn't have to make the grand decision every time I wanted to use a public rest room, go to the movies, ride the bus or have a soda at a fountain. I asked my sister to tell mother that I was going in the army but not to tell her until that night. I also asked her to tell mother if she told that I had forged the papers and lied about my age they might send me to prison. Mother took it very hard but she didn't try to make the army send me back home, as she knew that I had to do something to get away from Stockton.

Mr. Cohen had once said it would be best if I never came back to Stockton; at that moment it didn't sound like a bad idea. I would go away and get lost in the army. I had heard that the army wasn't segregated and that everyone was treated equally, I even believed it for a while.

I got to the recruiter's office early, and he was waiting for me. He told me I was the only one from Stockton to go that day. The other boy hadn't passed the test. I was glad that I was the only person from Stockton to go because I didn't want any strings that would tie me to Stockton ever again.

The drive to Jasper took about thirty minutes. We talked about what job I should apply for, and I ate it all up with big expectations. Everyone who has ever heard of all the promises a recruiter can make, knows how hilarious it can be. At Jasper we met the other two people that were going.

I thought Stockton had a lot of Jim Crow signs but it had none compared to Jasper. The "white only" sign were on every bathroom, water fountain, restaurant and everywhere the public would congregate. When I went inside the courthouse I used the white only restroom even though I didn't have to do anything. I suppose I just wanted to try out my newfound freedom. When I came out, nobody gave me a second look, and I thought segregation was over for me. One of the people that were going with me was black, and he wasn't from Jasper either, and when he asked for the colored restroom, he was told that it was outside and around back.

I began to have conflicting feelings about my so-called "newfound freedom." As we I sat on the public benches waiting for the bus to take us to Fort Jackson, I realized Harry, the black recruit, would have to ride in the back of the bus. I had only known him for less than an hour, but we were talking a mile a minute about going into the army and the things we would do on our first leave. The white recruit was from Jasper and was talking to his family and was out of our conversation. The bus finally came, and as I expected, Harry went to the rear. I went as far back as I legally could and was two seats in front of him. The bus was almost empty and Harry refused to talk to me anymore. I only wondered why for a short time. The law of segregation had separated us, not just as passengers on the bus but as humans also. I found that the laws of segregation were going to be awfully hard for me to follow; I had made my decision and was going to stick with it. After all, I didn't make the rules and had tried to live by the other set but that didn't work either. I began to hope that Harry and I wouldn't be assigned to the same unit because I was a little put out with him for not talking to me after we got on the bus. Later that day I realized he was probably quite upset with me for not sitting with him or him not being able to sit with me. We both had very little to say about the matter.

When the bus stopped at Orangeburg I got off and stretched my legs. I had a change of heart about going into the restaurant when I saw the white only sign on the door. I walked around the station while some of the other passengers got something to eat. Somehow the sign took away my desire for food. After all, I had seen them all my life and they still meant the same thing that it meant the day before. As we were getting back on the bus, I met Harry at the door. He smiled and said "This is our last freedom for the next two months." I realized he wasn't angry with me; he was just following the rules. I felt guilty for doing things that he couldn't do.

We got to Fort Jackson around four that afternoon and were put into the reception center. Harry and I stayed in line and talked all afternoon and had supper together. I'm sure we thought we would never have to worry about segregation again. Harry's last name was Washington, and we were separated that night by alphabetical order. I never saw him again but I have often thought about his being the first person I refused to share a seat on the bus with of my own accord. That was a decisive moment for me and the memory of that incident has remained.

I was sworn in three days before my sixteenth birthday and was assigned to the 101st Air Borne Division for basic training. (In 1954, the 101st was only a training unit.) I stayed in the reception center for three days. I wrote Mother and told her I was doing fine and not to worry about me, I also sent her a picture of me in fatigue uniform.

We were promised if we didn't screw up we could get a weekend pass after the fourth week. During the coming weeks, we became a bunch of super troopers, passed the Saturday morning inspection and got the pass. I took a cab from the Post that took me into town.

I was going to hang out in town but as the cab neared town I told the driver to take me to the bus station. I bought a ticket to Stockton and got on the bus and started for the center or rear section of the bus. When I saw that the very front seat was empty I sat in it. I thought "Why the hell not, I'm a soldier now?" I had begun to get accustomed to living as just a person; I doubted if anyone would recognize me in uniform anyway. When I got to Orangeburg, I got off the bus and used the white entrance to the restaurant, ordered a hamburger and coffee and decided not to see the signs anymore. When I got back on the bus, some new passengers were getting on. I noticed one of my old teachers from Seaside High school was getting on also. When she went by the front seats I held my head down and hoped she wouldn't recognize me, and she didn't, as she went to the rear of the bus and sat down. I had the urge to go to the back of the bus and sit with her as one of my favorite teachers, but decided to let things remain as they were. The bus driver never would have allowed it anyway. When she got off at the next town and still didn't recognize me, I laid my head against the seat and went to sleep.

When I woke up we were getting closer to Stockton and my little ego trip began to fall apart. I asked myself "What if the police are there to meet the bus?" They usually were because they had nothing to do anyway. Cab drivers, police, and other townspeople would be there to meet the bus when it came into town. I looked back and saw no empty seats near the rear of the bus. I decided to get off the bus on the north side of town and walk down a side street to the bridge and try to hitch a ride. That proved to be a bad decision.

As I got off the bus, about six or eight other people got off also. They were all black and most of them were females coming home from college. I began walking along with them and not saying anything. I was in a hurry to get home and I was trying to get around them. It was nearly ten o'clock in the evening, very dark, and someone to walk along with didn't seem like a bad idea. They were beautiful girls, which made the idea even more attractive.

After a few blocks, a long black Buick sedan pulled up beside us and stopped close to me. The driver yelled "Hey Marine, get over here!"

I knew he was talking to me, but I asked him "Do you mean me?"

The driver yelled, "Who the hell do you think I'm talking to? You are the only marine over there, aren't you?"

Pointing to my Screaming Eagle patch, I told him, "I'm not a marine, I'm in the army."

They put the inside light on to get a closer look at me and to let me see what they had inside. I couldn't figure out what they wanted, so I stood there getting very scared. Finally after giving me a complete visual, the one in the back seat asked me,

"What are you doing walking along with those nigger gals?"

I started to run but they made sure I saw the double-barreled shotgun between the two front passengers. I also saw the white hood I had heard so many dreaded tales about. The one in the back held up the hood with eyeholes in it. All of the other people had gone, and I felt a cold chill begin to come on. I began to tell myself, "I'm going to have to lie my way out off this one, fast.

"I wasn't walking with any niggers; I don't like them any better than you do."

I told them I had just gotten off the bus and was on my way down town. The driver asked me,

"Why didn't you ride the bus all the way down there?"

I told him "I thought that was the only stop in Stockton and had gotten off by mistake; I 'm going downtown to get a cab."

"Where are you going in the cab"?

"Out on the Island," I told him

"Gull Island?" he asked.

I agreed with him, because to say Seaside would have meant a new set of questions.

They wanted to give me a ride downtown to the cabstand but I told them I needed the walk after the long bus ride. They weren't too impressed with that answer and the big one in the back seat with tobacco stained teeth told them that he still thought I was after one of those "Nigger gals." I pointed my thumb at my chest and asked, me? I wouldn't mess with one of them if they were the last ones on earth."

He gave me this speech about, "I don't know where you are from, but around here we don't walk or be seen with niggers. If you want to do it, you better get your ass back up north or stay on Gull Island with the rest of those bastards."

When they drove off, I was frightened out of my wits and thought, "Welcome home." The night was as black as pitch and every sound from the bushes made me want to run. I tried to stay as calm as my young years would allow. I had always thought soldiers were brave and feared nothing, but I found out the uniform didn't make me feel any more secure. The Buick came back around a few times to check on me. Each time I was relieved when they didn't stop and demand that I get in the car for a ride to the cabstand, or God only knew where. They finally stopped coming when they knew for sure that I was headed to the cabstand. I was relieved when I saw that the stand was closed, as the black cabs wouldn't take me and it was also illegal for white drivers to pick me up. I walked to the foot of the bridge in record time. All I needed was for my favorite cop to see me walking the streets at ten o'clock at night, alone. I would have to go through the third degree all over again.

As soon as I got to the bridge and stuck my thumb out, a man from one of the white families on the Island stopped and gave me a ride all the way home. I was relieved when a white person picked me up. While walking downtown I was worried about the group in the Buick seeing me not go to Gull Island but to Seaside. I didn't want them to see me get into a car with black people, given that they had that double-barreled shotgun ready to use on someone.

I didn't tell anyone about the problems I had in town. For a lot of my younger years I always considered my problems to be only my problem. Also, I didn't want most people to know about them; I was afraid people would see me as some sort of freak. Mother was nagging me already for being in the army at such a young age without telling her. If she learned what happened, it would have been all she needed to go and raise hell with someone. In spite of my being very tired from basic training and the bus trip home, it took me a long time to fall asleep. I decided not to take the bus home again or come home at all until I found a better way to travel.

Mother also had a new friend for what seemed like the tenth time in less than a year and we didn't get along at all. For the next few weeks, when I got off the post I found some hangouts around Columbia. I had no trouble getting into any of the bars because my ID card said I was nineteen years old. They never checked anyway.

Chapter 12

MY "WHITE" ARMY YEARS

I went to a lot of shows at the clubs on post and had eased my mind about going back home. In 1954 they had some white girls from town to come in and do a night show, and didn't allow any blacks in the club. It's hard to believe, but the army said that blacks couldn't be in the club. Many of the black men were not long out of Korea and they turned the place out. Some probably got busted and kicked out, but I'm sure it was worth it to them. A good friend and neighbor of mine told me the army did it to them all the time in Texas, and it almost always started a fight. I left the club with a sick feeling in my stomach. I was still having a lot of conflict in my mind about passing. The high mental price of it was just too high to pay.

I learned that a black sergeant from Seaside was stationed at Jackson and went home about once a month. I got his address from his family and when I got some time off I looked him up. I found his company but he wasn't there. I was told he had to be back at seven, and I waited two hours until he got there. I hadn't known him before, and when he saw me it was evident his family at Seaside hadn't explained me to him. From the expression on his face I got the feeling he lost the desire to take a passenger to Seaside. He did finally say that the next time he went home he would let me know.

I was surprised the next Friday when he came by and said he was going home on Saturday morning, and if I wanted a ride he would take me. He came to pick me up about ten o'clock Saturday morning. Some of the other people from our company (they were all White) asked if they could get a ride into town. He said "yes" and we all headed into town. We made idle talk and all seemed well. When we got to the bus station to drop the other guys off, we decided to use the restroom before we started the trip to Seaside. We got out of the car, and knowing that I wouldn't be allowed to go into the colored section, I followed the other people from my company into the white side of the bus station. Fortunately I got back to the car before he did, or I'm sure he would have left me.

I was sitting in the car when he got in. At first he didn't say anything to me. He floored the car and headed out of town toward Stockton. After about thirty minutes he turned to me and asked, "Why do you hang around with those cracker boys?" At first I was shocked, and I was also mad as hell. I hadn't yet learned that sergeants weren't God and held my peace. I would settle down, get the ride home and not worry about his feelings. After a few more questions, I told him I didn't hang around with anyone, they were just guys from my platoon and we knew each other. I told him, "It was you that gave them the ride." The rest of the trip to Stockton was made without much conversation. When we got to the Island he loosened up a little and we started talking. I told him I knew his younger brothers from school and had been in the same class with one of them. When he dropped me off, I tried to get him to take gas money. He told me to wait until we got back to Jackson and give him ten dollars.

On Sunday afternoon he never came to pick me up. I waited until late afternoon and the only bus to Fort Jackson had gone. I had to be back on the Post and in bed before midnight or I would be AWOL, (absent without leave) which could have meant six months in the stockade. We drove over to his parents' house and they told me he left around noon that day.

I went to the bus station and asked if they had a bus to Columbia that night or even early in the morning. I also had a neighbor waiting to take me. We also had gathered enough money for a cab if all else failed. Everyone thought it was a dirty trick and just couldn't figure out why he did it, but there was never a doubt in my mind as to why he didn't pick me up. Finally the attendant at the bus station said that he had a bus that was going to Charleston for repairs and he would let me ride that one. He called the station in Charleston and told the attendant to hold the Columbia bus until I got there. He said that he knew all about being AWOL and would help me in any way that he could.

I got to Fort Jackson that night at 11:45 and was just pulling the blanket up on me when the CQ came around and made bed check.

I had made it in spite of the sergeant. I never saw him again and was pleased that I didn't. I again told myself that I wasn't going home again until I had enough leave time to get home and back with a lot of time to spare. In later years I wondered if he was angry with me for using the white only rest room or was he afraid to have me ride in the car with him. There could have been severe repercussions if the wrong crowed or the wrong police wanted to make life miserable for us. I understood why the incident angered him. I was a basic private and he was a Sergeant E-6 and was a decorated Korean combat veteran. On the post he would be my superior, but off post, according to the law, I was somehow supposed to be superior to him. I wonder if he realized that I was a victim of the same system and felt victimized as he did.

After the trip with the sergeant from Seaside, I decided I was ready to leave the south. As a matter of fact, I had to leave the south and its segregation laws, or as that famous policeman from Stockton would have put it, "Get in trouble there boy."

I stopped coming home on long weekends and settled down to getting through basic training. I found that no matter how physically fit I was from working on the farms; I still lacked the maturity of most of the other people in our unit. At sixteen, I wasn't prepared for the rigid mental pressure of army basic training.

Preparing for the inspections kept us up all night. Even after the lights were turned off, we still worked to be the best and not get restricted. When we weren't preparing for inspections it seemed there was always someone with enough energy left to keep the rest of us awake.

One morning it began to take its toll on me. I came out of the barracks for the morning formation and as soon as I got off the step, I went down and out like a light. I came to on the way to the hospital. The doctor said I was suffering from total exhaustion and would have to take a week away from basic training. That meant I wouldn't get out of basic for at least another month while they recycled me to another unit. I told the doctor there really wasn't anything wrong with me. I told him I had stayed up all the night before and would be fine in a couple of hours. He finally agreed to let me go back to my unit after a clerk called the first sergeant and told him I would be on quarters for that day. When I got back to the company, the first sergeant called me in and gave me a massive ass chewing for not getting to bed on time. It was Friday, and he restricted me to the company area for the weekend and my restriction turned into a long weekend. Being the only one in the barracks for most of the time, I slept through most of the weekend. I admitted to myself that I had a lot of growing up to do. I would get to bed on time, eat all that was there for chow (I had lost fifteen pounds) and stop worrying about anyone learning my true age or race. After that, basic training became bearable.

There were always little incidents to remind you that segregation was alive and well. You could almost relax or even forget it for a short time, but it always came back in its cruelest form. One weekend in our advance infantry training unit, we were all on restriction for doing poorly on tests the week before. On Sunday morning when we were beginning to enjoy our morning nap, the first sergeant called us out for formation. I thought, "what now?" I could hear the griping throughout the barracks. When we got outside and in formation, out front were this white civilian man and woman, a military and a civilian police. The first sergeant yelled out,

"I want all Negroes out in front of the formation."

I couldn't believe what I was hearing but decided that I wasn't going out front and it wasn't "passing" either. A few other black soldiers refused to move as well, and the first sergeant had the MP (military police) come and get them. The white woman came out and looked all of the black soldiers over and didn't recognized anyone and the group took off to harass another company. The sergeant told us to fall out and go back to the barracks. Nobody, black or white, seemed to have appreciated what had been done.

I later realized that someone was watching the first sergeant. One of the black soldiers had turned him in and brought a case against him. I missed the first sergeant from the company shortly after that morning, but never gave much thought as to what happened to him until three years later. I was in Columbia getting some paper work done with the VA (Veteran Administration.) when I saw this police officer that looked familiar. I turned around, went back and looked at his nametag, and it was the first sergeant from basic training. I asked if he had once been the "Top" (first sergeant) for "D" company at Fort Jackson.

We went to a spot for coffee and I asked him why he had given up the army. I remembered him having around fifteen years in. He started telling me one of the most racist stories I had ever heard in my life, and I had heard a lot.

He told me, "Some nigger Captain from CID (Criminal Investigation Division) framed me on some drummed-up charges, and they busted me down two stripes and I wasn't going to stay around when niggers could control my life like that. Here, as a police officer, I'm in charge and I'll get even with that black-son-of a bitch if I ever see him in town."

I asked him how long had he been a police officer. He told me "About two-and-a half-years." I realized that was about the same time I was in basic at Fort Jackson. It never occurred to me he had been taken out of the company for that infamous Sunday morning formation.

He asked me, "Are you looking for a job"? I told him, "sort of."

He told me to put an application in for the police department. "They are really looking for people. All you have to do is just keep these niggers in line."

I decided right then and there I didn't need to be on the Columbia police department.

He said he was only going to be there for another six months because he had a job opening coming in his hometown in Mississippi. I finished my coffee and said so long to him. I left with a sick feeling in my stomach.

On reflection, I realize that someone was always watching, maybe not always able to do anything about it, but watching anyway. Evidently he had done something similar before. The CID waited for the chance to hang him and when he called the formation on that Sunday morning, they nailed him. Even when we are unable to do anything to stop people like the first sergeant, karma will often prevail. I suppose I was quite naive to believe the soldiers that were singled out had done nothing about it or had allowed it to be dropped. I remember this one black soldier who was a lot more mature than the rest of the company. He looked to be in his late twenties, knew all of the drills, took charge of the barracks he was in and helped all of us with our problems. He was one of the men the MPs came into the formation to get. After talking to the ex-first sergeant it didn't take too much imagination to come up with the best probability as to which soldier was the CID agent.

We were given a two-week leave after basic training. Reluctantly I decided to come back to Stockton, primarily because I had nowhere else to go and my family was there. I hitchhiked from Columbia because I didn't need the hassle of the bus. Being in uniform and carrying the duffel bag, I had very little trouble getting a ride all the way into Stockton. The ride put me off at the foot of the bridge and I waited for the bus to take me over on the island. It was unmercifully slow but I knew it would eventually take me right to our house, and the next time I would have to move the duffel bag would be the last. The bus had a new driver this time so I sat on the front seat to keep from having to go through the explanations.

I had begun to realize that segregation was everywhere, and I had to start doing what made life possible for me. I never really intended to live in Stockton anymore and didn't really care what the people on the island thought or said. I got on the bus around noon on Thursday, and there were very few passengers. I was tired from the party the night before and lugging the duffel bag from Columbia. I leaned against the window and went to sleep. When I got near my stop someone woke me up and asked, "Are you Mary's son?" I told the woman I was, and she told me the next stop would be mine. When I woke up, I realized I had made it all the way from Columbia without any problems, and I also realized if I just went "white," a lot of problems ceased to exist, even in Stockton.

To avoid being seen and harassed by the police in town, I stayed on the island for two days and began to get restless for excitement, so I went to Rice Patch. There I stayed with my aunt Ester for most of the two weeks. I met a couple of fine girls who weren't related to me. Finding someone at Rice Patch who wasn't a relative seemed impossible at one time. The two weeks seemed to go by too fast, and I had to return to Seaside. When I got back to Seaside, I opened my mail and found orders for Alaska. There was a joke in the army at the time that if you were sent to Alaska or Greenland, you were sent home on leave and were sent your orders by mail. They just didn't have the heart to see a grown man cry.

I went back to Fort Jackson and was put on a C-47 troop carrier for the trip to Fort Lewis, Washington, for processing and to be put on the ship for Alaska at Seattle. A lot can happen to a person in a very short time. I had taken my first airplane ride, come across country, was processed out and was on a ship bound for Alaska, all in less than two weeks. I was also as sick as a dog; I had also discovered seasickness. I never had any duty aboard ship because I, along with about twenty other people was lodged in the brig. We weren't confined; they just used every available bunk for carrying troops. The brig was against the bow stem of the ship, which is the worst area when you have high seas. They never even scheduled any duty for us. I guess they knew from prior experience that army troops against the bow would never be able to do it anyway.

Alaska on that January day in 1955 was the most beautiful sight I had ever seen. It also meant my getting off that ship. We came into Wittier and the seals and walruses, which I had never seen, seemed to be everywhere around the ship. The mountain peaks seemed to reach the sky and it was snowing as was usual in Wittier. We got off the ship with bag and baggage, and headed for the train that was waiting for us. Even though it was early afternoon, it was already dark and the whole area was one large sheet of ice. I fell down at least a dozen times before reaching the train. All at once the beauty seemed to have turned into a beast. That was my first lesson in learning that Alaska could be very unforgiving.

I got to my unit around eleven o'clock and thought I was going to freeze. The only cold weather gear we wore was long johns and overcoat. I sat beside the oil-fired heater thinking, "For two long years I have to be in this God-forsaken place." When I finally got undressed and went to bed, it was after midnight.

My "White" Army Years 115

The next morning I was issued what was to become a pair of skis. They were unassembled, a real basket case. I opened the box to see two of what I took for skis and a bag of screws, leather straps, and two tubes of ski wax, one fast and one slow. I thought about throwing the fast tube away because I knew for sure that I would never need it. I dug deeper in the box and came across the instructions on how to put it all together. I looked at the instructions and realized this little boy from the warm coast of South Carolina was going to catch hell even putting the skis together. I hadn't given much consideration to riding them down some hill at speeds approaching sixty miles an hour. I sat around the Quonset hut all morning and with some needed help from some of the older troops, I got the skis together around noon. I was assigned to a heavy weapons platoon, and was informed by one of the other soldiers with a grin on his face, that I would have to learn to carry the heavy machine gun while skiing.

That afternoon someone got the bright idea to go on an overnight bivouac. It had been planned in advance but I wasn't sure I was supposed to go. I was issued all of my arctic gear and was told to be ready to go out that afternoon. The other soldiers were looking at me with a sly grin on their faces. I was put in a set of harnesses with two other men, and we hooked up to a sled that carried an eleven man squad tent, stoves, ax, shovel, gas for fuel, the thirty-caliber machine gun, a large box of ammunition, and a lot of other things that we never used. We started out around four o'clock in the afternoon and it was already dark. I was put in the third man position in the team, which meant I would be next to the sled and if I fell down, the sled would ram me. The experienced skiers were always put up front. I learned later that was the best way to do it.

It seems I fell on my behind at least every ten feet as we started out. The other team members began to get impatient as the rest of the company began to move away from us. They started getting on me about everyone leaving us behind.

I yelled back from a sitting on my behind position, "Let them go, I sure as hell didn't ask to come out here."

The number two man in the team asked me, "Where are you from?"

I told him Seaside, South Carolina, and I was sure no one had ever heard of the place, but he laughed like hell and said to the lead man, "Another damned Geechie boy!"

The lead man said, "Watch your mouth there man," and I detected what was left of a Gullah accent. The lead man told me he was also from Seaside and instantly started to guess which one of the white families I was from on the Island. To end the conversation, I told him I had come there from somewhere else and had no other relatives there. But after that it was always "home boy," and we were the two "Geechie boys," as the highlanders of South Carolina called us. But you could always get a fight out of Jimmy, the other soldier from Seaside, if you called him "Geechie boy." It would usually be an ass kicking. This one guy knew Jimmy would break his behind, but he never stopped calling him "Geechie boy." Jimmy stayed on his behind but they remained very good friends. As we got farther into the woods, the solid ice disappeared, and with the powdered snow, I began to get the hang of it. We finally made it to the area with a lot of pushing, helping me up, and "Come on home boy," from Jimmy. We formed a relationship that night that would last a lifetime.

The mess crew was already there with hot chow, and gas lanterns for light. I took my mess kit out and got in line. When I was served, I looked around for a place to sit. When I finally sat down to eat, the food had already begun to freeze. It had only taken about three minutes in the sub-zero temperature for the mashed potatoes and gravy to freeze. That was lesson number one. Get it and wolf it down right away. As they put it in your mess kit, take it out and eat it. Later in Alaska I spent what seemed like hours with a can of sterno sitting on a ski, while trying to thaw out a can of sausage patties. I couldn't stand the stuff but that was chow, take it or leave it. As I tried to warm the can, only the gravy melted and I used my finger to get as much of it as I could before the column moved. I often ate as much of the gravy as I could sop with my finger. I used my bayonet to dig the patties out of the can and ate them frozen, or held one in my mouth until it thawed.

The next morning was a bright and sunny day. After wolfing the morning chow down, we hooked ourselves back to the sled and started back.

Someone came up and said, "Let's go back the hill route so we can get some hill work in."

Jimmy looked back at me with his usual smile and said, "Homeboy, you are going to love this."

The tail man, Al, was from Canada and a great skier. Al told me to just try to hang on and ride the hills out, which didn't sound all that impossible.

After about ten minutes of flat country, I was learning to barely stand up on the skis. Finally we came to a power line route that as far as you could see was nothing but up and down, up and down, in a never-ending series of hills. I thought to myself, "No way." When we got to the first hill, Al fell in behind the sled to break, in case we picked up too much speed. I fell about halfway down the hill and the whole team went into a tailspin. When we finally got to the bottom of the hill we were a mass of skis, ropes, and sled. The other two men put it on Al, but I felt guilty because it wasn't his fault. As soon as the sled started picking up too much speed to suit me, I fell on purpose before we got to the bottom, and I nearly broke my neck. I learned from that experience, as Al had told me, it was best to try and ride it out. Climbing the next hill proved to be worse than going down.

About halfway up the hill I had a tantrum. "Get me out of these straps, I ain't no dog, I can walk better than I can get around on these torture boards!"

Finally the guy who had suggested that we take the hill route came over to me and asked, "Do you really want to try it without the skis?"

I said, "Yes, anything."

"Where are you from?"

I told him, "South Carolina," which he thought was funny. He helped take the skis off and said, "Okay, take off."

I had totally under-estimated the depth of the snow. He smiled again as I stepped off the skis and went waist deep in the snow. Not to be outdone, I decided to go up the hill anyway. After about ten minutes of pawing, kicking, and gasping for air, he looked down and asked, "Do you want them back now?" I held my head down to keep everyone from seeing what a grown man looked like when he had just been beaten into total submission, and said, "yes." I had just learned lesson number two. I had to learn to ski. There was no other way to get around in the woods while pulling a sled. As he helped me put the skis back on, his fur hood came off and right in the middle of his cap sat the silver leaf of a lieutenant colonel. I thought "Oh shit! I have done it now."

The colonel started talking and showing me how it was done, and after awhile he asked, "How long have you been here?"

I wanted to say, "All damn day sir," but I considered myself on his little dirty list already so I answered, "Yesterday morning, sir." At that moment even the colonel put a smile on his face, and I kept wondering, "Why am I not getting the joke?"

"You mean you have never been to ski school?"

I told him I had never seen skis until yesterday morning. He went to the platoon sergeant, still smiling, and told him to take me out of the harness. I later learned that it was a joke to take the new guy out and put him through the hills before he had a chance to go to ski school. The next winter I was number one man in the team when we took some poor guy out from Savannah, Georgia, and put him in the number three position. We rode his butt all the way out and back and no lieutenant colonel came to his rescue. I'm sure that he caught someone the next time some new meat came into the company. The next winter I made the battalion cross country ski team. One day I was doing a downhill race (I had learned to use the fast ski wax) with a team and we were leading in the competition. As we went zipping past the colonel he yelled, "I see you finally got it down Carolina!" The colonel was from northern Wisconsin and never let me live down the time I wanted to try it without the "torture boards."

Getting to know Jimmy was good, but it also presented a problem for me. I now had someone from the very island that I was getting away from and was passing for white. Passing had gotten rid of the racial problems I had in the south. Jimmy and I got along excellently, but I knew it was only a matter of time when he would write home about my being from the island and someone would tell him about me. After about three months, it never came up so I decided to stop worrying about it. We became really good friends. The two of us, along with two other white guys made a super ski team. Al was from Canada and was a whiz kid on skis; the other soldier was from San Francisco, and Jimmy and I were from Seaside South Carolina. We often went to town and hung out together.

One day Jimmy told me he had another brother in the army and he was coming to Alaska, and were trying to get into the same unit we were in. I started worrying all over again that I would be discovered, because Jimmie said his brother had just left home from a thirty-day leave and Jimmy had told him all about the two of us from the island being in the same company.

I lost my wallet one day and a black soldier from our unit found it. I had a picture of my younger brother and sister in it. When Charles found the wallet, he went through it and found the pictures and showed them to most of the platoon. I found out that day why I didn't want to be discovered as being black. Charles made the biggest issue out of it. "Man, I know damn well you ain't white, yet you hang around with them crackers and them white joints in town." Some of the black guys started avoiding me after that. It seemed that I was an embarrassment to them, but not Jimmy. He acted as though he had never heard about the pictures. One day this white guy from Mississippi came right out and asked me, "Are you colored or white?" He told me if I was colored, he didn't want to go into town with me anymore. I decided to try and put the whole thing to rest that day. I told him I was white, but I didn't want to go into town with him anyway if he had to question me about my whole life just to ride the bus into town with me. I had a lot of things I wanted to tell him but tried to bury the incident as quickly as possible. After that, he just avoided me as if I had smallpox. Charles was transferred out of the company shortly after the incident and the whole thing sort of blew over. The only people who let it concern them were a few black and white hard cases, mostly from the south. They just had to draw that distinct racial line.

Jimmy's brother, Frank, came into the unit a month later and was altogether a different person than Jimmy. One night in his very first week, he was on CQ and came down looking for someone to clean the orderly room. He came into our hut and pointed at me and said, "I want him."

When I got to the orderly room, his very first question was "Why do you hang out with those white boys?"

I told him that I also went into town with his brother Jimmy and he didn't seem too upset about that.

Frank was a drunk, and he gambled most of his money away. "Lets go into town this weekend together," he suggested.

"No, because I have something to do on the base this weekend,"

"Probably with some of those crackers."

I told him "As a matter of fact it is, and if you have nothing else for me to do, I'm going back to my area."

He wanted to ask me a lot of questions but I would only talk to him about what I came in there to do. After three times of his doing the same thing to me, I decided I would put an end to it. I finally had enough of his bullshit and would fight back. I felt he was trying to blackmail me. If he kept it up, I would bring the whole thing into the open and take the matter to the CO or the IG (Inspector General). I figured he had a lot more to lose than I did. I knew that our racist company commander would just love to bust him. Frank, like me and every other black soldier, hung around with or at least had conversation with white people. It was just when I did it that it seemed to upset everyone. The segregation issue for the most part disappeared when we were in the barracks or working together. We all wore olive green fatigues. The only time people wanted to segregate themselves was when they went into Anchorage, only because black and white soldiers often had different interest. We all went to the movies and restaurants and traveled together, but it was just when I did it that seemed to offend certain people, blacks more than whites.

"Passing" is one thing for which you will never be forgiven, and blacks were the least forgiving with me. Let's face it; I would catch hell trying to pass as black. A person that had never walked in my shoes could never understand what my life was like. I learned to do what was comfortable for me without ever looking at a person's

ID. I just wasn't going to be a slave to the people who only saw a person's race. In South Carolina we were not only segregated by race, but there was an unwritten law that segregated me by color. A lot of white people were very uncomfortable when I associated with black people. The law didn't apply here; it was just that the people wanted to segregate themselves and they wanted to segregate me from everyone else.

Jimmy left Alaska when I had still another year to do. He came home and visited my family but I never heard from him or anyone in the company about it. About five years later I met him in one of the neat little joints on Seaside. He had moved away and was home on vacation. We drank a pint of Johnny Walker Red for old times and had a long talk. He had known about me after about two months, but saw no reason to mention it to anyone. Somehow I knew that he did, but we got along great anyway. He had about the same view as I did about the situation. He said he knew right away that I never could have made it in the company if I didn't pass for white.

The CO was a refugee from the Klan. I had known this and managed to stay out of his way, but I constantly watched his actions. He made no bones about not liking blacks; at least he didn't when there were none around. We had a black lieutenant in our unit and I once heard the CO (company commander) refer to Lt. Able as "That nigger lieutenant," while in the presence of NCOs (non commissioned officers.)

Jimmy said he told his brother not to come into the unit because of the CO, but he came anyway. He was like the parents at Seaside Elementary. He just had to see what I looked like, and he put himself to a lot of trouble to find out. Jimmy also told him about me but couldn't get him to understand. He said he told Charley he knew my family and we came from a real "cracker family" and that put it to rest. He told me that was when he realized that I had to do what made life livable. Jimmy, Charles, and I had always been good friends until he found I was black. After Charles found the pictures he turned against me altogether. Jimmy said the situation with me was starting some friction in the company. He put an end to it by saying he had written home about me and my family. I realized then that he was probably under as much pressure as I was for sticking with me, but he never let me know it. I told him I bet a lot of times he wished that I had disappeared, and he jokingly said he did.

About half way through the pint of Scotch, he asked me' "You SOB why did you keep the pictures when you knew that they would expose you?"

I told him, "The pictures were of my sister and brother and I wanted to keep them. Later I sent them home and told Mother I didn't want them to be damaged.

Jimmie and I met every year or so after that and remained very good friends until he was killed in an accident a few years later. I lost a very dear friend. At the time he was the only person who understood, and I have met very few since Jimmy who did. Frank was let out of the army on an early release and went home shortly after Jimmy left. The matter with me was very quickly forgotten for the most part, and I settled down to do the other year in Alaska.

In summertime in Alaska, we traded our skis in for mountain climbing equipment. I somehow managed to master that easier than I did the skis.

One day as we were rappelling down what seemed like a bottomless cliff, I looked down and saw the chaplain standing at the bottom looking up. We made jokes as we always did with him. When we got to the bottom, I laughed and said "You can go home now sir, we all made it." The chaplain and the first sergeant both had serious looks on their faces and called me over. The chaplain told me my brother Mark had been killed in an auto accident and I would be given emergency leave to go home. I tried to control my emotions but I openly sobbed in front of the entire company. The army put me on a hop out of Elmendorf Air Force Base that night, and I got home two days later.

I got hops all the way to Charleston and was still in winter uniform on that 90 degree June day. I was sitting in operations half asleep when an air police came over and woke me up and asked, "Why are you in winter uniform soldier?"

I told him, "I don't want to get pneumonia and must keep warm." He didn't think that was very funny and could have written me up and put me through a lot of delay. I told him I was coming from Alaska and that was the proper uniform. I apologized to him and the desk sergeant. I showed them my emergency leave orders and after giving me a good ass chewing, Sarge gave me a ride to the bus station in Charleston.

It had been almost two years since I had ridden the bus in the south, and had given very little thought to the segregation laws. When I got to the station and saw the signs, it all very quickly came back to me. I asked myself, "So what's it going to be, white side or black side?" The white side was closer and was cleaned more often so I opted for it, and when I came out of the bathroom I went into the restaurant and ordered lunch. I hadn't had a decent meal in two days. When I finished eating and the bus was ready to leave, I got on early, chose a seat in the front area, and settled down for the trip to Stockton. When I got to Stockton, I called a cab that took me home to Seaside. The white driver was surprised to see all of the black people standing around when he dropped me off. He began to try to figure me out, but I was already home and he had just broken the law. The driver took the money and didn't say anything, but if dirty looks could kill I never would have made it into the house.

Chapter 13

THE SUMMER OF 1956

After the funeral I had another twenty-five days of leave. I went to Rice Patch where I knew some girls and spent most of my time there. I met this girl in Ritter who was very dark, beautiful, and daring. Carol and I quickly got to know each other and started hanging out together. One night we stopped for gas, and it pissed off the local crowd to see us together, and that fed her ego. For a while I thought it was going to get us in trouble. A couple nights later we stopped by again. This time it was Saturday night, the natives were restless, and they got mean. I came outside after paying for the gas and ran to the car. I jumped in before they could get turned around and slammed the high performance Chevy to the floor. They chased us for about ten miles at speeds that kept the speedometer pegged and my heart doing double time. When we came to Rice Patch I saw some people that I knew and slid to a stop, and they went by. The next night Carol told me she had never been to a drive-in movie. Blacks couldn't go to the drive-in at Ritter and she wanted to go before she had to go back up north. I said no at first because no crowd was going to work me over just to see a drive-in movie. She told me she would hide in the back seat until we got inside, and promised not to get me in trouble with the law. She promised to make it worth my time if we went in. Her promise sounded like it would be worth all the trouble in the world.

On the way out o the theater she waved at the attendant and he tried to stop me, but I sped out of the theater. It almost scared the pleasure of the night out of me. After a few minutes and we weren't being followed, I felt we were safe. She wanted to go again the next night but I told her, "Lets find a safer place because I'm sure the attendant will remember this red and white Chevy convertible if we go in again." She jokingly asked me to put the top down when we were in the theater. Carol always wanted to do something to get even with them for chasing us the night before, but I had no desire to be the bait. Carol had grown up in New York and was spending a few weeks with her grandmother at Ritter before going back to college in Orangeburg. She just didn't understand the complications in pissing off the local red necks. At Stockton we could always go to the drive-in theater. I told her I would take her to Stockton and we could go there. She told me, "It won't be any fun if we don't piss them off." Carol insisted that we had to go to the theater at Ritter; she said she wanted to screw me on the very front row at Ritter with the top down on the convertible. She said, "That will give them crackers a movie they will never forget." The idea sounded great but there was no promise in the world that would persuade me to do it. I knew she was only kidding when she said it but I still shudder when I think of what would have happened had we gone through with it.

I spent another half-hour trying to talk Carol out of wanting to go back into the theater. I knew if we were to go back in, she wouldn't just sit there and watch the movie. She would have to do something to piss off the pickup crowd that had chased us the night before. Even though she had my head in the clouds, common sense and fear of white people who drove pickup trucks and carried shotguns in the rear window, kept me from agreeing with her. I finally started the car and headed away from town. I drove for a few miles in the direction of Rice Patch while thinking of something to do, or at least a safe place to park. Carol finally got over not going in the theater and told me she wanted something to eat. My heart skipped a beat when I thought she would ask me to go back into town and get something from a "white only" drive-in that we passed.

I reluctantly asked, "Where?" She thought for a while and said, "I know a place that we can go. If you go in it will be worst than us going into the drive-in theater. My aunt owns the place and the club is built onto the house. We could go into her house and she could get something for us."

I thought, "A few minutes ago she was ready to get us both lynched by the people in the theater."

Even as I was thinking, she slipped across the seat, bit me on the neck and said in her low sexy voice, "It's not me I'm worried about, but I would have to cut the first mother's throat that laid even a little finger on you."

"Why don't you go inside and bring something out and we will sit in the car and eat. You have to slow down now; you have to turn onto a dirt road up ahead. I have only been there once, so I have to look for the road; that's it, right there."

I put the clutch in and to keep from taking my arm from around her, she put the transmission in reverse. We drove for about a half-mile down a dirt road that was full of holes and tree roots that kept me shifting between first and second speed.

"Slow down now, you have to turn again, right here."

I turned onto another dirt road that had never been maintained, I left the car in first gear as I eased across the tree roots and in and out of holes. We met another car on the narrow road that seemed too small for even one car. I managed to ease over far enough for it to pass. As soon as we got straight in the road, we came to a small stream that crossed the road and formed a large water hole that had hogs sleeping in it. We again had to turn out for the hogs that didn't even bother to look up from where they slept. As the head lights bounced up into the trees, I spotted the eyes of a raccoon in the Spanish moss that hung from the huge oak trees that the road weaved itself between. The raccoon would wait until the crowd was gone, then it would come down from the tree and retrieve any scraps of food that were left after the party was over

We finally came to the combination joint/house and had to make our way around people as I drove to what looked like an empty parking space between two trees. I eased the Chevy between the trees and as the headlights came into the space, I saw a man coming from behind one of the trees. I thought that he was zipping his pants up after taking a leak until I saw the woman going in the opposite direction. When the man gave me a dirty look and swore profanity at me, I knew that I had broken up his fun for a while. I felt bad about cutting of their fun and immediately turned the headlights off. I turned the ignition off and the radio died. As people went in and out of the building, they left the door open and I could hear bits and pieces of "Please, Please, Please" by James Brown, and "Its Too Late" by Chuck Willis. As soon as the engine died and we got over ruining the night of the couple from behind the tree, Carol slid even closer to me, and we wrapped up and swapped spit for a while until she said, "If we are going to get something to eat, I better get it before I mess up my hair any more than it is already."

I gave her some money and she got out of the car and went toward the club. We were parked about seventy-five feet away from the building. Carol followed the string of twenty-five watt light bulbs that hung from the trees to create a path of light to the building. My eyes followed her almost six foot frame and I anticipated what might happen as the night grew. What Carol did for the jeans and blouse, no designer would ever be able to equal. As I watched her stroll almost out of sight, I said almost too loud, "Damn, what a woman!" It was about ten in the evening when I turned the radio on and hoped that WLAC in Nashville would play something appropriate for the mood, and for the time I was looking forward to having. In about fifteen minutes I saw Carol coming back and my eyes followed her as they had on the trip into the house. When she got back into the car, she gave me her beautiful smiled and said, "I hope you like pig feet; they had that or chitlins, and I know you folks don't' eat chitlins." She also had a pint jar that was about two-thirds full of moonshine whiskey that looked crystal clear when I turned the inside light on to examine it. I took a sip of it and it must have been one hundred and fifty proof. As I gasped for breath, Carol handed me another pint jar that was full of grape punch.

"All of the sodas were gone and it was all Ethel had to chase it with. I like it better with punch anyway, tonight we are going to get drunk down-home style."

We sat in the car and rolled the windows up to keep the mosquitoes from eating us alive. We ate pig feet, potato salad and drank moonshine whiskey that we chased with grape punch, and the DJ supplied the blues. We threw the bones from the pig feet out the window and sat the pint jars on the dash, and met in the middle of the seat. The high that was coming on from the shine and the gel and grease from the pig feet made one hell of a kiss. We held it until she asked me to undress her; I unbuttoned her blouse and unhooked her bra. She knew how to press all of my buttons. I wanted to tear her clothes off, but managed to maintain control. She had me to the boiling point but I took precious seconds to get my clothes off, and we went after each other like wild animals.

About an hour later, we came up for air and a shot of shine. The June night was hot, but we hadn't noticed it until that moment. The car's windows were all fogged over and we were both soaked from perspiration. The grease and gel from the pig feet and from anything else that got on us, made a hell of a mess. Carol poured the little bit of punch into the jar that held a lot more moonshine, and we killed it. Carol came over to me and whispered, "And to think, I wanted to go to some cracker drive-in theater." The shine had us both high, and we giggled, wrestled and made love for a long time until we finally went to sleep, or passed out. When we woke up, we were on the bare metal under the back seat. Somehow the seat had worked itself loose, and we had gotten behind it. I turned the inside light on, found my watch, and saw that it was after two in the morning.

"What time is it?"

"Two-thirty," I told her.

"My grandmother is going to be worried sick, she always told me to be in by twelve."

We fumbled around and found our clothes. I was about to get dressed when Carol said, "I have to go to the pump and get washed up before I get dressed."

Only a couple of other cars remained and they were on the other side of the building. We went to the pump with our clothes in our hands. I found a bar of lye soap and water to prime the pump. I pumped for her as she lathered herself, and when she finished, I threw water on her with the pot that held the primer water. She in turn pumped for me while I took my turn. Even though it was in June, the cold water almost took my breath when she threw it over me. We put on our clothing and went inside for me to meet Carol's aunt. Everyone had already left and the joint was closed.

I had always pictured anyone who was an aunt, as prune faced, fat, and with at least five screaming kids chasing her around, but not Carol's Aunt Ethel. Ethel looked to be in her late twenties or early thirties and was built like a brick outhouse. She had on a very thin gown that I could see straight through. As she moved in and out of the light I could see that she had absolutely nothing under it.

"You better go home with me and tell Grandma that I was with you." Carol told her,

"She already sent Junior down here to see if you were here, and I told him to tell her you were here and that you could spend the night."

Ethel pointed to an open bedroom door. "You can sleep in that room and he can sleep in the other one."

When Carol went into the other room, Ethel caught me staring at her when the light was hitting the gown just right. She made no effort to move and I fell into a trance. She looked at me, smiled, and pulled the gown tighter across her beautiful breast. Ethel and the moonshine whiskey had my pulse doing double time. I started a conversation with her to change the pace.

"Are you Carol's mother or father's sister?"

She hesitated, then said, "Neither, I'm married to Carol's mother's brother who is in Korea for a year; he has been gone for nine months, and it's about to drive me crazy."

Carol finished getting the bed made for me and went into the other room and went to sleep. I sat and chatted with Ethel for a few minutes and started to go to bed also. Ethel was sitting on the couch with me; I thought she was much too close with Carol down the hall.

"Want something to drink before you go to bed?"

I really didn't want to but I decided not to sound anti-social and agreed to have a small drink with her. Ethel went into the kitchen and came back with a quart of Scotch, two glasses and some ice. She must have rearranged the gown while she was in the kitchen, when she came back, the drawstring that gave it any respectability at all was now loose and about eighty percent of her boobs were showing. She sat the scotch on the table and I poured myself a small drink and put a lot of water and ice in it. Ethel poured herself a big one, added a little ice, shook it around, and downed it in one gulp. "I only have one a day, might as well make it a good one." I took another hit from the bottle and began to feel another high coming on. I decided I had better stop right there and go to bed. I half staggered into the room and took my clothes off, and instantly fell asleep.

I was just getting into a deep sleep and thought I was dreaming when I felt someone in bed with me. She was biting me all over my chest. I put my arms around her, pulled her closer, and she got hotter and hotter. Her perfume was different from Carol's, and when she whispered,

"Wake up soldier boy, you have some more business to take care of." I knew Ethel was in bed with me.

I never had a chance to say no even if I wanted to. For a millionth of a second I thought about Carol sleeping in the other room. Ethel assured me she was out for the night. I got the bottom part of my underwear off and as I worked to get my T-shirt off she crawled on top of me. That night I learned there is a very thin line between torture and pleasure. She bit, scratched, and cursed me out at least five times, and then settled down into total beauty until we heard the roosters crowing outside. We were totally exhausted and lying very still for what seemed an eternity until Ethel snuggled up to me and whispered,

"Now that should hold me for another three months until Tommie gets home."

She kissed me lightly and got out of the bed. I decided what I had been through tonight would last me for a while also. I was badly in need from being in Alaska for the past eighteen months, where the only thing available was a very expensive quickie from prostitutes, which I never ventured into. Ethel gave me the experience all seventeen year olds should have before venturing into manhood.

It was Saturday and we slept until around noon when people had begun to come to the club. The jukebox was already going full blast and I had slept through most of it. Carol, Ethel, and I met in the kitchen for a very late breakfast. Ethel now had on a gown that kept everything hid. Carol was already dressed and looked like the doll she always looked like. They both went about the morning as if nothing had happened the night before. I finally relaxed when I realized that Carol had slept through all of the noise that Ethel and I made in the wee hours of the morning.

After we had eaten, I took Carol to her grandmother's house where she took a bath and changed clothes. I finally convinced myself I had better go back to Seaside and let Ron know his car still had four corners on it. I also needed to let mother know I was still alive and well. I knew Mother would be worried, especially after having just lost Mark in an auto accident.

As we drove the sixty miles back to Seaside, very little was said until we got to Stockton. It was tomato picking time and the trucks and tractors held the traffic to a snails pace as we came through town. When we got to the intersection before crossing the bridge to the Island, there was a cop directing traffic. As we approached, he held up his hand for me to stop. There were about ten people waiting to cross. As we came to a halt, the cop directed them to cross. As they crossed, they glued their eyes on us as the Chevy's exhaust echoed between the buildings with Carol and I in the front seat sitting really close. The pedestrians' eyes stayed glued on us as they crossed and one couple got their feet entangled and almost fell.

In a voice that was too loud for comfort, Carol said, "Look where you're going, you son-of-a-bitch."

I was afraid they had read her lips. I didn't need to get involved with the Stockton police so I said a little prayer for the light to change. After what seemed like an hour but was only a few minutes, the policeman waved us through. When we got on the bridge and over the water, Carol said, "Let's put the top down." I was glad she hadn't thought of it earlier as we came through town. On the island

I knew we would meet very few white people, and most of them would know me anyway. I also would have welcomed the chase with the top down on the Chevy.

Just as I predicted, mother was worried sick from not knowing where I was. Ron wasn't worried about his car being out of his sight. When he saw Carol, I got the reaction I expected from brother Ron, he winked and said, "I'll bet you are having some fun with that?" I assured him that I was and knew he would want to hear details later. I considered it a small price to pay for the use of his car. I took a bath, changed clothes and prepared to take Carol back to her grandmother's house. The weather looked like we might get a thunderstorm so I put the top up without any objections from her. On the way back to Ritter, she told me she had to leave and go back to New York on Monday morning and wanted me to take her to the bus station at Ritter with the top down. At first I thought about using another car that wasn't convertible, but I told myself, "What the hell, she deserved at least that." She had tried in every way possible to get even with the whites for stares, not being able to go to the theater, chasing us and just driving pickups with shotguns in the rear window. On the way back to Ritter, I stopped at a cousin's house, and he wasn't home. Carol was getting hotter and hotter, I drove the car behind the house and again we took everything off and climbed into the back seat. When I got back to her grandmother's house, I stayed for a couple of hours and drove back to the Island to let Ron use his well-needed car.

When I picked Carol up on Monday morning, I already had the top down and she was dressed for the occasion. Carol was a girl with class even when she wasn't dressed. Her parents were well off and she wore nothing but the best. She had on designer "peddle pushers" and a sweater. She had her shoulder-length hair in a loose ponytail with a scarf that matched her sweater and pants across the top and tied under her chin to keep her hair in place while riding in the convertible. I think Carol was a little disappointed when all we got were stares on the way to the bus station, but not me. I stayed at or slightly above the speed limit because we were running a little late. When we got to the station, she only had time to get her ticket and get on the bus. As the bus drove out of sight, I got butterflies in my stomach. I started the Chevy and went in the direction of Rice Patch. When I came to the dirt road that led to Ethel's house, I took it, and for the next two days she finished teaching me about the birds and the bees.

In the past weeks the two women had turned me totally wild. The time was my debut, my baptism and an introduction to a world that I had never known before. I loved every minute of the excitement. They taught me all about the birds and the bees, manhood and how to make the best of it. After spending a couple of nights with Ethel, it was all I could take for a while.

I took the car back to Ron and spent some time with Mother. Ron wasn't upset with me for keeping his car away for as long as I did. On Friday he told me he had to work on Saturday and I could use the car if I wanted to. I didn't have anything planned but I took the offer anyway. About midday Saturday, I washed the car and took a bath. In 1956 it was popular for service men to wear uniforms. I put on a neatly starched and pressed khaki uniform, filled the car with gas, let the top down, and left home. I didn't have any particular place I wanted to go. Some of Ethel's in-laws had come down for a couple of days so it wouldn't make sense for me to head in that direction.

I just wanted to ride for a while. I took some back roads and after a time I came into a town about the size of Stockton. It was about sixty miles away, and far enough where I didn't think anyone would recognize me. Even though I didn't need gas, I didn't want to try to find gas at night in a strange place. I stopped at an old country store and gas station combination and went inside and got a beer while the attendant filled the tank. When I came outside there was another red and white Chevy convertible parked beside Ron's car. Behind the wheel sat a very petite blond girl with a cute face and smile.

When she saw me, she yelled, "Where are you going soldier boy, I like your car, it's just like mine."

I asked her, "Shall we mate them?"

She gave me a cute little smile and said, "They both might be girls."

I told her, "I know for sure this one is a boy; I looked under the hood this morning."

After a few minutes of small talk, the smile remained on her face. I could see she was beautiful, witty, had a great personality, and could be a lot of fun. She told me they always had a party at the lake on Saturday night and asked if I wanted to go.

"I'll be ready as soon as I get a case of beer," she said.

I asked her if there was another place we could go. The Stockton police had taught me very well about the repercussions of talking to southern white girls. Being in her presence was enough to drive any man out of his wits. I could tell she was willing to be picked up. From the tone of her voice, I knew she didn't want to go to the lake; she wanted something different tonight. I came over and sat beside her in her car, still looking in all directions and my legs getting weaker. After a few minutes, she said, "Mama and daddy are gone to Atlanta for the George and Alabama football game and wont be back until tomorrow, we can go to my house." No way in hell was I going into the house with her. We drank a couple of beers and I could feel a buzz coming on. It was getting dark and we moved the cars around beside the store. With the two beers and being out of sight of people who came in and out of the store, my knees began to remain steady. We were sitting closer now, and her perfume was driving me to the boiling point.

As we were getting closer, she asked me, "Do you want some moonshine?"

I really didn't want any moonshine but I would have agreed to almost anything to get away from the store and out of sight of the public.

"I know this old nigger man out in the country that sells it. When I drink it, it gives me a warm feeling all over, and I get a wild feeling."

I didn't want any of her friends from the lake crew to hang out with us so I told her to park her car and ride with me. I also considered the probability she had a jealous boyfriend. If anyone recognized me and I had to run, I knew Ron's high performance Chevy would get it done and I would be driving.

When we got to the house that sold the whiskey, I stayed in the car. At first I didn't think he was going to sell it to her.

He asked, "Who is in the car with you? I done tell you people I don't sell anything."

I stayed in the car and didn't say anything.

I overheard her tell him, "He's an army man, he doesn't live around here. You know that I wouldn't do anything like that to hurt you Uncle Jake, Daddy would skin me if he found out I was going to drink some of it, it's mostly for him."

I got out of the car so he could see that I was in uniform. He left and in a few minutes, came back with a pint of moonshine in a scotch bottle. We took a sip of it and chased it with a swallow of beer. That was enough for me, I had to drive, and after a sip of the whiskey I knew I was going to have a lot of fun with this little white girl before the night was over.

I asked myself, "Why the hell not? They wanted to make a white boy out of me, so why not live up to their expectations."

I drove back to the store where she got her car; we drove to her house and parked behind a large barn. Every time I stopped, the mosquitoes would catch up with me. There was a huge full moon coming over the horizon that illuminated the area and I could see the farm implements. When I saw large tractors and combines parked around the barn I realized that it was a big business. I put the top and windows up leaving only enough opening for ventilation. She parked her car in the driveway and came over to where I had parked. We sat in the car and took another small sip of the whiskey and began giggling and touching. After some time we began to wrestle. She put an arm around my neck and tried to wrestle me down to the seat. My face was on her breast and I eased my hand under her bra. To my surprise she gently pushed me away. As I was beginning to think, what now, is it bad timing or did I try to move too fast?

She sat up, unhooked her bra, and said, "It's too tight anyway." While the moon cast light through the windows, I saw white breast and pink nipples for the first time, and it excited me even more.

We took off everything we weren't born with and went after each other with a passion. She was in great physical condition and came on to me as if she still wanted to wrestle. After the second time around, I tried to punish her for every time the police in Stockton told me, "You're going to get in trouble boy."

I wondered what kind of grudge she might have been carrying, because that little girl put as much on me as I was trying to put on her. After what seemed like a very long time, we relaxed, and a stiff breeze was blowing the bugs away. I moved the car out to the edge of the pasture and put the windows down. We put our clothes on, snuggled up and went to sleep.

I woke up around five o'clock and the uniform was in a mess. I got out of the car, stretched, and relieved myself. While I was asleep she went into the house and took a shower. When she came back to the car, I told her it was time for me to go. Even with the sun coming up over the horizon and creating long shadows over the pasture, she sat on the trunk of the car and wrapped her legs around me and did me as she had before. That night, I found out why the Stockton police considered it so precious and wanted to keep me away from it and keep it, "White only."

When I came through Stockton it was around seven thirty and the farm trucks were beginning to slow the traffic, and my former shadow was directing it. In the past weeks I tried to avoid him. I didn't want to have to deal with him in any way. He had been the most vocal when they strongly suggested I not come back to Stockton. I knew there wasn't a whole lot he could legally do to keep me from coming back home, however, he always reserved the right to make life as miserable for anyone as he wanted to. I came to the intersection and was just about through when he took a quick glance in my direction; the expression on his face read in bold print,

"I can't believe that damn nigger came back here."

When I got through the intersection I smiled and said to myself, "I'll bet you would have had a stroke if you had seen me last night." I felt vindicated.

When I first met Nancy I wanted her as a grudge thing, but before the night was over, I felt very close to her. I gave her my military address and we stayed in contact for a time. She wrote some of the sexiest love letters that I had ever read. She was twenty-one and a junior at UNC. I was seventeen, black, and a corporal in the Army. We stopped writing to each other, and I didn't hear from her until a year later when I was about to get out of the army. I got a letter from her that was post-marked at Lexington, Kentucky. It had a picture and a short note saying she was enrolled in medical school and was married to a doctor, she also made a note for me to look on the back of the picture.

It read, "Thanks for the last fling, had a great time, I'm a better woman because of it."

She had a little smiley face on it. I read the letter over a couple of times and tore it, and the picture up and threw them away. I'm sure it was her way of telling me not to try and find her. She knew that I knew where she lived and it was time for me to get out of the military.

Chapter 14

SEATTLE: OH WHAT A TOWN!

The summer of 1956 was over too soon for me. Carol went back to Long Island and I was assigned to Fort Lewis, Washington. We kept in touch for a while but dropped it in a few months. I was receiving love letters from Carol and Nancy, one white and one black, and it kept a smile on my face. I learned from Carol that summer you must fight the system in any form you can. I later learned she was arrested and jailed on one of the freedom rides into Alabama in the 1960s. I often wish I had the spunk and guts she had. For a long time whenever I did something I considered passing, my mind always went back to Carol and the back seat of the red and white Chevy convertible and the fact she would have disapproved of me passing.

When I got to Fort Lewis, Washington, I was assigned to a training unit as a cadre. We had a few weeks before the trainees came in and this gave me some spare time in the evening. I enrolled in school in Tacoma, Washington to get my high school diploma. Finishing high school was one thing Mother made me promise her I would do, in return, she wouldn't tell the army I was under-age and have them put me out. Going to school was the best thing I could have done. I met a lot of people from all over the Northwest, including girls. Meeting girls gave me a chance to practice what Carol, Ethel and Nancy had taught me over the summer. Going to school was altogether different than it had been in South Carolina. The class with all its colors and ethnic groups looked like the United Nations.

I again became the all-American white boy there. I lived totally as a white person for the time I was there and life became a lot easier. I dated only white or Indian girls and decided to stay away from black friends. Every time I tried to be black, it always ended in disaster and I had to go through the whole problem of rejection again. I decided to be nothing but white forever, and all my racial problems disappeared. I even became an Elvis fan. Every time I would hear one of the blues songs from the little hole-in-the-wall joint at Ritter, my mind would always go back to Carol, Ethel, Nancy, and the summer of 1956.

I did what most young men do at the age of seventeen: I worked all day at the post, went to school at night, and drove the fifty miles to Seattle. We would drag ourselves back to the post around three in the morning. I remember one week I had gotten only about five hours of sleep in bed for the whole week.

One morning the first sergeant called me in and asked,

"Did you get into any trouble in the past week or months?" I couldn't think of anything, and told him, "Not that I know about."

He told me the regimental commander wanted to see me.

I asked him "What for?"

"I have no idea, they didn't tell me. The sergeant major sent a memo saying the regimental commander wanted to see you at ten o'clock this morning."

All sorts of thoughts began to run through my mind. The first sergeant and I spent some time trying to figure out why the colonel wanted to see me. I wondered why didn't he send the information down through the chain of command? I didn't think the age thing would make a difference at this late date. I had recently applied for a secret clearance and my next thought was, "It must be the race thing." The first sergeant was as curious as I was. He checked my haircut, and found I had missed a spot while shaving. He asked me "Do you have a clean Class "A" uniform?" I assured him I did.

While driving to Regimental Headquarters, I got stuck in traffic and had more time to think than I needed. I thought to myself, "Now what, just when I was getting my life together, the race thing was coming up again." When I got to Regimental Headquarters and reported to the sergeant major, his first question was,

"Why does the CO (commanding officer) want to see you?"

It was my turn to say, "I have no idea."

I sat down and waited until the sergeant major motioned for me to come with him. Still very scared, I reported to the colonel and gave him my best salute. When the sergeant major left the room, the colonel told me to have a seat. Seems as if he let me sit there and sweat as long as he could.

Finally he took a letter from a drawer, looked it over and asked me, "How do you and your mother get along?"

I told him "fine."

"What about the rest of your family?" Curiosity was killing me, and again I said, "fine."

The colonel got up from his chair, pointed his finger at me and asked, "Why in hell don't you write home?"

I thought, "All this for not writing home?"

Mother never heard from me after I boarded the plane for Fort Lewis. She was worried because she had recently buried one son and watched me board an airplane and hadn't heard from me in four months. Mother called the Red Cross and they told her if anything was wrong she would be notified. I really didn't think the local Red Cross chapter tried to locate me. Mother asked the VA Service Officer for help, and when he located me, he gave her the regimental headquarters phone number. As luck would have it, the colonel answered the phone, and the shit hit the fan for me. The colonel wasn't upset with Mother but he sure was with me for not writing home.

He told me, "Mothers get awfully worried and we create a lot of problems for a lot of people when they don't hear from us."

The colonel gave me a fatherly lecture on appreciating our mothers and dismissed me. When I got back to the company, the captain and the first sergeant were waiting for me with paper and pen. I was told to write a letter home every day for two weeks and give it to the first sergeant or the CQ (charge of quarters) to drop into the mailbox. After that incident, I made it a point to write home on regular basis. Now that my son is a military officer, I know how Mother felt, but I will never call his CO on him.

From staying out too late, not getting enough sleep and too much drinking, I began to get in trouble with the army. In the past I always tried to be the best soldier I could be. As a good soldier, I considered the restriction unacceptable conduct. I wasn't doing my duty and was restricted for two weeks, which probably saved my butt. What created the biggest problem was, the section I had in the training unit was about fifty percent Puerto Rican. They all claimed not to speak English when it was convenient. I just wasn't experienced enough to handle them. The first sergeant told me he had another soldier in another platoon that was well educated, was born in Brooklyn and spoke excellent Spanish. The first sergeant asked me if I wanted him transferred to my section.

When Receio came into the section he solved the language problem, but we kept detecting a fight breaking out within the group. For the life of me I could not figure out what the problem was. I even had Receio try and find out what was going on, but they wouldn't tell him either. They had quickly branded him as not being one of them. One day I over-heard them call this one guy "Smith," and the fight started. Receio and I figured it out at the same time. The one they called "Smith" was lighter in complexion than the others and had reddish straight hair. They were calling him the "Englishman." I had a good laugh about it for a while but later realized what Doncell was going through and I put an end to it.

Afterward, "Smith" and I became friends, until one day I called him "Smith" and he went racing off to the first sergeant and told him to, "Please inform me his name was Private Doncell and not Smith." The first sergeant never could figure out why he would get so upset over a simple thing as being called "Smith." I understood very well, and that night I apologized to Doncell and made sure I never did it again. I told the others if I ever heard it again I would send the person down to see the first sergeant. Receio knew how to get instant quietness, just walk in and start swinging. It always worked and I got off the First Sergeants dirty list. I only had to do a week of the restriction, and then it was back to Seattle and Tacoma.

After a couple of months at Fort Lewis, Newell Philbrick came into our unit. Philbrick grew up on his family ranch in Montana and was drafted into the army at twenty four-years old, which made him a few years older than most of us. We never let him live it down; neither did he let us live down the fact that we were "just kids." He was one of the most fun-loving people I had ever known.

We told him, "You cowboys only get to town once a month and when you do, you get wild, so you better take us along to make sure you can find your way back home."

I probably did more growing up around Philbrick that year than I had ever done before. Maybe it was just the age in my life or the fact that he was six years older than me. He became like a big brother. My ID card said that I was twenty-one but I never told him that I was only eighteen. If I had, he never would have taken me into town with him. There was just no way that I was going to let him call me a kid. He had a car, which gave us transportation into town. It also allowed us to go to the small towns away from Tacoma and Seattle and into the back roads where we found some very exciting little joints to hang out in. The back roads took us away from all of the regular GI hangouts, which gave me a chance to see how people lived away from South Carolina without the segregation problem. Passing wasn't legally necessary, because the law didn't apply here. I thought a lot about how different things were here than they were when I was growing up in South Carolina. Philbrick was white and my very best friend, but he never learned that I wasn't white until twenty years later, which I will explain in a later chapter.

The things we did in fifteen months can't be told, because now our wives would throw us out. One Saturday night this other guy from Montana came to visit Philbrick and we all went out. The two of them kept bragging about how the people from Montana could out drink anyone from all of the other states, and especially South Carolina. Like a fool, I took the bet. After about an hour we stopped at our regular Saturday nightspot. It was in one of the smaller towns away from the Post. They always had square dancing and Philbrick was an excellent square dancer, or he at least had the guts to get out on the floor and we didn't. He always managed to get me connected with a girl before it was time to go. I was still shy, didn't know how to dance, and I didn't inherit rhythm. I also hadn't had a lot of experience at meeting girls.

Before we got to the club, I drank about half of a fifth of a scotch, and should have stayed outside. When I got inside, I started pestering people. I wanted to dance with everyone that night, even the ones who didn't want to dance with me. The reserve cop who was always on duty was the biggest man I had ever seen. He must have been at least six feet six and all muscle, but very friendly.

He came over to me and said, "Don't you think that you have had enough fun for tonight?"

I sort of staggered back, looked up at him and said, "You overgrown son-of-a-bitch, who the hell do you think you are talking to?" This guy would make Paul Bunion look like a wimp. He didn't like it too well and started to unbuckle his club. Philbrick just happened to see the incident and came over and told the cop he would take me outside and not let me come back inside. He agreed, and they took me out to the car where I instantly passed out. When I woke up about five in the morning, they had been to a whorehouse. They spent all of their money, took my wallet, emptied it, and made a list of what each person took, and I slept through the whole thing. I will never bet on who can drink the most liquor again. They never let me live down the night the cop at the Old Mill was going to work me over. I still have fond memories of "The Old Mill" in Puyallup, Washington.

One of the girls I met in Tacoma was Native American and had grown up in Montana. Philbrick had a date one night and had dropped me off with Marla and her brothers. They were huge guys. We rode around and had something to eat, and were supposed to meet Philbrick at a service station at midnight. We got to the station about ten minutes early. We were sitting and wondering if Philbrick was going to make it there on time. Rob was saying, "Those cowboys never know when to come back when they get off the place." A couple minutes later, Philbrick came screeching into the station with a carload of guys right on his bumper. He slid to a stop; got out of his car and headed for our car with four guys right on his tail while his date was sitting there looking very scared. When Marla's two brothers and I got out of the car, the four people that were chasing Philbrick stopped dead in their tracks when they saw that he was with us. Seems that Philbrick's date had a boy friend that didn't believe in sharing. We followed him to take his date home and had a good laugh about it as we drove behind them. Marla summed it all up when she said; "I guess the Indians saved that cowboy's ass tonight." From then on, every time he would bring up the incident that happened at the Old Mill, I would bring up the time we saved his ass in Seattle.

One night while riding around in Tacoma, as a spur of the moment thing, we decided to take a leave and go to Montana. We both were flat broke but decided to go anyway. Early the next morning we went to the orderly room and put in for a ten-day leave. We had to get our clothes from the cleaners and couldn't leave on the day our leave was granted, and that night one of the cooks gave us a key to the mess hall. We went into the mess hall and took cold cuts, bread, and a quart of apple butter. We left Fort Lewis early the next morning and ran out of food around noon. We ate apple butter sandwiches for the rest of the trip. Even today I can't stand the smell of apple butter. When we had traveled for most of the morning, we remembered we hadn't given the key back to the cook. We didn't worry about it because all of the cooks had keys.

Philbrick lived about thirty miles from pavement. The gravel road was a series of hills and turns that he took at speeds I felt would surly put us over a cliff before we reached the ranch. About halfway to the house I managed to catch my breath, and told him, "I now realized why cowboys only go to town on Saturday night, and usually only once a month in the summer time. We got to the ranch at two o'clock in the morning and were all out of apple butter sandwiches.

We were there for about eight days and found we didn't have enough time for him to help his father get the hay in. We called the CO back at Fort Lewis and got an extension on our leaves. That weekend we went into town for the Saturday night fling and started out about three in the afternoon. We went into Rosebud, had something to eat and started doing the bars, or I suppose I should use the singular form, because the town only had one bar that I saw. At nine, I was beginning to get drunk. It seemed everyone was buying me a round but they weren't having as many, I felt obligated to be sociable and drink all of them. Philbrick left me with a "Real good friend" of his and took off with a girl he hadn't seen in some time. I soon realized that he had set me up for the worst drunk of my life. I decided to play along with the game and went into the rest room and threw it all up, and came back almost sober.

After a few more drinks the bartender called me over and told me they were trying to put one over on me. I told him I had figured it out by now and that explained my frequent trips to the restroom. He gave me some sort of concoction that was supposed to keep me from getting drunk, and told me he was going to make mine light. The joke was now turned around. When the drinks came, I popped them down all at once and pushed my glass down the bar and waited for it to be filled again. Once the woman behind the bar gave me one that was full strength, I popped it down and it almost stretched me out. The bartender saw the look on my face and looked at me as to say, "Someone slipped on that one." I headed to the John and got rid of it before it had a chance to settle. Around midnight, the bartender and I were the only sober people in the place. They had all given up and decided to tie one on themselves. The whole crew decided to come out to the ranch for breakfast as soon as the bar closed. Philbrick and I went out to make preparation for their coming. We got to the ranch about two in the morning and waited outside while his mother did the work that we were supposed to be doing. We were hoping they wouldn't show up. About three in the morning, I saw a line of cars that seemed to reach back to the pavement. When everyone got there, we all went inside and Philbrick's mother made breakfast for everyone. After we had eaten, they told me about the joke and how it had failed, and they thought I could drink with the best of them. I never told them any different. A man came up to me and said, "Let's drink to that, and I agreed. He took a half-pint bottle from his pocket and poured me a shot. I don't know until today what it was, but it was lights out for the rest of the night. I slept until around noon and woke up without even a headache, but everyone else was sick enough to die.

Philbrick traded his car while in Montana and I enjoyed the return trip to Tacoma. We traveled during daylight hours and I had a chance to see the Northwest for the first time. We drove the trip East at night and I didn't see much of the countryside. Eastern Washington at that time was mostly two-lane road, and it seemed to be all one large wheat field. We never said much to each other on the way back. I was totally overtaken by the vastness of the countryside. We traveled for what seemed hours without seeing anything except an occasional passing car. The combines kept the ball of dust going as they labored in the enormous wheat fields to get the crop in before the rains came. The radio in the new car was excellent, and we listened to pop music of the fifties all through the state. We often looked at the speedometer and found it to be on speeds approaching one hundred miles per hour. I did a lot of day dreaming on the trip. I would get out of the army, move to Eastern Washington and find work on one of the wheat farms with all of its open spaces and where people were few and far in between. I told myself I would never return to the South. I had all but forgotten about segregation until I began to feel the freedom of the open country and how good it was to feel really free. But times like that always reminded me that I could never really feel free as long as I had a family that couldn't ride the front seat of the little ragged bus as it crossed the bridge to Seaside. I am sure Philbrick did a lot of thinking on that trip also. We usually ran our mouths constantly when we were together; even he was over taken by the vastness of the countryside.

Philbrick was the first white person I would trust enough to accept as a friend. The trip back to Fort Lewis was one of the most peaceful moments of my life. I again renewed my decision to remain a person, not just a white person or a black person, but a simple member of the universe. I thought about telling Philbrick about the whole race thing, but decided against it. I thought about all the problems that it had created when anyone found out before. I asked myself, why bring it up when life was just becoming livable? I had never in our friendship heard him use the word "nigger" or refer to a black person in a negative way. I thought, "Why destroy a good friendship," a thought that I kept for twenty years. We got back to the post at night, and were dog-tired from the trip. We went to bed and stayed in for the next couple of days to get ready for an inspection. When it was over, we went back on the town again.

After we had been back in the company for a week, an up-roar started about a key to the mess hall being missing. We didn't say anything; neither did the cook that had given us the key. We all pretended we didn't know anything about it, even to each other. One day when the company was in the chow line, the famous first sergeant came into the mess hall and said, "I know some of you have a key to the mess hall. If the person who has it comes forward and give it up, we wont do anything about it." Philbrick and I were standing in line together, and wouldn't dare look at each other. Nobody said they had the key, and the first sergeant started the search. I didn't know if Philbrick had the key on him or not but I couldn't stand it any longer and I looked at him; he opened his mouth and I saw the key. I thought I was going to faint from fear, but he remained very calm and put his hand to his mouth as to cough and took the key out. When the line moved up to the next flowerpot he forced it into the soil. We couldn't eat lunch that day. We both got our trays and sat down to eat, but after a few minutes, we dumped the food into the garbage. That evening at the formation, the first sergeant announced, "I'd like to thank whoever put the key in the flowerpot, however, if that person had another key made, I will find out." He never had to worry about that, because we both had learned a lesson. Even the cook who gave us the key was surprised when it turned up. He told us he never worried about it because he thought we had thrown it away. Philbrick, I hope it is safe to tell about this after more than fifty years.

The cop at the Old Mill had forgiven me and allowed me to come back inside. I sat down and started looking about the room to see if any girls looked available. As I searched the room, I saw a girl looking in my direction, the expression on her face said, "Why not ask me?" She was very quiet, alone, and appeared to be shy. I felt the same description because I had never learned to dance. I was afraid to move because the Paul Bunion cop was still keeping an eye on me. I finally got up enough nerve to walk over and talk to him. I let him know I had learned my lesson and was embarrassed about the whole thing. He took his eyes off me and started watching another potential troublemaker.

I crossed the room to where the girl was sitting. There was an empty chair, and I asked her if she was keeping it for someone. I was surprised when she smiled and said, "Yes, you." Susan and I sat together for about ten minutes not saying too much, just making small talk. We were watching the crowd wind up for what was going to be a long Saturday night. She told me she was from a small town in Northern Idaho. Her strict parents had never allowed her to go dancing, and she had never learned. I told her I didn't know how either but if she was willing we could give it a try. The crowd was getting large and the lights were turned down. No one would be able to see if we were dancing in "proper form" or not. Most of the people were wrapped up and doing something that resembled what we called a "slow drag" back at Seaside. We went on the floor and wrapped up like everyone else, and did a slow drag to country music.

Susan lived in Seattle, and was a secretary for a large overseas shipping firm. She had her own apartment, worked hard, and was very intelligent and forgiving. She was just a beautiful person. At first we started seeing each other only on weekends. After a few weeks, we wanted to see each other every night. Philbrick found a hot spot there also and started going almost every night. Again we went back to the old system of getting off work, heading for Seattle, and getting back to the Post around three in the morning. We usually stayed over in Seattle on weekends.

After one of our long weekend love making sessions, I asked Susan if she wanted to get married, and she said yes. I would get out of the army, go home and visit my family, a plan that I'm sure never materialized for a lot of young couples. Susan wanted to go to South Carolina with me, but I didn't know how she would react when she saw my family. We flew out to Spokane one weekend, and Susan's parents met us at the airport and took us to their home at Little River. We were there for three days and I fell in love with her parents and the town, very small, up in the mountains and very quiet. We decided we would move back to Little River to live when we got married. Susan was to stay in Seattle and work and I would go to Mississippi to a cousin that lived there and was passing. David, my cousin, told me I should be able to find a job at a new metal fabrication plant. We made plans to meet again at Little River and be married for Christmas. We spent a lot of time in the mountains. We went skinny dipping in the icy waters, and I thought I would never be able to have a sex life again. Susie was a person who just loved everything about nature. We picked berries, walked and talked a lot while we were there. Sometimes we would buy beer and take it as far as we could find roads that would take us up into the mountains. We often sat and drank a six-pack in a couple of hours and allowed the effects to wear off before we started back down the winding roads that would take us back into town. She never wanted her parents to know she drank beer. I often teased her about returning to the country and becoming a totally different person than the person I knew in Seattle. It was great to see a person in total charge of their direction in life.

We flew back to Seattle and I stayed at her apartment that night, and Philbrick picked me up the next day. I went back to the post and began to get strange feelings when I thought about getting married. I wasn't having thoughts about not getting married, but how would I support a wife. I had never had a decent civilian job, and didn't know if I could even hold one. My biggest fear was, Susan was white and I had never told her that I was black or about my family background. That was really the only reason that I felt I had to go away after I got out of the army. I would write and explain it to her, and she would have time to think it over. If she still wanted to get married, it would be her decision. I was at a point where I wouldn't trust anyone, not even a woman that I wanted to marry.

Susan often said she felt there was something worrying me, and there were times when I would shut her out of my thoughts, and there were other times when I seemed to hate all people. I realized that it was all coming out after almost three years of passing. Now it was again becoming a problem. I never wanted to disown my family or even marry anyone who couldn't get along with them. I was also very aware of the pains that would come from rejection. Susan began talking about coming down south to live because she had grown up in cold country and would rather live down south. One day when we were out in the field and I had nothing to do, I sat around all day and decided to tell her that night. I made all sorts of plans on how I would tell her. I took the bus to Seattle on Friday night so I wouldn't have to be with Philbrick if everything went wrong. When I got to her apartment and she met me at the door, I knew I was never going to be able to tell her, at least not that night. She was dressed in a very thin gown that made her look totally inviting and her perfume just seemed to pull me into the room. She had prepared a special dinner of baked salmon for us, she said I seemed depressed lately and she wanted to cheer me up, and find out what was bothering me. At that time I never could have told her anything, and that night she really cheered me up. About three in the morning I woke up and she was already awake. I told her that I was getting out of the army in a few weeks, and I felt insecure about getting married and not having a job. She assured me that wouldn't be a problem, but after that night I knew I would never be able to tell her because I didn't want to go through the rejection.

I went back to the post that weekend more confused than I had been before. I was getting out of the army in a few weeks and didn't know what I was going to do, or where I would go. I didn't want to go back to South Carolina. I planned a year earlier to go and stay with David in Mississippi." David told me not to tell anybody about him, because he had never told his wife or children, and if they were to find out he was afraid that it would destroy his family or even get him lynched. My final choice was to remain in Seattle and get married but I really didn't want to get married until I felt more secure. Looking back, I was only eighteen years old and had done a hitch in the army, but how secure could I have felt at that time with all the decisions facing me. Philbrick left the company to go to Yucca Flats atomic bomb testing range. If I had another month to serve, I would have been sent there also. With Philbrick gone, rides to Seattle weren't as plentiful as they were before. Susan had a friend with a car and some of her girlfriends were going with guys at the post. They would get together and come out on some nights. I told her the trips were too much for her when she had to work the next day.

Finally I was sent down to the separation station to be processed for discharge. I still didn't have any idea where I would go or what I would do. I learned early in the army not to volunteer for anything. To keep busy while at the separation station, I volunteered to paint a fence that formed the parameter of the compound. I painted every crack and post-top. I dug dirt from around the bottom of the post and painted underground, but time still seemed to drag along. We couldn't leave the area while we were in separation. I wanted to get to Seattle one minute, and the next minute I didn't. After the third day Susan came to the post and found me. She spent most of the night out there with me but I never could bring myself around to tell her my situation. That night we said our good-byes and still made plans to get married in December, and Susan still wanted to come down south to live, which aggravated the problem even more. She was in favor of my coming south and finding a job and getting settled. Coming south was the most frightening thing for me, but staying in Seattle made me feel too insecure. In 1957, it just wasn't thought of for a wife to work and pay the bills and the husband to be unemployed.

Chapter 15

THE DREADED RETURN TO THE SOUTH

I was discharged the next morning and didn't know what I would do or where I would go. A white guy in our company who I had known since basic training was getting discharged the same day. We talked about traveling together on the way back to South Carolina and keeping in touch. I said okay but really didn't mean it. When I met him at the airport, he asked for a ticket to Charleston, South Carolina. I made up my mind and asked for a one-way ticket to Jackson, Mississippi. I told him I would visit my cousin in Jackson and we would drive to South Carolina. When his flight was ready to leave, we shook hands and he said, "Look me up when you get there." I agreed, but that was the end of our relationship. He sent me a Christmas card from North Carolina but I never answered it. Now I wish I could get in touch with him. We came in the army the same day, went through basic together, were in the same company in Alaska, and were sent to Fort Lewis at the same time. His serial number was only one digit lower than mine. Because of my fear of rejection, I dumped a lot of very good friends over the years.

When I arrived in Atlanta the segregation sign didn't bother me for the first time in my life. It didn't bother me when the black people were sent to the "colored" area. By now I had begun to feel totally white. I was somewhat surprised to find the signs didn't bother me. It had been three years since I had spent a lot of time under the segregation laws, and there weren't as many signs outside of the southern states. For a while I even felt superior or at least more fortunate than the average black person. I felt above all the black people who had to obey the "Colored only" signs. I stayed over in Atlanta for three hours and decided if I were going to live in the South, especially Mississippi, I would have to be all white and never think about the black plight. I had made my decision and was going to stick with it, no matter what.

When I got to Jackson the signs were more obvious than in Atlanta; they were everywhere. I told myself, this was the South and I must live with it. I would only be here for a few months, and I would be gone. They could work it out the best they could, and it was no concern of mine. Sometimes I felt they deserved each other.

David and his wife met me at the airport and took me to their home near Meridian. When I got there, I called Susan and she was still anxious to come down south to live. I told her, "I will look for a job tomorrow and maybe we won't have to wait until Christmas." We talked for about thirty minutes that night and I went to bed with a positive outlook for finding a job the next day. I lay awake for two hours and became more confused than when I was in Seattle. I was very lonely for Susan, and when I thought about being back in the South I got a sick feeling in my stomach.

I had enough money saved up to buy a car, or at least make a down payment. I needed the car to get around and look for a job. When I sat behind the wheel, my first thought was to start it up and head in the direction of Seattle. I couldn't have both, the car and the move to Seattle. Early the next morning David took me into Meridian to the apprentice school at the metal fabrication plant. They only took about two a day, and were only taking people for the welding school. They gave me a card and told me when my number was called, come into the office and they would start me on a machine. I went every day for a week and waited for my number to be called. By the end of the week I noticed the number didn't mean anything. If someone knew you, you were put in the school. I realized it was a waste of precious time and started looking elsewhere. I finally got a job on the freight docks of a trucking company. The pay was $125.00 per week, and in 1957 that was good. I was paid $140.00 per month while I was in the army. I was there for two weeks when the foreman told me he would have to let me go because I was non-union, and the union was on his back. I told him I would join the union because I wanted the job at whatever the cost.

"That won't work, even if you could get into the union, you would be the last person to be sent out."

I drew my pay and early the next morning I was out looking again. I spent three more days chasing leads from the employment office. Once I was sent out to a job to drive a laundry pick-up route. The driver had to be at least twenty-one years old. I had no problems because my driver's license said I was twenty-two. I showed the supervisor the license and he asked

"Are you married?"

I said "no"

"Our policy is to only hire married men."

No matter how I tried, he wouldn't give me the job. I was out at six the next morning and was in town at seven waiting at the door of a cabinet company where I had seen a "help wanted" sign in the window the day before. The owner was the first to get there.

He asked me, "Are you here about the job?" I told him I was if it was still available.

"If you waited at the door for an hour and a half, you deserved the job."

They turned two people away who came in about ten minutes later. The next day, they put me on the graveyard shift. (Midnight to eight o'clock) The company had about two hundred cabinets to build for a food store chain, and we had plenty of work. We had to cut plywood, nail and screw it together, then take it to another shop where we painted and completed the whole cabinet from a pattern. Building the cabinets wasn't a problem for me, just a lot of physical lifting because we had to get our own material from the warehouse. All of the other men who were there before me went in pairs to get material, but none offered to help me. I didn't need any help because I was in excellent physical condition and looked at the trips to the warehouse as a way to stay in shape.

There was only one black person there before I came. The guy was a wiz at building cabinets and he always kept to himself. He went to the warehouse alone to get material. He wasn't in very good physical condition and it usually took him a couple of hours to get his material set up, but still his production was ahead of most of the others.

I waited for him to go out to the warehouse one day and I went behind him. I asked him about he and I getting together when we came for material. I was surprised when I found a person could be so professional in their work and yet so humble in dealing with another human being, one who he thought was white. He said, "nosa," and I let it drop. I thought he just hated me for no reason except he thought I was white, and I had no problem relating to that. After a few meetings in the warehouse he would smile when we met in the morning. James told me he was the only person that started with the owner that was still there. On another trip to the warehouse, we met again. This time I was tired, and I'm sure he was also because we had been putting in a lot of overtime. He was stacking three quarter sheets of plywood on the dolly, when one of the white guys came in and told him,

"I need that thing."

He took the dolly, along with the plywood that James had struggled to get down from the stack that was well above his head. James seemed to take it as being all in a days work, but it angered the hell out of me. I had promised myself I wouldn't get involved in any racial incidents because I always came out the loser. James took another sheet of plywood from the stack and was struggling toward the shop when I came up behind him and took the tail of the load.

He looked at me and said, "I don't know where you come from suh, but if you want to stay outta trouble you better leave me alone. I been doing this for nigh on to thirty years, and it aint killed me yet, and it aint going to kill me now."

The foreman watched the incident and when James left, he came over to me and asked,

"You Yankee aint you, you talk like one. Are you from New York or some place?"

I told him I came there from Washington. It took a couple of minutes to explain to him I meant Washington State and not D.C. A crowd had gathered for break time and he felt he had to impress the others.

"Yankee boy, one thing you gotta learn, down here we let niggers do their own damn work and ours too. If you don't like that you better get your ass back up north."

It pissed me off to the max but I managed to keep quiet while the others all agreed with him, and James kept driving nails. He would pause between strokes of the hammer to get bits and pieces of what was being said. Somehow the hammer didn't have the almost perfect rhythm that it usually had. The next day I met James in the warehouse again. I asked him if he wanted me to help because the stack was again well above his head, he gave me a very short "no." After he had gotten the plywood down, he paused for a few seconds to catch his breath and told me,

"You aint helping me by stirring up all that mess, that is just how things are down here, so don't bother me anymore."

I didn't get angry with him but was saddened when I realized I was creating a bigger problem than the one he already had. I would never be able to solve the racial problems by a simple humanitarian gesture as helping him with a sheet of plywood. James never stopped speaking to me. After that it was always, "monin suh," At least he wasn't angry with me, I kept my greeting to a simple "mornin."

The foreman and I stayed in some sort of argument after the incident in the warehouse. I knew sooner or later I would have to leave the job or fight him, or both. I asked to be transferred to the middle shift. When I got to work that afternoon he also had asked to get on the same shift and was there with a nasty smirk on his face. I needed to work but I realized they were getting me in the same position they had James.

One night the foreman told some of the other workers, "Nigger lover over there want to go back to days"

That was about all I wanted to take from him, but there were too many of them and I knew they would join in to help him. Not out of loyalty or they liked him, but to kiss his butt to keep their job. I retaliated in the old Seaside phrase that always started a fight, "your mother," only I added "loves niggers also." I really used another word for love. It took me about two seconds to realize I probably shouldn't have told that white boy that in Mississippi. The place got really quiet and I geared up for the fight. I kept my eyes on a short piece of oak two by two on the table. The owner came in and we let it drop for then. I wasn't afraid of the whole bunch whipping my behind because if there was one thing I had learned at Seaside and being in the army, was how to fight and also to take an ass whipping when I had to. I would at least let them know they had been in a damn good fight. I also learned to give it all I had with whatever means available. I started to leave right then but it was Friday night and payday. I decided to stick it out for the rest of the shift and get my pay and then leave. I told myself I was getting awfully tired of Mississippi anyway. After break that night everything seemed to be going smooth, too smooth. I went to the warehouse to get material as usual and was getting plywood from the stack when James came up to me and told me quietly but very quickly, "They talkin about beatin you up tonight"

I started to leave then but I figured it would be at midnight when we got off. I wanted my pay, which we usually got at the eight o'clock lunch break, but most of all, I wanted to get that little wimp of a foreman alone before I left. I wanted to put the ass kicking of the century on him. I decided to take my chances and wait until after the pay envelopes were given out. On Friday nights, all of the crew would leave the shop to eat out, except the foreman. He always stayed around to answer the phone or call someone. I knew he would make some little nasty remark when he gave me my envelope and that would be my cue to start it with him.

The envelopes were given out as usual, but I didn't get mine. I waited until all the others had gone. Even James left that night, and as I expected the foreman stayed. If he had given me my pay I would have left along with everyone else. I saw the envelope on the desk and realized the plan was to keep me there after work hours, and they would all get a piece of my behind.

I went into the office and told him I wanted my pay, he stood up from the desk and said,

"You'll get it when I'm damn well ready to give it to you. I would have fired you when you first came here but that damn Italian Yankee owner wouldn't let you go. He claimed we were short-handed."

I told him, "Your troubles are over, because I'm leaving as soon as you gave me my pay, and if you don't give it to me, I'm going to kick your little wormy ass and take it anyway."

He was about 5'7", and I doubted if he weighed 150 pounds.

"I would like to see you try!"

He came charging into me at 6'and 195 pounds and in top physical condition at nineteen years old. I met him head on with a fist in the face. I picked him up and slammed him into a pile of sticks and scrap lumber that fell down on top of him, and he never moved. I was disappointed when he didn't put up more of a fight than he did after all the mouth he had given me earlier. I picked up the envelope from the desk, yanked the phone cord from the wall and ran outside. I almost panicked when I remembered I had to boost the car's battery before I left for work that afternoon. I fumbled with the key as I tried to get it into the ignition. I finally got the key in and pressed the starter button, and the engine turned about a quarter of a turn and came alive. I sat there for another ten precious seconds and short-stroked the accelerator; I wanted to make sure the engine wouldn't die when I started to leave.

If they were to come back, I knew they would get together and there would be no telling what they would have in store for me. I wasn't too concerned about them calling the police, they would want to catch me and take care of me them-selves. I slowed down when I got near David's house. I slid to a stop and hid the car behind the house, left the engine running and went inside. I quickly told David I was leaving. As I grabbed what little belongings I had, I told him some of what happened. I stuffed everything in the duffel bag and threw it into the trunk of the car. I kept my voice down to just what it would take for David to understand what I was telling him. I didn't see any need to wake his wife up and have her ask a lot of questions and upset their lives. I could see panic coming into David's face. I slowed my packing long enough to assure him that they hadn't followed me and they had no way of connecting me to him. He pitched in and helped me finish packing,

I backed the car from behind the house, turned it around and threw gravel on the house as I floored it to get back into traffic. I wasn't worried about the group from work looking for me in Meridian. I had Mississippi tags on the car so they would think I lived somewhere around town and would look for me the next day. I had news for them; I was never going back to Mississippi.

I drove the fifteen miles to the Alabama state line with the flat-head Mercury engine wound out to the maximum. About four hours later I was crossing the Georgia line and had slowed down to the speed limit.

I finally figured out why everything seemed so quiet and reached for the radio. I played with the dial and I finally came across WLAC in Nashville and a homesick feeling came over me. The feeling was more than homesickness; it was also a feeling of freedom. Mississippi and Alabama had great blues and gospel stations and they always reminded me of home. For the short time I had been there I would never allow whites to catch me listening to the black stations. I was having enough trouble getting rid of what they considered my "Yankee accent." I listened to the black programs, but I did it with the windows rolled up very tight and always turned the radio off before opening the doors. After a couple of weeks I forgot about the black stations altogether and found another station.

As I drove along I began to realize what had happened to David. He had tried to totally erase his past. We had grown up together and were very close as young boys at Rice Patch, but now he was a total stranger. At first I considered it was that we both had grown up and had different interests, but as I got to know him again it was evident that he was trying to totally eradicate his past. Often I would talk about something that happened to us as children. He never wanted to talk about it. He found me listening to the local Sunday morning black gospel program and asked me to turn it off. That is when I realized that we would soon have to go our separate ways before I got him into serious trouble. Even though I had played the passing game for over three years, I had never played it with a wife and three kids in Mississippi. I had very little trouble understanding where he was coming from, because I had been there also.

David Kaiser, like me, grew up black. He went into the air force with another cousin that was somewhat darker than he was, and it was detrimental to both of them. The darker cousin had very little trouble while they both were stationed at Maxwell, but he couldn't reject a very close friend, cousin, classmate and just plain "homeboy" so he caught hell as well. He requested duty in Korea to relieve some of the tension. David also later served in Korea, when he came back to the states, they sent him back to Maxwell again. He simply told the air force he wanted out, and they honorably discharged him. When he got back to Maxwell he had already learned if he was to survive he had to pass for white. He married his Mississippi-born blond-haired and blue-eyed girlfriend, and they settled down to live as a southern white family.

Now that I had put Mississippi, Alabama and the complications of trying not to get David into trouble behind me, I began to feel better. I raised the volume on the radio and listened to the DJ as he blasted away with the blues. The blues and R&B had a powerful effect on blacks in the South. Most people my age often tell me they have had some great times in the back seat of a car while the DJ supplied the "Blues for the moods."

Even as I drove along I really didn't know where I was going. I had enough money with my week's pay and what I had saved when I was in the army to get back to Washington State. After a few minutes I decided to go to South Carolina and visit my family for a few days before going that far from home. I told myself it probably would be a long time before I got back to the east coast. As I drove along I thought about spending a couple of weeks doing odd jobs in Stockton. I could make more money for the trip. I also considered, "Where in hell would I find a job in Stockton that would pay me anything?" After an hour I had totally confused myself and still didn't know what to do.

About twenty minutes into Georgia, I picked up a cop on my tail. I was driving right on the speed limit and didn't give it much concern. After following me for about ten minutes, the cop put the red light on. In the distance I saw a light that I took for a service station. I put the turn signal on to indicate I was going to stop. I must have angered him because he started to honk the horn and never stopped until I was at the station. The building had a small light bulb over the front door. He walked up to the car and asked for driver's license and registration.

He looked them over and asked, "Do you know why I stopped you?" I told him that I didn't.

"Speeding," he said.

He put the light in my face to make sure that I didn't look drunk.

"Speeding hell, you were back there for over ten minutes and I would be a damn fool to speed knowing you were behind me."

I shut up when he said, "Just keep running your damn mouth boy and I'll close it for you."

I asked him as quietly as I could, as I didn't want to upset him "What's the fine?"

"Thirty-four fifty," he told me. (I just had to ask him what the fifty cents was for.)

He told me the fine was thirty-two dollars and I had a two-fifty night hazard. As the red light on his patrol car came around at regular snappy intervals, I kept getting glimpses of his face and I could see I had probably pissed him off. As I got more glimpses of his face I could see he had a wad of tobacco in his jaw, from which he had allowed the juice to run down his chin and it had dried into a nasty looking crust. His stomach resembled a large pouch in front of him that covered his belt buckle by at least four inches. He wore his pistol in a sagging manner and he kept pulling it up along with his pants. His shirttail was about half out and it made the task of keeping his pants up even harder. After he told me to shut up, I started saying "yasa and nosa" to him, and he stopped punishing the wad of tobacco and the evil in his face began to disappear. He now kept almost perfect rhythm with the chewing on the tobacco and the flop, flop, flop of the windshield wipers on the patrol car. The wipers made a screeching noise as they kept up the losing battle of keeping the windshield clear of the rain that had been with us for the past ten miles. He wore no hat, and the steady light rain had wet his hair and it had begun to fall down into his face in a black and gray mass. The rain had also begun to melt the crust that the tobacco juice made. He set the scene perfectly by leaving only the parking lights, windshield wiper and the flashing red light, brought me to the very eve of vertigo. Couple that with his twisted tobacco stained teeth, he was one hideous looking sight in the dark of the night as the red light flashed around and around. He was almost humorous, but I was in no mood for jokes after the past twelve hours.

He told me if I didn't pay the fine he would have to lock me up. I looked at my watch and saw it was after two in the morning. The rain had now started coming down in sheets, and the thought of driving the early morning shift through the rainstorm was more than I cared to think about. I needed a place to sleep for the rest of the night because I was getting awfully tired from working the night shift and driving since about nine that evening.

I shrugged my shoulders and told him, "I don't see how I can afford to pay you thirty-five dollars and get a room at a hotel also, so I guess you will have to lock me up."

I also seriously doubted the existence of a place in town to sleep except the jail or in the car. I knew for sure he wouldn't allow me sleep in the car in his town. That turned out to be my first and last time in jail ever.

He told me to turn around and follow him to the jail. As I put the car in gear to get turned around, he told me, "Now don't try any smart-ass trick like trying to run away from me. He tapped the hood of his car, smiled, and said, "There ain't no car around here that can get away from this Ford."

I assured him I would be right behind him. I followed him to one of the County's finest jails at Salem Georgia. When I got to the courthouse, I pulled into the first available parking space and turned the engine and lights off. The deputy got out of his car and came over to me; the water was now topping his shoes but it never seemed to bother him.

He yelled over the sound of the spattering rain, "You can't park there, that's' official parking only!"

I tried to restart the car but the battery had finally died, and when I pressed the starter button all I got was the rapid clicking sound of the solenoid. I told myself if the deputy wanted the car moved tonight, he would have to do it himself. The worse he could do was to lock me up, and he was doing that already. I got out of the car, and while dodging the ankle deep puddles; I made a hundred-yard dash to the door of the courthouse. The rain never seemed to bother the deputy or he was just too heavy to run, as he didn't even try to dodge the puddles. When he finally got inside, he was soaked, making him look even sloppier than he had earlier. I headed to the lighted area of the courthouse where I found a dry version of the one who was following me. This one was friendlier than the one bringing me in.

When I walked into the office he looked at me in my half-soaked state and put a grin on his face. "Come in the house and pull up a dry chair," he told me.

The deputy that brought me in entered the room with a sour look on his face.

"Write him up for speeding, sixty in a fifty-five mile zone, and then lock him up."

The one who was in the building when I came in was the jailor.

He told me, "Empty your pockets on the table so I can see what you are carrying around with you."

When I put my wallet on the table he thumbed it open and saw the stack of bills, and said, "If I were you I wouldn't take all of that money in there with me."

The deputy that brought me in found new strength to get angry with me all over again when he counted out three hundred and sixty dollars.

"Boy you mean to tell me you have all that there money and won't pay your fine?" On the advice of the jailor, I decided to check my wallet into the office safe, along with my three hundred and sixty dollars.

The jail was in a separate building behind the courthouse. The deputy told me the jail had a buzzer that I could signal if I needed him. When I saw the inside of the jail I almost decided to pay my fine right then. After listening to the rain still coming down in buckets and thinking of the dead battery in the Mercury, I decided to stay the night. There were no bunks in the place, just a lot of mattresses in piles. I pulled the top mattress back on one of the piles and found a layer of bed bugs. The deeper I dug into the pile the more bed bugs I found. The jail had no toilet; what was left of the toilet bowl was over in the corner smashed into little pieces as if some disgruntled inmate must have decided to take his frustrations out on it. Where the toilet once sat was a four-inch drain with a piece of plywood over it. Everyone relieved himself in the hole and it didn't have any water to it. The whole building was about twenty-five by twenty-five feet. There was a cage in the middle of the room; inside the cage was an older man who looked to be in his late fifties and black. He was sitting on the bare concrete floor without any cover. Inside the cage was a bucket with a top for him to relieve himself into. There must have been at least twenty army surplus blankets scattered around the room.

I asked him "Why don't you take some of these blankets and make a bed for yourself? Why sleep on the floor with all the blankets lying around?"

I began pushing blankets through the bars to him but he told me "They won't let me sleep on them."

I asked him, "Why not sleep on them tonight and put them out in the morning?"

There was a young white boy in jail, and even he agreed to let him sleep on the blankets for the night. We pushed about five blankets into him but he wouldn't use them.

I finally sat in a corner and was just about to go to sleep when the jailor came back to check on us.

When he saw the blankets in the cage, he asked "Who put dem blankets in there with that damn nigger?"

All fingers pointed to me and I said, "I did."

He yelled to me, "If you don't want to get in there with that nigger, you better get dem damn blankets outa there."

I told the man "You better give them back." Again I realized I was only making things worse for him, and I would be gone tomorrow; the whole thing was probably embarrassing to him.

When I saw the man in the cage sleeping on the cement floor, I lost the desire to sleep. I thought about the jailer allowing me to use the mattress and blankets, but wouldn't allow him to sleep on them. The white boy, Jason, was talking a mile a minute. I asked him what was he in there for.

"Speeding."

"How much time did you get for speeding?"

"Sixty days"

I asked, "Damn, in here?"

"You think that's bad, old Sam in there is doing six months."

After the jailor refused to allow the older man to sleep on the blankets, I couldn't sleep on them either. I couldn't allow myself to feel superior to him. I walked around the cage a few times and thought, "What a hell of a way to treat another human being." I finally sat in a corner on the concrete floor and tried to sleep.

Before the jailor left he said," I'll turn the lights off when I leave."

The only light we now had was a dim night-light over the door. I never gave any thought to his turning the lights off until later when the young boy said, "I sure wish I had asked the jailor for some water before he went home."

I never realized when he left there wouldn't be anyone to take his place. I asked the boy, "Are you saying there isn't anyone in the office, suppose someone get sick?"

He shrugged his shoulders and said in his slow southern drawl, "Tough shit I suppose."

With the lights off it became even creepier than before. I was just about to nod off when the man in the cage was turning over; he must have had a lot of pain. I could hear the moans and groins as he tried to find a comfortable spot to get some relief. I don't think he ever found a good spot. Throughout the night I could hear his moans. I caught catnaps and tried to find peace within. I woke up about four o'clock when he was trying to turn over again. He said in a low and pleading voice, "God please help me." Neither God nor anyone else came to his aid that night, not even the jailor. I sat there and try as I might I couldn't go to sleep. I came to the conclusion that I could never become a white person. The price was just too much to pay. The time I spent in Alabama, Mississippi, and Georgia was some of the best therapy I ever had. Some might say it was the worst, including my psychiatrist, and I still disagree with her. Sometime that morning, I also had stretched out on the cement floor; even at my young age, I was very painful when I stood up.

The next morning, the deputy brought breakfast and a bucket of water. He opened the cage for the man to empty his bucket and to pour the five gallons of water down the drain. Breakfast was a slab of half cooked salt pork and grits with pork grease for gravy. The food was in a tin pan that was rusting around the edges and a galvanized spoon to eat it with. That's when I realized I had better pay the fine and get out of there. I also realized that it had been almost twenty hours since I had eaten anything, but my stomach was still saying no to the deputy's breakfast. I asked Jason if he wanted mine because his had disappeared as soon as it was given to him. I told him, "I just don't have an appetite for breakfast this morning." As he inhaled what had been my breakfast he smiled and said, "By God you'll eat it if you stay in here long enough." He sat the pan down and came over to where I was sitting on the pile of mattresses.

"Got a cigarette?" he asked in his slow whining accent.

I took my pack out and shook one out to him. He took it and turned toward the man in the cage in anticipation of the light he knew would be waiting for him.

"Sam in there ran out of cigarettes fore I did, but I had to share with him to get mine lit. That fat-ass jailor never would give me any matches, said I might burn the place down. Now how in hell can anyone burn down cement and iron bars?"

The boy was talking so much he was beginning to get on my nerves until I realized he probably needed someone to talk to. Sam hadn't said anything since the jailor locked me up the night before.

"Betcha we have chicken for dinner tomorrow; we always get chicken on Sunday."

I soon realized he had probably been in there for a while. I asked him, "How long have you been in jail?"

He took another long drag on the cigarette as if to try and suck the whole thing down his throat. As he spoke, a never-ending series of smoke rings came from his mouth in little choppy puffs.

"I have been in here for thirty days, that stinking judge gave me sixty. I have 'bout thirty more to do. That was the second time that fat ass deputy caught me. He never would have caught me this time, cept'n I ran out of gas. That's your Merc out there? What kind of mill you got in it?"

"Just a stock flat-head," I told him,

"What you need in that thing is a rocket eighty-eight engine. My brother got one in a fifty Ford and there ain't a thing in this county that can catch him."

Thoughts of who would I bet on in a race between the boy's brother and the Deputy ran through my head.

I smiled when I said, "No wonder the judge gave you sixty days."

"Can I have another one of your cigarettes?"

I took the pack out and shook another one out for him, and this time Sam took one also.

I started to put the pack back into my pocket but changed my mind and motioned for him to keep it. He and Sam had become friends or as close as were allowed. I was surprised when he split the twelve remaining cigarettes evenly with the black man.

"What the hell did Sam do to get six months, screw the judge's wife?"

Neither one of them thought that was very funny; no matter how the boy hated the judge he didn't like anyone making that kind of remark about a white woman. I am sure Sam knew better than to openly admit it was funny. I never did learn what Sam was doing time for. After another ten minutes of listening to the boy talk, I soon realized why Sam never said anything. To get the young boy started, a person would have to listen to him for the rest of the day.

I finally pressed the buzzer and the jailor came to the door and asked, "What's up, podna?"

"How much time will I have to do if I don't pay the thirty four- fifty?"

He hesitated for a few seconds to make sure that I was listening. He turned to me with a smile on his face and said,

"Thirty days."

I had considered doing a week rather than getting up off my hard earned thirty-five dollars. I could put some badly needed tires on the car for that much. I had nowhere to go and had all day to get there, When I was in jail in Georgia, only five people in the world knew where I was: me, the two deputies, the black man in the cage, and Jason. For a brief moment I considered the jail to be a good place to get lost. I sure as hell wasn't going back to Mississippi, and I had a lot of negative thoughts about going home to Stockton where I would become a victim of the system I left three years earlier. I felt as if I were on my way back to square one. I had just spent three years in an army infantry unit, so the jail wasn't the worst place I had slept in the past three years.

When the jailor said thirty days, I had a change of heart and told him I was ready to pay the fine.

He looked at me, spit tobacco juice on the floor and said, "I figured you would sooner or later. We have our ways to make sure you pay."

On the way to the courthouse he backed away and held his nose in a mock gesture that I didn't smell too good, and said, "I guess we can at least offer you a shower for your money."

I am sure it was very obvious I needed one. When we got inside, he gave me an old shirt for a towel and pointed down the hall to the shower. I went out to the car and dug out clean clothes. The shower would at least have hot water, and I was beginning to not be able to stand myself. I turned the hot water up as hot as I could stand it to try and kill off the bed bugs and hoped I wasn't covered with cooties. I examined myself and didn't see any.

I was surprised to find all of my money still in my wallet after what the deputy said about having ways to make sure I paid the fine. Even today I tell myself that was a dumb thing to do. Some jailors probably would have shot me for a lot less than three hundred dollars at that time, especially if he knew I was black.

I threw the new blue jeans along with shorts and T-shirt into the trashcan that was outside the bathroom door. I hoped somehow they would infest the whole town with bed bugs. I slipped into the khaki pants without underwear and put on a fatigue shirt that still had corporal stripes on it. I washed my tennis shoes while I was in the shower, and when I came out of the bathroom I had them in my hand and was bare footed.

I stopped by the jailor's office and asked him if he would give me a boost to help get the car started.

"I can't use the county's car to boost you; it's against the law. The service station won't open until nine. The best thing for you to do is buy a battery from the Western Auto store when it opens."

As bad as I hated to admit it, he was right. I just wanted to get the hell out of his town. I borrowed his knife to take the stripes off the fatigue shirt after he told me, "If you are out of the army, you aint supposed to keep dem stripes on your shirt." He also was a corporal.

It was about eight-thirty when I went outside to sit on a park bench and wait for the Western Auto store to open. I could see the sign about two blocks down the deserted street. After sitting there for a few minutes, I decided I should at least try and see if the car would start. I ran over to the car, got in and pressed the button. This time I didn't even get the clicking sound. The waiting no longer seamed unnecessary or a waste of time. I sat on the bench and tried to relax in the quietness of the morning. A few people began to move around when the time got closer to nine, but I saw no one at the door of the Western Auto store. Merchants were now out front cranking their awnings in place in preparation for the heat that would soon be upon us. I started the slow walk down to the Western Auto store about five minutes before the hour.

The quietness was broken by a sound that I had heard many times as I grew up at Rice Patch, the sound of a mule drawn wagon. I was surprised to see a mule-drawn wagon in town in 1957. As the wagon drew closer I could see its occupants were black, a middle-aged man with a new pair of bib overalls and a white shirt was the driver. Behind him sat what I took for his wife and seven children. As he approached each one of the merchants, he, his wife and children all bowed their heads and went through the motions of tipping their hats. The merchants all gave the same response in a voice that was too loud for the quietness that was about us, "Good morning John." They all sounded as paternalistic as your grandmother would when you came to see her at age five. The mule was well fed and was slick as glass. The wagon was an almost new Wagoneer, which I recognized as being one of the higher priced ones when I was growing up at Rice Patch. His family was well dressed in good clothing that looked well pressed and spotless. The merchants would respect him as long as he didn't show any sign of moving up to their level.

The man was probably in a lot better financial condition than a lot of them were. I remembered a lot of other families at Rice Patch having the same problem. Even when a man worked his butt off to make a better life for himself and his family, he had to appear poverty stricken or the next time he went to the bank for a loan, his credit wouldn't be any good. The man in the wagon knew the rules and accepted them as a way of life, and would do anything to keep them happy. The system was devastating to the black society, for we had to kiss ass every time that we needed anything that the whites were in control of. The whites had the money, and they were in control of everything. The wagon probably cost almost as much as a new Ford. If he ever needed to borrow money for the farm, the banker wouldn't pass up the chance to tell him, "You don't need that car." As long as he drove the wagon into town, and he, his wife and children waved just right, he would always have credit. In most cases he would also be required to pay a higher interest rate.

When I got to the Western Auto store, the owner wasn't there. I sat down on the sidewalk and waited. When the owner arrived ten minutes later, his shirt was already wet around the armpits from perspiration, and a spot covered most of the back of his shirt.

"Sure is hot," he said.

I made the proper response when I said, "Yep, sure is."

"What do you need?"

"A six volt battery."

"Let me get opened up and I'll be right with you."

He took the crank out for the awning and began to crank it in place. He was already out of breath from the walk to the store; I reached for the crank and finished putting up the awning. A radio had been left on in the store over night and I was able to listen to it while I waited for him to come down. The DJ's wife must have recently left him, because he alternated between Hank Williams and Kitty Wells with only their greatest tearjerkers. The owner finally got opened up and went behind the counter and asked,

"What kinda car you got?"

"1950 Mercury"

"You from around here?"

"No, just passing through, I spent the night in your county jail."

"Probably said you were speeding."

"Yeah, how did you guess?"

"That fat ass Harvey is going to give this town a bad name, he stops every out of state car that comes through here. Are you from out of state?"

Again I asked him, "How did you guess?"

"You got money left to pay for a battery?"

"Yeah, they left me a little bit, felt sorry for me."

"They don't usually leave you with very much. I have a battery that's guaranteed for twenty-four months and one that is guaranteed for thirty-six month, which one do you want?"

"The one that costs less,"

"The twenty-four month one is fifteen dollars, you got that much?"

I took my wallet out and paid him for the battery, he took it out to another man who had now come in to work.

"I'll let Robert take it back to the court house and put it in for two dollars." "Sold", I told him, and gave him two more dollars. On the way to the courthouse, to make conversation with the man I said,

"Man that jail is one filthy place."

The man looked at me with a snarl on his face.

"You shouldn't do anything to get locked up fer, keep your ass outa trouble and you won't have to be put in thare. I ain't ever been in trouble myself."

I kept my mouth shut until he had finished putting the battery in. I was glad when he didn't have to boost it.

I left the courthouse about ten thirty that morning. I wanted to get out of town as quickly as possible so I didn't try to find a place to eat. I also made sure I didn't speed. About ten minutes down the road I looked in the rear view mirror and there he was, right behind me with a disgusting grin on his face. I thought for sure he was going to stop me and get another piece of the three hundred dollars he knew I had. He followed me until I came to a county line sign. I was relieved when he waved to me and turned around.

I drove until about four o'clock in the afternoon. When I reached Savannah, I realized I wasn't going to make it home without getting something to eat. I drove to the bus station restaurant and decided I had better use the white side for the last time for a while. My next stop would be Stockton, and home, where a lot of people knew me. I had enough dealings with the police to last for a few days. After eating, I went outside and sat in the car for about an hour. I really didn't want to go back to Stockton, but it suddenly occurred to me I didn't have anywhere else to go. I found myself thinking about all of the problems I had with the police at Stockton. I felt I was back to square one and would have to swallow a lot of pride. I also thought of the Island, away from the crowds and it's slow pace of life, after all, it was home. I would be there for a few weeks and I would be on my way back to Seattle. I had some mustering-out pay coming, and with what I had, I would take a chance on starting somewhere else.

I took my slow time in driving the last leg of the trip home. I stopped a lot and thought about what I would do when I got to the Island, none of it sounded very pleasing. I got home that evening around six o'clock and was ready for bed shortly after. I decided to take it easy for a few days and do nothing. I slept until around ten the next morning. When I woke up, I felt the security of home around me and began to relax for the first time in three years.

Chapter 16

BACK TO SQUARE ONE

As the days passed at home, I found I didn't want to leave the house for anything. I was content in staying inside with all of the doors closed. I seldom bothered to crank the car. I had lost all desire to go to the movies or into town. I didn't want to take the step backward to going around to the back door at the theater again where I would have to tell them "I'm colored." I wrote Susan often, and every time I got a letter from her it depressed me even more. She always talked about joining me down south but I knew now the only way we were going to get married was for me to go back to Seattle. I sat down and wrote her a letter that explained the whole thing to her. I told her if she wanted to call it off, I would understand. I got a letter from her in a few days saying, no matter what my family background was it didn't make any difference to her.

She wrote, "You should have known better than to go back down south in the beginning."

She wished I had told her all about it before I left Seattle. Also, it had taken a load off her mind because she knew there was something bothering me and no matter how hard she had tried, I would never let her inside of my thoughts. She asked me if I wanted her to send money for the trip to Seattle, but it would have to be my decision. I don't know why, but I never answered her letter. I didn't want to screw up her mind the way mine was at the time.

I finally went out and bought a pint of good Scotch and drank it all that evening. I was as sick as a dog the next morning, but I had done some serious thinking the night before. I made up my mind to stay home for a while and find a job because Mother was out of work at the time and she needed some assistance. I would help her until she went back to work at the navel base and I could also save some money to leave again. I went out to find a job in Stockton. I went to the employment office to apply for compensation. At that time it was given to veterans as an adjustment to civilian life. Mine was $26.00 (about $125.00 in today's monetary conversion) per week, which wasn't very much even for 1957.

When I filled out the application, it had the ever-present race block. In South Carolina, I was required to put colored or N for Negro. The person's attitude changed entirely when he looked at my application.

"We don't have any work around here for you. Why did you come back to Stockton? You probably won't like the wages here."

I really didn't expect to find a job in Stockton but I did want the compensation, I filled out the job application and gave it to him. He took it and saw the wages I had made in Alabama and Mississippi and asked again,

"Why the hell did you come back here?"

At that time I had begun to wonder the same thing. He looked through his files and I'm sure he came up with the crappiest thing he could find. He finally pulled a card and gave it to me. I didn't know if he was trying to see if I could read or was ashamed to tell me what it was. I took the card and read where some family wanted someone to plant grass in their yard. I wanted to do something, and he was totally shocked when I told him I would take it.

I went out to the house and met the wife of the family. She showed me what she wanted done and where to get the grass. The area was a new development, and the people who bought the homes were doing their own lawns. When I got through with the first house, the whole neighborhood wanted theirs done also. They all agreed not to tell the people at the employment office and I became self-employed for the rest of the fall. I enjoyed the work because

I had no boss and I was able to set the wages. I used my car to bring grass from the Island and bought tools to chop the soil, and drew the twenty-six dollars also.

The army kept writing and reminding me that I had some reserve time to do and it seemed as if they weren't going to let up. I went to Charleston and checked into it. The person on duty told me I was supposed to have been there three months ago. He assigned me to a unit and gave me a lecture about not missing any meetings, and if I did they would send me back to active duty. I came back to the Island and tried to find someone to share a ride with. All of the people I asked said they would be going on Thursday night. My information said I was required to be there on Tuesday night. I would have it changed to Thursday at the next meeting. It just didn't make sense for me to drive the fifty miles alone when they had two cars from the Island going on another night.

When I got to the meeting that night, I asked the sergeant if I could get mine changed to another night. He said, "This is the only meeting night for whites. The niggers meet on Thursday."

I could not believe what I heard, and it totally surprised even me. This was the army reserve we were talking about, not the local social fish fry.

I sat through that meeting and decided it would be my last. I was telling one of my friends from the Island what happened. He always came up with a joke about anything racial and said,

"I always wondered what happened to all of those white dudes that got out of the army. I thought they only made us attend the meetings so they could keep an eye on us." He almost rolled in the sand from laughing at my predicament.

"Man you better not ever go on the rifle range with them, they might find you out and use you for target practice. You should go and spy for us."

I told him no thanks, and decided not to go to any more meetings no matter how much the army wrote me. If they pressed it, I would tell them to integrate it and I would attend. Six months later they wrote me and said that I was only on standby reserve and wouldn't have to attend any more meetings. I was sort of disappointed. I wanted them to raise hell with me about it. I asked a man that was going in the late 60s; he told me that it was still segregated. It was illegal to have a by-racial militia in South Carolina. I'm sure that it was illegal in all of the Southern states, and a lot of others as well. During the segregation era South Carolina didn't allow blacks to join the National Guard. A lot of white men took advantage of the law and joined the guard and were very often exempt from active service. As in most cases, that was another great injustice to black men, a double whammy.

When it was too late in the season to plant grass, I began to feel the need to find another job or "hustle." Whatever the hustle would be, it would have to be as close to self-employment as possible. Being away from Stockton for so long, I really didn't think I was ready for the type of job or supervision I would get in town.

One morning while having one of our many bull sessions while sitting under our favorite oak tree, an older man was trying to borrow money from someone in the crowd to buy an outboard motor for his boat. He wanted to start crabbing to make some money for Christmas. The weather was still warm enough, and if he worked fast he could pay the money back before Christmas. He said that he couldn't borrow the money from the bank or a loan company because he didn't have a job. The only work he had ever done was working the river, crabbing, picking oysters or shrimping. He finally got around to asking me. I'm sure he thought I was the last person who would lend it to him because I was fairly new to the Island and he didn't know me. I knew him to be a hard worker so I asked him if he would be willing to take on a partner, one who didn't know anything about crabbing. He said he would, but didn't think I was serious. As we talked, he found out I was serious and most of all, I had the money we needed to buy the motor. I went into town and bought a good used outboard motor and we formed a partnership. He told me what I would have to do and the equipment that we would need to get started. Seemed that the boat and motor weren't the only thing we needed. We soon put together all the equipment that we would need.

In 1957, the crab trap had either not been invented or at least had not found its way to Seaside. We used the old method that had been around for generations. We bought a fifteen hundred foot line that we tied pieces of fresh salted cowhide or "bull nose" to. We laid the line out in the water, waited for about an hour, and rowed the boat backward while the other man used a net to take the crabs off. The operation was repeated all day, depending on the tide. We caught a barrel or sometimes up to three barrels. We then took the line with the bait up and went home. After four or five days of using the same bait, it really began to smell. The crabs didn't really begin to bite until about the fourth day when maggots got into it, and after a few more days even the crabs couldn't stand it. We took it off and started over again with fresh bait. The smell would stay in your hands for days, and no matter what you put in the wash, your clothes always came out smelling like "bull nose."

The freedom of the river and not having a boss was worth any hardship the bull nose might have presented. Like any other business, the buyer always had the upper hand. The company we sold to also sold the bait, line, or anything we needed. They also sold the gas for the outboard motor. We sold the crabs for a nickel per pound. The line cost a cent per foot but it would last the whole season, and even at that we managed to show a small profit. I was still getting the $26.00, so we struggled through that winter and the spring of 1958.

The guy at the employment office always came up with a new way to put me through the third degree. After a few weeks I became just as much of a hard ass as he was. My argument was, "You give me a job that I can live on or keep that measly twenty-six dollars coming." They always tried to send me out on some yard job for a day to rake leaves to keep me from getting the check. For a measly twenty-six dollars a week, he tried every rule in the book on me. He constantly sent whites out on good jobs. He also found work for other blacks, but he either didn't know how to classify me as a working person or wanted me out of Stockton altogether. He often let me know by asking me the same old question, "Why did you come back here anyway?" The worst thing about the whole question was I didn't have an answer for him. One morning he sent me out to a job at a radiator shop. I got there about nine o'clock and the owner asked me if I could use a torch. I told him I could, and he told me I was hired. I had long learned to ask about the pay before hiring on with anyone because it could be full of surprises in South Carolina. I asked him what the job was going to pay. He stuttered around for a while and didn't want to tell me.

"Let me see how much you know and then I can tell you how much I can pay you."

I insisted that he give me some idea on what kind of pay I could expect before I got started. Finally he told me that if I wasn't afraid of work he could start me off at fifteen dollars a week. I told him I wasn't afraid of any work and I could lie down beside it and go to sleep at that price.

I went back to the office and told them the pay wasn't enough, and there was no way in hell I could afford to work for that kind of wage even if I was willing to. He said,

"We have a lot of people doing it now, but you think that you are above those other people out there on that Island. You either take the job or we will have the check cut off."

As we were talking, the man from the radiator shop called and they had a discussion about me not taking the job. They were discussing ways to get even with me. When he got off the phone he told me to wait a few minutes until he talked to his supervisor and find out what to do about me not taking the job. I somehow got the feeling that it was all a set-up to keep me from getting the compensation check. The clerk came from the back office in about ten minutes and all the people who he had the big meeting of the minds with, were with him. The one that I took for the big boss was about six foot four and well built. He was chosen spokesman for the group, and he wasted no time in getting to the point. He started in by saying,

"In using the guidelines of the Compensation to Veterans Readjustment Act is, if at anytime you refused to take a job it would be grounds for termination of the compensation."

At first I even tried to reason with them about why I should work for fifteen dollars a week when I'm getting twenty-six anyway. At that time in my life I had become the world's biggest nonconformist. He told me, according to the guidelines I was supposed to work for that and they would pay me the eleven dollars to make up the difference.

I asked him, "Why not have me work for the guy at the radiator shop for nothing while the Government paid me the twenty-six dollars."

His face turned to the color of a beet, He said, "I'm tired of you talking back to me."

For a while I thought he was coming from behind the counter after me. I had my hand in my coat pocket on my "bull nose" cutting buck knife and it was as sharp as a razor. I'm sure I would have gutted him if he had made the mistake of trying to punch me in the face. Fortunately for both of us, he controlled his gestures. He told me he would give me one more chance to keep it from being cut off if I went and took the job at the radiator shop.

I told him "Go to hell, my last job paid me $125 dollars a week and I would be a damn fool to work for fifteen. Let's stop kidding, if at any time you can come up with a good job with good pay I'll be very happy to take it. The army gave me a copy of the guidelines for getting the check when I was discharged, and in the future all I want to do is come into the office and sign the form and leave, so I can look elsewhere for work."

Mother was having about the same problems with them. I told them, the next time mother came in, she wasn't going to take any maids job because she was going back to civil service in two months. I told him, "Mother has earned every cent that she is having to kiss your behinds to get, and if it wasn't for people being unemployed you would have to go out and rake leaves yourself.

He was as angry as a wild bull in a cage, but he remained behind the counter, and I kept my hand on the knife. I thought he was going to have my check turned off, and I really didn't care. He turned the color of a beet again and threw the pen on the desk but didn't say anything. I signed the form and left the office. The next week the $26.00 came in the mail as usual. I went to the office and took Mother with me, only this time a clerk shoved the forms and a pen to us. We signed the forms and Mother looked at me, winked and we went home. I caught the next tide and went into the river to get two barrels of crabs. That was my last trip to any state employment office. I didn't have the ability to work for anyone, and never did acquire it.

Chapter 17

MY "BLACK" ARMY TIME

When I first came back to Seaside from Mississippi, and not answering Susan's letter, I was in a state of depression. I hated almost everyone and stayed inside with a case of flu that I just didn't seem to be able to get rid off. My sister Rose was living at home also and she had a friend who kept coming over from next door, she was very attractive and didn't seem to be offended by my unkempt ways. I seldom shaved and had let my hair grow really long, mostly because getting a haircut was always a big problem at Seaside. It was in the same mode as trying to figure out which john to use. I finally gave up and grew a DA (ducks ass) style. Linda, the girl from next door, kept coming over every evening. She and Rose talked and giggled, as young girls did. After a couple of weeks I started joining in the conversation, and when I finally got over the flu I found myself making sure I would be there when it was time for her to come over. After another week of waiting for her to come over, I started going over to their house with Rose to watch television. Linda suggested a haircut and I found a black barber and got a haircut and a shave and looked like a totally different person. I became a friend of her brother, and that gave me an even better reason for going over. After a few weeks, Linda and I became really close. She would tease me a lot and of course I ate it all up. When I came in from the river I always stopped by her house. If she didn't see me she would come over to our house, supposedly to visit my sister Rose, but I knew better. We became very close, and by Christmas we were going together.

Linda was a senior in high school, and her mother finally allowed her to go out with me. We were very happy just riding around the Island and talking to each other for hours at a time. We spent almost all of our free time together, and I began to come out of my "shell," as she referred to my withdrawn ways. When I first started going with Linda, I had a lot of things to sort out in my life. I was at a stage where I didn't trust anyone. Having just gotten out of the army, tried living in Mississippi, and converting back to black society, I developed a complete hatred of the white man. I had tasted the ideas of freedom, but it had a lot of strings attached. The system wasn't any different than it was in South Carolina. I had just gotten over a time in my life where I had almost forgotten I had grown up as a black person. It only took Mister Jim Crow a very short time to remind me how cruel it could be, and I didn't want to be a part of it. I was having a lot problems adjusting back to the segregated south.

Linda stuck with me through my adjustment period and helped me get through a lot of mentally depressing times; she is still my life support system after fifty years of marriage.

We were both very happy in the spring of 1958. Linda was getting out of high school and we were dating. I noticed her mother had begun to give me the cold-shoulder treatment. One afternoon I asked Linda if I had done something to make her angry with me. She explained that her mother was beginning to fear for her life when she was riding around with me. I understood why she would be worried but it didn't help our situation any. We kept to the Island and away from town but nothing would ease the fears of her mother. One day Linda told me she was being sent to Boston. I knew why but I also knew it was going to tear us apart and I would never be able to stay at Seaside without her being there. We found that her mother wasn't going to give in and change her mind or get over her fears no matter how much we talked to her. I decided to take another hitch in the army and would leave the same day that Linda left to go to Boston. There were no decent jobs to be found in Stockton. I felt the town had won again. I imagined the smile on the face of the clerk at the employment office when he heard the good news. In June 1958 I had a new engine installed in the Mercury and drove to Fort Ord, California.

This time I decided to do the army hitch my way. The last time I didn't get a school and spent all of my time as an infantry machine gunner. Most important, when I filled out the application, this time when it came to the "race" block I wrote in "neg." I decided then that was all I would ever put in it. The recruiter caught it right away and asked,

"You sure you want to do that?"

"That is what the state of South Carolina said I am and I have no problems with it."

He put a strange look on his face and said, "It's your funeral."

At the time I resented him for saying what he did, but in the next three years, I often wondered if I had done the right thing.

I told the recruiter I wanted to be sent to the 6th Army Area. (West coast.) When I got out of mechanic school at Fort Ord, California. I was assigned to Fairchild Air Force Base near Spokane, Washington (in the army but on an Air Force Base.) I was only a few miles from Susan but decided to let it die. I was very lonely for Linda and couldn't sleep, eat or keep her out of my mind. Finally Rose heard from her. She sent Linda my address and she wrote and said she was having the same problems. We wrote each other every day for the next two weeks and decided to meet back at Seaside and get married. Her mother wasn't as afraid as she had been now that I was out of the South, and I'm sure my having a steady income had a lot to do with it. I took a short leave and came home. Mother had to get her marriage certificate to prove that I was Negro, because a birth certificate wasn't made when I was born. She went to the courthouse and got all the identification I would need to prove I was her son and Negro. The judge that married us really hated to do it, but it was legal. He insisted that I kiss Linda in his presence. I guess he just wanted to see what it would look like. I remember looking at him from the corner of my eye to get his reaction. I saw he didn't like it, so I decided to give him an eye-full. I slipped my hand down on Linda's behind and not letting go until I was sure he had all he could stand.

I was told I would probably be at Fairchild for only a few more weeks. We decided Linda would stay home until I had a more permanent assignment. I went back to Fairchild alone.

There was a rule in the army that you were allowed only one permanent change of station in any twelve-month period, but I had five that year. I would spend time at Fort Ord, Fairchild, McCord AFB, the Presidio at San Francisco, and finally Germany. I became the army's hot potato. My old records caught up with me at Fairchild and everyone noticed that they were different this time, and even now they had a lot of "Caucasian" spots in them and also a lot of "Neg" spots. To the army it probably didn't matter a hell of a lot but every personnel clerk was having a fit with it. I began to get the feeling that all of the commanders thought I was sent there to check their compliance policies, but most of all they were afraid some officer would use the "N" word in my presence. There solution was to ship me to someone else. From Fairchild AFB, I was sent to McCord AFB, and after about a month, the personnel clerk said I had to come in and sign some papers. I got out of formation and went to the office. When I got there, the CO and the personnel officer were there also, but the clerk did all of the talking.

He asked me, "Just what are you, colored or white?"

I told him Negro, and asked him if he would make me a new 201 file to reflect only Negro because it was getting to be a problem for the army. The next week I had orders to transfer to San Francisco. The CO had solved his problem. Instead of making me a new 201 file, the clerk just scratched through "Cau" and put "Neg" above it, which made matters worse, but it didn't really bother me. I considered it was the army's problem, and I left it alone.

While driving down to San Francisco, I had a flat tire and developed a hernia while changing it, and I would have to go into the hospital when I got to the Presidio. I didn't like the Idea of having the hernia but was glad I would have to go to the hospital. I didn't want to be operated on but after the surgery I wouldn't be sent overseas for at least six months. I hoped I would be able to remain in one unit and bring Linda out to San Francisco with me.

I checked into the unit at the Presidio and went to the hospital the next day. I was put on "no duty" status for a week until they had an available bed. While waiting for space at Letterman General Hospital, I found out I didn't want to stay there either. The CO was an absolute loser. He was a captain who had been passed over the maximum amount of times. I found out he was from Alabama and the first sergeant was from Mississippi.

The first day I was there, I was told, "Get your ass upstairs and into a Class "A" uniform, the company commander wants to see you NOW."

I changed into a neat uniform and went back to the orderly room and waited with what I must admit, a very poor attitude. He finally told me to come in and have a seat. He asked, "Why do I have to get all of the Germans in the army?"

I wouldn't dare tell him that I wasn't German. I had heard that one before and wasn't going to bite and have to explain my racial makeup to him. When I told him about having to go in the hospital for the hernia operation, He said,

"That's all I need, a unit with everyone on quarters."

I was assigned to 6th army headquarters maintenance shop to work on Diesel generators. I wouldn't be doing any work before the operation, and it would be a while before I returned to duty, but I drove to the shop everyday. I went in and met the maintenance sergeant and told him I had been assigned to his shop. I told him I was going into the hospital to have an operation and would be there for a while. The master sergeant told me he knew I was coming as the personnel sergeant had told him the week before. He then came right out and told me, it would be best if I just stayed there at the shop. Sergeant Jones suggested I stay away from the orderly room until after the operation and move off post as soon as possible. At first I didn't know what he was talking about, and I'm sure I looked puzzled. He then told me,

"They were going to send you straight overseas, but after surgery they can't send you anywhere for six months." Sergeant Jones told me he knew what I looked like before I came to the company. He told me to stay out of their way as much as possible. I thanked him and spent the next week with sergeant Jones, and doing paper work. He was a master sergeant who had been in for eighteen years and was black. He said that the personnel sergeant told him all about me, saying to him, "He is just here to cause trouble for us."

The personnel sergeant was also black. I went into the hospital on Monday morning and had the hernia repaired. I left the hospital on Friday and was given twenty days convalescent leave. I took the bus home to Seaside, and Linda. We decided as soon as I got back on duty and was able to drive that far, I would come back for her. With any luck at all I would be in the same place for some time. I caught a ride back to San Francisco with a friend from Seaside who was stationed at the Oakland navy base. I stayed in the barracks for the next month and met the personnel sergeant. The guy was the most insecure person I had ever seen. I was an embarrassment to him. He often hung around the gay bars in town, which partially explained why sergeant Jones didn't like him either. I made up my mind to put up with his little nasty remarks for the month because I wanted to move off post and the CO would have to approve it.

One thing about people not knowing that you aren't white is you can listen in on all sorts of little sneaky plans. I overheard the first sergeant tell a white sergeant that there was an E6 promotion coming down and he would get it and not, "That one in personnel." I laughed to myself when I heard what the first sergeant said. I had learned long ago not to carry messages because I always came out the loser. In most cases, it was just talk anyway.

One night I was in the shower when Brown, the personnel sergeant, came in and finally wanted to talk. He asked me, "Why did you come to this company?"

I asked him, "Why the hell did you come in it?" I came here for the same damn reason we are all here, because Uncle Sam sent us.

"He really did think I was sent there for some strange purpose. He said, "Man you know damn well you aint colored. I'm going to find a home for you" (overseas.) I told him, you can't find a damn thing for me for the next six months."

I just couldn't pass up the chance to tell him what I overheard, and I smeared it on heavy.

"You better find a home for your black ass while you are at it because they don't like you a damn bit better than they like me. The next SFC stripes are going to a certain white guy with far less time in grade than you.

If anybody knew information like that, the personnel sergeant would, I teasingly said,

"Just wait and see."

He wanted to swing at me, but he knew that was what I wanted him to do. Two weeks later the white sergeant put on SFC stripes, and Brown just knew I was a spy in their midst, or I could have never known that information before he did. I just had to take one more dig on him. One morning I sat and waited for him to come out of the mess hall. He was walking in my direction with an urge to kill look on his face. Just before he got to me I stood up and almost blocked the walkway. I smiled at him and said, "I told you so."

After a month, I put in for a leave to go home and get Linda and Vicki. I was never told whether the leave was approved or not. I went to Sergeant Jones and asked him to see if he could find out what was going on. He came back and told me they would only give me ten days and I wasn't allowed to drive that far on a ten-day leave. I would have to show the first sergeant an airline ticket before I could travel that far from San Francisco. I told Sgt. Jones to tell them I would take the ten days and let my family fly out to San Francisco, and I would stay around town. He cautioned me about traveling that far by private auto in that many days were against army regulations. I said, "yeah, I know," but that afternoon I went downtown and rented an apartment.

The next day my ten-day leave came through. Sergeant Jones brought the leave papers around noon. I was let off early from the shop, and I headed east. I suddenly realized that I only had sixty dollars in my wallet and had two worn tires, but I also had a new spare tire. I ran the numbers through my head and decided the sixty dollars would probably be enough if all went well. I kept telling myself if I needed money for anything I would have Linda wire some in a town ahead of me. For now, I just wanted to get as far away from the army post as I could. I drove all that night and everything was going smooth. The worn tires were showing no sign of giving out, so I kept driving.

Being away from the army gave me a new feeling of freedom. I drove all the next day. I stopped for gas, checked the tires and splurged a few dollars on a loaf of bread and some cold cuts. I rested for a couple of hours in east Texas, and started driving again about seven that night. I kept hearing about a storm heading east. Every time I stopped the rain would catch up with me and I would start driving again. I caught short naps in Louisiana but the rain kept pushing me. I stopped in eastern Louisiana and got some French coffee that looked like mud and chased two No-Doze pills with it and started the final leg home. At least the rain would keep the tires cool and cut down on the wear. The rain kept me pushing the Mercury as long as it and I could stand it. I got home about three o'clock Friday morning, just over forty-eight hours after I left San Francisco. I was very tired and the No-Doze and coffee had me too nervous to sleep. As I pulled the covers up and snuggled up to Linda, the rain came down in sheets. I snuggled closer and said, "Let it rain, I'm home."

I woke up around noon, checked my wallet and found I had two dollars left from the sixty I left San Francisco with. My gas receipts added up to fifty-four dollars. I went out that afternoon, put tires on the car and made preparations for the trip back. Linda was excited about going to San Francisco. This would be our first time away from home together. I stayed home an extra day to get as much rest as possible before we had to make the dreaded trip back.

We left home on Sunday morning about eight o'clock. All of Linda's family gathered around to see us off and I could still see the fear in her mother's face. We said our goodbyes on the bright and sunny morning. I was rested from the trip home and now the trip back to San Francisco didn't seem quite as impossible. We were enjoying the drive and I had plenty of time to get there. All we needed was a little luck and the Mercury staying together. We kept to the speed limit, especially in Georgia. I remembered what happened there before. I was now for the first time traveling with a wife and daughter and didn't want to put them through the hassle of me going to jail.

It was a new life for me to be traveling with a family; I was excited about us having a chance to be together. I would get off from work in the evenings and have someone to come home to. Our daughter Vicki was curled up in the back seat of the car seeming to be as happy as we were. I kept teasing her about having the most comfortable spot in the car and doing the most complaining. We had enough food to last for about two days. Linda's mother had made a lot of doughnuts. We fried chicken, and my mother baked cakes and pastries. They all gave us a happy send-off. We all knew that in 1959 places for blacks to eat on a trip were few and far between.

I was rested from the trip home but decided to look for a place to sleep when we got to Jackson, Mississippi. Before we left home someone had given us a copy of the "Negro Travelers Guide," (A small publication with a green cover that listed restaurants and lodging for the black motorist.) Because of its green cover it was often referred to as, "The green book" Linda had taken it out and found a listing in Jackson, and we planned our first stop. We stopped someone on the street and they gave us directions to the Jones Hotel. It was only about four blocks away. Now, I thought to myself, if they don't try to send me to the ones downtown I should be okay. When I went to the desk and asked if they had any vacancies, the clerk was very polite and asked how long we needed it for.

"Just for tonight," I told her.

"Do you want a crib for the baby?"

I said "yes," and went over to the area where they were stored, but the clerk said "Someone will bring it up and set it up for you." The service at the hotel was excellent, and that would be the last time we would find anyone who would allow us to stay at his or her hotel for the rest of the trip. We have always thought very highly of the Jones Hotel (The real name of the hotel) in Jackson, Mississippi; it was like a honeymoon for us, and the only place that would let us in for the duration of the trip.

We got an early start the next morning and were in Louisiana before noon. I checked the Green Book to find something hot to eat but found no listing. Linda opened up our food box and we ate donuts and chicken. When we finished eating, we washed it down with Nehi strawberry soda. Linda had just finished putting everything away and was feeding Vickie when I saw the state trooper pull in behind us. The trooper put the light and siren on and held it screaming until he drove us almost onto the sidewalk of Monroe, Louisiana. It seemed as if the whole town very quickly gathered to see what the siren was about.

The trooper came to the car and jerked the door open. I scrambled to get out before he would physically take me out. He slammed me against the car, patted me down, and began a never-ending series of questions.

"Where are you from boy? Who is that woman you have in the car with you?"

I told him she was my wife.

"What state were you married in?"

After about five minutes of screaming at me from only inches from my face, he finally got around to asking me for some identification. Whites were on one side of the street and blacks were on the other side. I looked in both directions to see if I could get support from either side, but I saw none. About half of either side had a grin on their faces. I also saw a lot of people who had a sad and inquiring look. I knew there wasn't anyone who would ask the state trooper why he was keeping me pined to the car for no apparent reason. Finally he allowed me to stand on my own and away from the car. I held my head down to avoid eye contact with him and to look as humble as I thought he would want me to. Looking humble was another one of my southern survival skills that I learned in earlier years; let them feel superior. I had to use all of them with the trooper. I finally got enough nerve to try and lead the conversation as much as I would be allowed to. I asked him if there was a military base in the area. The only military base I knew about in Louisiana was Fort Polk, and I didn't have the slightest idea where it was located. I thought to myself, "God let be just around the block or at least just outside of town." I wanted to get to some federal property and do it quick.

At this stage in my life I was used to and knew most of the answers to the questions and harassment to which I was subjected to, but this time it was serious. The trooper was a professional. He knew all of the many ways to make life as miserable as possible for blacks, the kind of law I had seen work before. I had been well trained by them to keep my mouth shut. They could mean real trouble, especially when you were away from home and no one knew you. I now had a family and didn't want them subjected to all of the harassment. I suppose the only thing that kept it from being worse was he directed all of his questions to me and allowed Linda to remain in the car. After about ten minutes he told me it was illegal for a white man and a "colored" woman to ride in the front seat of a car together. I told him I knew about the law and wasn't breaking it because I wasn't white. This had in the past calmed the situation, but I got the opposite reaction from the trooper because he didn't believe me.

"Let me see your damn driver's license."

I gave it to him and he saw it was from California and didn't have race on it. He looked at me and then at the description, and said,

"Boy, your eyes ain't brown, they look green to me."

I told him "The department in California wrote the information in and I had never really looked at it." That turned out to be the wrong answer. He gave me a lecture about "Checking behind those dumb-ass queers and cock suckers in California, they might put anything on it."

For the first time in a long time I was afraid. I decided I had better try to come up with something to get away from this town, this state, but most of all, this state trooper. If he took me away from the crowd there was no telling what he might do. Worse, if he kept me here, there was no telling what this crowd might force him to do. I very gently told him I was in the army and was going to be late if I didn't get on my way. I told him if he would let me get in touch with any military installation and sign in it would be okay. He thought for a moment and I could see I had probably won a stay. He asked me to see my leave papers. I had to dig them out of the trunk of the car and he seemed to be getting restless so I kept talking to him. I told him if I could get to a military base I could get my pay and pay any fine I had gotten.

I finally got my leave paper out and showed it to him. I told him I had a day of grace and started to explain the day of grace to him. That turned out to be the wrong thing to do. He pushed me back against the car and again got angry, and started shouting from about six inches from my face.

"I don't need you to tell me about any god-damn day of grace, I was in the Marine Corps in Korea and I know all about that bull shit."

He again allowed me stand away from the car, and he settled down. He didn't say anything for a while, which was more frightening than when he was screaming in my face. He seemed to believe me or just didn't know how to handle me now that he knew I was in the military and I wasn't white. I could tell he just didn't want any trouble with the military or the government in general. He finally let up and told me there was no fine, and to get back into the car. I very quickly put all of my belongings back into the trunk, making sure I left my leave papers out where I could get to them if I needed them again. I sat behind the wheel and was getting ready to crank the car when he held up his hand for me to wait. He came over and pointed to Linda and said,

"Make sure she sit over there by the door."

I'm sure he would have told me to have her get in the back seat but there was no space on the rear seat.

When I pulled away from the curb he pulled in behind me and followed for about ten miles. He pulled off when another cop took his place, and he followed me until another one relieved him. The relay went on all the way to the Texas border. As I drove along with the state troopers following me I was very afraid. I kept asking myself "When is it going to happen?" Each time I crossed a bridge or had a deep embankment off the side of the road I became more afraid than before. My feet and legs were shaking so much I could hardly control the pedals. I also felt ashamed and belittled in the presence of my wife. I knew I must look brave or Linda would start to panic. So far she had remained strong, I am sure to keep me from going into a panic. Once I saw a trooper coming from the opposite direction. As the trooper approached, I closed my eyes and waited for the sound of shots. I looked in the mirror and saw him turn around and replace the one who was following me.

I could tell the troopers who carried the most hate inside from the distance they would follow us. The ones with the most hate rode my bumper and I could see the expression on their faces. The troopers who stayed off my bumper kept a neutral expression. To them they were just doing the work of the State of Louisiana, and the Lord. I was relieved when I didn't see any Texas troopers waiting for me at the border. It was about four o'clock in the afternoon when we crossed into Texas. I was totally wiped out from a very bad case of fear, nerves, hunger, anger and fatigue.

I drove until about ten that night and couldn't make it any further. I pulled off the road and drove a few feet on what appeared to be an abandoned road. Later I woke up from the roar of a mile long freight train. The lights were shining straight through the car. At first I panicked; there wouldn't be time to move the car, and even if I did, I could very easily drive onto the track. I realized I had put the keys in my pocket when I went into the trunk for blankets. As the train approached, a very calm and peaceful feeling came over me. I realized if we were on the track, there wasn't anything I could do about it. I thought, "At least we all would be killed at the same time." I asked myself what had I led Linda and our daughter into. I should have left them at home. At least Linda wouldn't be left to raise our daughter alone. No more state troopers, no army to have to go back to, no more headaches when I needed to ride the bus or make up lies to keep the Klan off me. For the first and only time in my life I thought death would be better than life. I also thought about what my father's suicide had done to us as a family. The train finally roared past about fifty feet away. The peace remained with me for a few minutes but now it was different. I wanted to live more than I ever did before. Life seemed more precious than it had in the past. That night, on a lonely road in Texas, I promised myself I would never let anyone or anything drive me to that level again. I've had low and high points, but never again did I ever think that death would be better than life.

I began driving around six that morning. We dug through the food we had and didn't find anything we wanted for breakfast. After we had driven for about an hour I saw a sign that said "Breakfast, take it out or eat it here." I parked the car a block away and walked back to the restaurant. I ordered as much as I could on two plates and took it back to the car. That would be our last hot meal for the duration of the trip to San Francisco. The potatoes, sausage, eggs, and hot biscuits really hit the spot, even if I did have to swallow my pride to get it. We had baby food for Vicki and were able to keep it warm by putting it near the car's heater ducts. In the daytime we put the jar near the windshield where the sun would warm it.

We drove to Fort Worth and looked in the Green Book and found a listing for a restaurant and hotel combination. I found the place and their sign said barbeque ribs were their special. It looked very attractive and we could smell the aroma of the roasting meat as we drove into the parking lot. We went to the entrance and saw the doorman at the door. I didn't have the slightest idea there would be any trouble getting served. The doorman took one look at us and asked,

"Just where in hell do you think you are going? You know damn well we can't serve you in here; the police would be here in five minutes. They always come around anyway, and we have to give them sandwiches."

I tried to sound as "brother-like" as possible and told him

"Man I ain't white. You know damn well I wouldn't be traveling through Mississippi and Alabama with a black woman if I was white."

I asked him, "What about a room for tonight, or some sandwiches to take with us? We have been traveling for two days and all we want is some hot food, a shower and a place to sleep."

Other customers were gathering around and he ignored me. I knew better than to get into a shouting match with him, his job description probably spelled "B-o-u-n-c-e-r." Linda saw that I was getting angrier and angrier and she pulled on my sleeve and said, "Lets go." We stopped at a grocery store and got some bread and cold cuts and got the hell out of Fort Worth, Texas. We drove for an hour and parked near an abandon service station where we ate salami and cheese sandwiches and slept in the car. The barbecue sandwiches would have been better but we never had to kiss butt to get the salami and cheese.

The next day we drove to Amarillo and once more looked in the Green Book where we found that Amarillo had a listing. When I finally found it, I went inside and asked for a room. The woman said in a sleepy voice,

"You are in the wrong neighborhood man, you need to go downtown."

I told her I wasn't white; I just wanted a room for tonight and would be gone by six the next morning. I said, "Lady, I'm not trying to get you in any trouble. I have a wife and baby and have been driving all day. I'm very tired and all the hell I'm interested in right now is a place to sleep," but she wouldn't give in. I tried one more thing with her, saying, "The Green Book directed me here."

She said, "I don't know anything about any damn green book."

I really wanted to tell her to kiss off, but she kept one hand under the counter as she talked to me. I was sure she would have taken enough interest in me to call the cops or come up with a thirty-eight from behind the counter if she felt threatened. In disgust, I went back out to the car and looked in the book for the next place along our route and found that Amarillo had another listing. I spent another precious hour looking for it. When I finally found it, I was very disappointed to say the least. It was little more than a shack, but we were sleepy and it probably had hot water. This time we decided Linda would go inside. When she asked for a room, the woman said, "Yes we do." Linda came back to the car and we both started in with me carrying Vicki. When she saw me, the woman pitched a fit about not having any place for us.

"Them folks downtown would put me out of business first thing tomorrow morning if I let you stay here. When you married that white man you made your own bed, and now you must sleep in it. Just don't ask me to get in trouble for you."

As we were leaving, I took the Negro Travelers Guide and threw it out the window toward the steps. It had only been excess baggage for us since we left Mississippi. It would have served us better had we used it as toilet paper.

It was about two o'clock in the morning when we left Amarillo. I drove to a spot beside the highway where other cars were parked for the night and went to sleep right away. I almost froze but did manage to catch naps between Vicki's constantly waking up and the cold. I woke up about seven, and in spite of the night before I felt I could cover a lot of road that day.

We started out in flat country and I rested my heel on the Mercury's accelerator. It went flat out at eighty-five and stayed there for most of the day, and we made good time. At that stage we were ready for the trip to be over with. We only stopped for gas, picked up some cold cuts, and kept driving until about ten that night. That night we decided to stop and give it another night in the car. The Arizona night was cold so we took blankets from the trunk of the car and snuggled up in the front seat; even Vickie slept through the night. I woke up around seven o'clock and went to the public rest room at the far end of the rest stop, and my legs began to feel better. On the way back to the car I met Linda going to the rest room, we touched hands in passing and she gave me a little smile.

I told her, "Thank God this is the last day."

Even getting back to the army didn't sound too bad at the time. We left early that morning, anticipating San Francisco sometime that night, and again, I ran the car almost flat out. When we got to the Mojave Desert I put my heel on the accelerator again.

We were putting the incident with the Louisiana State Troopers, and not being able to find a hotel room that would accommodate us out of our minds. We were having fun just running our mouths with each other when we saw the, "Free Ice Water With Gas Fill Up" sign, and I pulled in for gas. The attendant put the nozzle in and started to pump, but when I asked him where the ice water was he told me,

"It's not for yaw'll, but if you are real thirsty you can get some from the stream out back."

I yanked the nozzle along with his hand away from the tank and told him to take the water from the stream and wash his filthy ass with it. He had put in a few gallons of gas and I wasn't going to pay him for it but Linda kept insisting.

She said, "Just go ahead and pay him and let's get away from here, because if you don't, that will give him the excuse he needs to have the cops pick us up."

I threw two dollars on the ground and left. I had enough gas to get to the next town where I filled up, took a short break, and settled my nerves as much as was possible.

We got to California's route 99 about three o'clock that afternoon, and I just couldn't go any farther. For the past ten days I had pushed myself to the limit and had to take a nap. We stopped at a roadside rest area and I instantly fell asleep. I slept for almost three hours and woke up feeling a lot better but this was going to put us in San Francisco late at night. I really didn't know where the apartment was because I had only been there once and was in a hurry. I had written the address down and went through the glove compartment and finally found it. We thought about staying on the road another night and going into the city in daylight. Even though I had the address, I didn't write the apartment number on my notes. We decided we had stayed too many nights on the road already and agreed that San Francisco would be our next stop. I would call in for an extra day of leave to get some rest before I went back to work. We started the final leg of our trip and got to San Francisco around midnight. I found the address but I was hesitant about going inside to find our apartment. I also discovered that the doors to the building were locked at night, and I didn't have a key. Just as I was about to give up and spend another night in the car, someone came out and I grabbed the door and went inside and up to the second floor. I tried the key in what I believed to be our apartment and the door came open. I found the light switch, turned it on, and home sweet home, we had made it. I left a set of fatigues there when I rented the apartment and was never in my life so glad to see them again. I knew better than to leave anything in the car overnight so we unloaded everything before going to bed. We got everything unloaded and into bed around two o'clock, and Vicky slept the entire time.

We enjoyed living in San Francisco. We were newly married and very happy with each other. In San Francisco we had very little, if any, resentment from the public. Linda found stores in the Fillmore district that had the meats and vegetables she was used to having back home. She even found collard greens that she was, and is still addicted to today. She seemed to enjoy preparing meals for her new family. I went to work at the shop and stayed away from the orderly room as sergeant Jones had suggested. I always looked forward to getting off and rushing home to Linda and Vicki.

We often visited Fisherman's Wharf, as we both loved seafood, especially crabs. Even the bull nose couldn't turn me against them. We spent most of our Saturday afternoons at the wharf eating crabs and just walking. We drove around and saw the whole San Francisco Bay area. Our apartment was very small but it was all we could afford on army pay. We had a small kitchen and a Murphy bed in what were a combination living room, bedroom, and a small bathroom. We both have a lot of fond memories from that little apartment at 1956 Post Street.

That trip totally changed my life; I was never able to completely put it behind me until later in life. I was able to put it in the back of my mind but there were times when it would resurface. I often dreamed about the trip, especially the incident with the Louisiana State Troopers and the car being stuck on the track and a train running into us. I became very hard and trusted very few people. Each time the trip resurfaced I would go into a hate-filled and depressed stage. I always tried to put it behind me as quickly as possible, and to keep my feelings from my family. After a number of sessions with a psychiatrist, I started to write and it slowly began to go away. Even today when I think about the idea that I could have been killed just for having my wife in the front seat of the car with me, I still get angry.

While at the Presidio, I got an infection and had up to ten boils on my buttocks at one time, and I had to go back to the hospital. I got rid of the first group and was about ready to return to duty when they came again. The doctors did allergy tests but couldn't come up with anything. They wouldn't let me out of the hospital to see if it was something at home or work that I was allergic to. The boils kept coming, and Linda couldn't come to the hospital to see me and I couldn't get out to see her. One night after all the staff had gone, one of the orderlies covered for me while I went home to Linda for a couple of hours. I only hoped what I had wasn't contagious but I felt I at least had to check on them. I had to kneel in the cab on the way to the apartment and I told the driver to pick me up in two hours. At first he wouldn't promise me, but when I told him what I was doing, he said he would be there in two hours. Linda was taking my not being there in stride and it made me feel a lot better. We both wished we had a telephone but also knew we couldn't afford one. When I came back downstairs the cab was there as the driver promised he would be. He only charged me half-fare for the trip back to the hospital. He told me he had been in the army once and knew what it was like. He had been off duty for over an hour and couldn't find anybody to come for me, but he had promised to come back. He dropped me off and wished me luck.

I checked back in with the orderly at the hospital and he said the night doctor had been there and asked for me. He told him I was out in the day room watching television. We both were scared because I wasn't supposed to leave the area. No one ever said anything to either of us, and the next day I figured the civilian doctor hadn't bothered to write it up.

The boils continued to come and the treatment began to get to me. The doctors wouldn't give me any painkillers because they thought it might spread the infection. Every morning they held me down, cut and pack the incisions with gauze so they could drain. I really didn't mind it because I would have put up with almost anything to get rid of the boils and out of the hospital. I ask them to stop holding me down, just to let me know when they were going to cut and I would lie still. The tall Korean doctor would always sit on my legs while one of the others cut. I never tried to move or fight the pain. The pain of the doctor sitting on my legs was a lot worst than the pain when they lanced the boil. Finally one morning they came around and the Korean doctor got ready to sit on my legs. I told him I would lie still if he would let me be, and if I were to fight, he wouldn't be able to hold me anyway. He got upset and sat on my legs as usual. I waited until they touched the boil with their hands and I flipped the doctor into the head of the bed and he got up with a nosebleed and fire in his eyes. They all looked at me and were trying to figure out what they should do about it but I stared right back with as much hatred as the Korean doctor had. I saw their officer's ranks, but I really didn't give a damn because every morning I had asked them not to hold me down. I could always say it was reflex, and I wanted to be kicked out anyway. At one time the Korean doctor wanted to tie me down but I was glad when another doctor told him, "Let's try it his way for a change." I bit into the pillow and the Korean doctor did the cutting that morning. I was determined not to move even when he shoved the wick as far as it would go and packed it again and we had no problems after that morning.

At one time the doctors thought I might have been getting the infections from the hernia operation. They did a lot of pushing and squeezing and didn't find anything. The major told me it was probably a case of nerves causing the boils, and they let me go as an outpatient. I went home and the boils began to go, and Linda took care of what did pop up with old home remedies. I went back on my regular appointments and they were relieved that Linda was taking care of me. They never did find out what caused the outbreak. The major asked me if there was anything worrying me. I said,

"The army, sir."

He laughed and said, "If that's the case, then I should be coming down with a very bad case of boils any day now."

One Monday morning Sgt. Jones told me,

"I guess they finally got you."

I didn't know what he was talking about until he showed me my orders for Germany. I looked at the orders to check the date. It was six months and one day from the day I had the hernia operation. That would be my fifth station change in twelve-months. I would have to make the drive back across country again. I was glad to get out of the unit at any cost. I decided I would start working on a way to get out of the army, even if it meant getting a dishonorable discharge. I wanted out and was fed up because it was costing me too much, not in dollars and cents but in mind and body. Even though they were giving me travel pay, it never would take care of everything.

Once again on a warm May morning in San Francisco, we loaded all of our belongings in the Mercury for the trip to South Carolina. This time we decided to take the northern route because we didn't get much of a kick on Route 66 on our way to San Francisco.

I was watching a documentary on television some years ago about a stretch of Route 66 being closed to make way for the Interstate system. I hate to sound like a spoilsport, but so be it. Along with the interstate system came motel chains and fast food restaurants that didn't discriminate. In South Carolina and throughout the South they all carried the "White Only" signs. Linda and I are both self-employed and understand and appreciate the small business concept, but we were glad to see the interstate system and the motel chains. The coming of the motel and fast food chains perpetuated the downfall of the local fleabag hotels and the white-only restaurants. In the past they turned a lot of business away because of race or color; somehow I can't sympathize with them. Often before the completion of an interstate system along a given route, a lot of small motels and restaurants would go up in flames. It's what is called here in the depressed shrimping industry, "friction fire." Friction between the mortgage company and the insurance company gets so hot it sets the building on fire. In other parts of the country the signs weren't always there, but the practice was very much alive throughout the country, yes, in your state too. In the South, at least you knew where you stood. In other parts of the country you sometimes assumed they just might accept you. Usually they very nastily told you that you couldn't sleep or eat there which made it even harder to accept. As it was with the gas station attendant in the Mojave Desert and the ice water, somehow I slipped and believed that California would be a little different.

We took US 50 out of Sacramento and headed east and had very little trouble traveling because now we didn't expect to find a place to stay over-night or anything to eat. We knew cold cuts and beans from cans would be the only things available. Vickie was now sleeping better at night and sleeping in the car for four days wouldn't be as bad as it had been in the colder month. We accepted sleeping in the car as the only method we had. With all of the conditions attached, we had a good time on the trip. I had a thirty-day delay in route from the army and we could take our time and see the country. Once we were refused gas in Missouri, but it had happened to us before and I wasn't surprised. I always started looking for gas when we got below half because that was a common thing to happen to blacks throughout the country. Somehow, you developed a sixth sense on which stations wouldn't sell gas to blacks and you avoided those stations.

My sister Rose was married to a soldier and her husband was stationed at Fort Campbell, Kentucky. We decided to spend a couple of days with them. I wanted to get into a shower and soak until all of the hot water was gone. We also needed to rest before we started the final leg home. We got to Fort Campbell around midnight, and even though it was a military base I was glad to see it. We called Rose earlier and she had a hot meal for us, and after a well needed shower, I sat down and ate like an animal.

The two days at Fort Campbell revived me to the point I felt I could make the trip to Seaside while stopping only for gas. I was well rested and had put the entire trip east behind me. I was also relaxed and in a good mood. I drove as fast as I could without getting picked up for speeding. Unlike the west, they enforced the speed limit in the East. All I would need to spoil a good day would be to get picked up for speeding.

When we got into South Carolina, I saw the old "Free ice water with fill-up" sign at an old country store. The store looked deserted, and I told Linda,

"Lets stop and see if it's for real."

Linda pleaded with me not to stop but I just couldn't pass up the chance to get even with he and the guy in the Mojave Desert. I had more than a half tank of gas, was almost home, and had been through it all in the past three months. I was sure there wasn't anything he could say that would anger me. I parked the car at the tank and laughed and joked with Linda until I was sure he saw us.

The old man finally came out and asked in a very paternalistic manner, "How much you want?"

I said "Fill'er up."

He turned the cranked to reset the pump and put the nozzle in the tank. Before he started to pump the gas I asked him

"Where is the ice water the sign said I could get with the fill up?"

He told me, "We don't have any for colored people."

He was almost polite when he said it as if I should know the rule, and he seemed surprised that I would ask.

"You can get some from the spigot over there by the hog shed if you want to."

I told him I had changed my mind and didn't want any gas. He yelled out and asked "Why did you get me out here boy, if you don't want any gas?"

I told him, "No ice water, no gas, it's just too hot to be bothered with just plain old spigot water." He started a roll of steady cursing and was still letting it out as I drove away.

We got home around ten o'clock that night and left everything in the car, and went straight to bed. The Mercury had taken us across country again.

I mention the Mercury here as I have before in the book, so here I suppose I should give it a favorable ending. I decided to sell it before I left for Germany. It was getting old and Linda didn't trust it anymore. It had well over two hundred thousand hard miles on it, and we decided to get what little money we could out of it. It had been as much a part of our lives as we were to each other. I had kicked it, sworn at it, and run it with my heel resting on its accelerator through most of the western states, and never once did it let us down. I still shudder when I realized how vulnerable we were while traveling across the Country in 1958. I don't want to think about all of the things that could of happened to us if the car had broken down in the middle of the night and on a deserted road in the South. At that time we never gave much thought to it. I never realized how ruthless people could be until we traveled together.

That was a new experience for us and we simply had no choice, as being in the military, I had to travel. Linda and I both have given a lot of thanks to God and our dedication to each other for keeping us safe during those days. We had used the car as a motel, living room, and restaurant in all of our travels, while it only asked for gas and tires, it always brought us home. The greatest feat it did was when it brought me across the Alabama state line that night in 1957. I sold the 1950 Mercury to a neighbor at Seaside, and two years later when I returned from Germany, it was still hanging on for dear life.

Chapter 18

GERMANY

When my leave was up I took a bus out of Stockton to Fort Dix New Jersey for overseas processing. Linda came down to the station to see me off at Stockton. I got on the bus and started to the rear, about halfway to the rear of the bus, I changed my mind and decided to sit anywhere I wanted to. I could see the smile on Linda's face as I sat down on the front seat.

While processing at Fort Dix I found I was one of a very few lower enlisted grades to have flight orders. I wandered if sergeant Brown had decided to do me a going away favor and hoped the plane would crash and burn. Whatever the reason, I was glad I didn't have to ride the ship again. While I was home on leave, Linda had talked me out of trying to get out of the army. At one time I had considered not reporting to Fort Dix and start working on a DD, (dishonorable discharge) but Linda reminded me of what it would do to me later. I was never known as a quitter, so I decided to give it my best for the next twenty-three months. I was going to stand up for myself a lot more than I had done before. If I couldn't remain in one company I was going to raise hell about it and they could throw me out. This was a bad attitude to have in the military to say the least, but I really didn't know what else to do.

When I got to Germany I was put on a train to Kaiserslautern. It was around three in the afternoon when I got to Kaiserslautern and no one was there to meet me as the sergeant in Frankfurt had promised. I told myself someone would be along shortly and I sat down at the bar in the train station to have a beer, then another and another. Around seven o'clock, I was loaded. I wasn't used to the liter bottle of German beer and it did a job on me in a hurry.

I couldn't speak German and nobody was there to pick me up. I tried to talk to the police but they probably saw me as another drunk American GI and didn't want to be bothered.

Around nine o'clock I was just beginning to feel a panic coming on when two MPs showed up on their rounds. I almost missed them as they were leaving but I ran after them and told them I needed transportation to my unit. The one in charge told me,

"Get your bags and hop in!"

I had never been so happy to see MPs in all of my life. When they came back inside with me to get my bags, they were talking with the German policeman and he was speaking English. I got into the back of the jeep and we headed out to my unit at Miesau. The driver floored the jeep after every stop in Kaiserslautern and made damn sure he hit every pothole in the city. The jerking of the jeep began to take its toll on my stomach. I finally tapped the one in the right seat on the shoulder and pointed to my bulging jaws, he instantly yelled for the driver to stop. I barely cleared the jeep before I spewed the beer beside the road. The two MPs thought it was funny that a newcomer to Germany had gotten involved with the German beer. They were more than happy they got me out of the jeep before I dumped it all on the floor. I felt a lot better after I threw most of the beer up, and to help matters, the driver eased up on the accelerator. I tried to stretch out and make myself as comfortable as possible in the crammed space in the back of the jeep. I tried to keep the khaki uniform as clean and wrinkle-free as possible. I never knew who would be at the company when I got there.

When I got to the company, the CQ (charge of quarters) woke the supply clerk up to get bedding for me. The supply clerk knew I was coming and had put bedding in his room earlier.

I attended formation the next morning and looked around to see if I recognized anyone from another unit. After formation

I went to the first sergeant and reported in. He told me my records were already there and the captain would see me shortly. I sat down to wait, and thought to myself, "Now what?" When I got in the CO's office I must admit I was in a very bad mood, but I also wanted to make a good impression. I stood there at a rigid position of attention until he returned my salute and told me to have a seat. I had been through a lot of company commanders lately and wanted to impress this one or at least get started on the right foot with him. I had lost a lot of respect for officers after the last two. I no longer respected or feared them as I did when I was in the infantry units.

Captain Garcia had a dark complexion, spoke with a heavy Cuban accent and was very professional when he talked to me. He welcomed me to his unit and suggested I enroll in another school while there. He asked me if I was going to bring my family over and if I were going to make the army a career. I told him I was undecided on both questions, even though I knew for sure I wasn't going to stay in the army any longer than I had to. Captain Garcia finally got around to asking me why I had been in so many units in the past year with out having any reason for transfer indicated.

"You must be very valuable for all of these units to want you," He told me.

I began to relax and decided to try and get it over with without getting into a long conversation or to make him think that I had a "problem."

I finally told him, "I was the army's hot potato, sir."

At first he didn't say anything, and I started to think maybe I said the wrong thing. After another minute of looking through my records, he looked up at me and said,

"I can see why," and his stiff face almost changed into a smile.

He never said anything else about my records. He asked me if I had any questions or problems. I told him I would like to remain in one unit as long as possible. He was still going through my record jacket when he told me he didn't see any reason why if I "soldiered" for him I couldn't remain in his unit for the next two years. He dismissed me but when I started out the door, he called me back. I turned around and answered, "Yes, sir?" He dropped the military look from his face as he said

"If at any time you have any problems in this unit, let me be the first to know."

I left his office with a new outlook, and decided to start soldiering again; the infantry units had taught me how to soldier, and most of the time I took a lot of pride in the military.

The next two years in Germany seemed the longest time in my life. I was married for less than a year and had been with my family for about three months when I was sent overseas. One of my biggest nightmares today is I am still in Germany and have two years to be away from my family. I have a lot of sympathy for the soldiers and their families of today when they have to be separated. I decided not to take Linda and Vicki to Germany with me. After three months, I settled down and decided to keep my record clean. I would take a leave and go home after the first year.

About a month after I came into the company, I was called into personnel. As I walked through the door and started getting all of the stares, I knew what the questions would be. The personnel clerk took my file out and called me over. He opened the file and pointed to the block that said "race" and asked, "Which?" I said Negro, and his next question was what I expected: "Why?" he asked me. I asked him "Why not?" but decided to keep our conversation professional military. He wasn't being rude about it. For the next week, in the back of my mind I expected to get orders to another unit, I was relieved when they never came.

What had happened to my records could be confusing to anyone seeing them for the first time, especially if the person was required to make a distinction of a person's race. If someone filled out a form on me while looking at me, or from their knowledge of what I looked like, they wrote in Cau. The forms that I personally filled out, I wrote in Neg, and the forms that someone found and corrected had a line drawn through Cau and Neg had been written in. The army required race be on all documents at that time, and mine had gotten pretty screwed up. Even our company roster had a column for Neg., Mongolian, and Cau. When the clerk at personnel looked at my records and the roster, he hadn't seen me. He looked at my file for the information and it blew his mind. Can you imagine how degrading it would have been considered to put Negro beside a white person's name? It could have destroyed the poor guy for life and they surely didn't want to "elevate" a black person to white status, so they called me in to find out.

At least they had given me the respect of calling me in and asking me about it. In previous companies, they would ship me out to another unit, where they also got confused and sent me in circles again. This time I insisted personnel make my whole record jacket over. There were things that just couldn't be made over, but as a whole we got it straight. I know by today's standards it is very hard, if not impossible to see why this was a problem. In 1959, the civilian and military forms had a place that asked for one's race. Maybe it was kept for statistical reasons, but I never could figure out why our company roster had to have a column that denoted our race. One night I was on CQ and was looking at the company roster and came across Tony's name. Tony spoke with a Spanish accent and was blacker than any other person in our company. I looked across to the race column and found he had Cau in the race column. I said to myself "No wonder the personnel sergeant had trouble figuring me out."

Even today, I challenge a white person to tell someone that is filling out a form on him to tell the clerk he is black. I know this to be true because it still happens to me. I recently filled out a form for my fishing and hunting license. I asked for the form because I wanted to fill it out myself. I often leave it blank because it's none of anyone's damn business what my race is. The retired marine, who thought he was still a drill instructor, insisted he had to fill out the form himself. He wrote white in the race block and threw it across the counter for me to sign. I threw it back to him and said

"You didn't fill it out right. Give me a new form, and I will fill it out myself."

I checked "black" in the race block, signed it, and gave him his copy and it really pissed him off. His face turned the color of an over-ripe strawberry and he was about to make some nasty remark until I held my hand in front of him and said,

"Don't go there with me," and he sucked it up.

If it had been the other way around, it would have ruined the average white guy's day. The belief is no one should want to, or admit to being black when he could be white. It is often taken as a rejection of the white society for me to admit that I am black. I still don't understand why South Carolina still has to have "race" on my fishing license.

My brother-in-law told me a good one about the old race confusion game. He was stationed in Korea for a year and was about to leave and be assigned to Fort Bragg North Carolina. He looked like the Filipino guys who he hung around with and had never gotten rid of his Gullah accent. When he went into personnel to get his records, the personnel sergeant tried to give him thirty days delay in route to go home to the Philippine Islands. He said he just couldn't figure it out because he had a leave coming when he got to Fort Bragg to get his family together, but this guy was trying to give him thirty more days. His Filipino buddies straightened him out when he got outside. Seems if you were Asian and stationed in

Japan or Korea and were being assigned stateside, you could get a thirty-day delay in route to visit your native country.

My brother-in-law said, "The nerve of that guy trying to send me to the Philippine Islands for thirty days after I had been away from my family for thirteen months."

He said he often used his Gullah accent to get into all sorts of places when he was stationed in the South, as they just couldn't figure him out.

In 1959, we had some minor racial incidents in our unit. Everyone was hoping they would soon go away, but they seemed to drag on. One day I found the root of the problem. This guy from West Virginia was always starting something between black and white soldiers. It was nothing you could really put your finger on or kick his behind for; he was just an agitator. He kept yelling out racial remarks in the theater.

"All right you niggers, sit on the back seats where you belong!" or "This is a white-only movie."

When the lights were put on, he always looked straight-faced and of course his buddies never told on him. I was sitting behind him one night when he looked all around him and didn't see any black faces and all of his buddies kept egging him on to say something. Finally he held his head down and yelled out,

"No niggers in the white section!"

I then knew for sure who was causing the problem. I decided to wait and see if it would just end on its own. He had caused a lot of friction in the company and some fights had broken out. The problem continued for about a month, and the CO finally assigned a black warrant officer to try and find the root of the problem. The warrant officer came to me at the shop one day. He called me outside and told me what he was trying to do. I got the impression he just wanted the whole thing to go away. I was surprised when he told me Captain Garcia told him if anyone knew who had started it, I would. He had the company roster with him and pointed to my name and then to "Negro" in the race column and reluctantly asked,

"Is that correct?" I told him it was.

He said, "I have seen you here for almost a year, and I only noticed it after the captain pointed it out to me."

Even with the captain telling him, he checked my nametag before he started asking any questions. I told the warrant officer about the incident at the theater and I knew who said it. He loosened up and told me,

"Simmons is asking for a special court martial in lieu of an article fifteen (The article 15 is the lowest form of the uniform code of military justice, usually 14 days restriction and company punishment) for fighting in the club when someone called him a nigger. I wish he would just go ahead and accept the damn Article Fifteen and lets get this bullshit over with. Captain Garcia wants to get it settled in the company if at all possible."

The next Monday morning they assigned the guy from West Virginia to our shop and put him next to me. I led him to believe that I was a racist white guy from South Carolina. It took him about two days to loosen up and tell me about all of the crap he kept doing in the theater. He also told me he belonged to some little clan group back home and asked me to go to the theater with him that night. I called Mr. Wilson, the black warrant officer, and told him what he had told me. He wrote up a statement and I signed it. The West Virginian made no bones about hating blacks and Jews. Even when they questioned him about it, he told them,

"Hell yes I hate them! You can do anything to me that you want to, but that won't change my mind."

The court-martial on the other guy was dropped and the guy from West Virginia disappeared from the company and in about two weeks, things settled down to normal. The most disgusting thing about the whole incident happened a few weeks later when the guy that was to have been court martialed came into my room. He looked at a picture of Linda and said,

"She is a little dark aint she man? I don't want anything to do with black women, they are too damn evil; they have to be yallah or white for me to mess with them."

I suddenly wished I had kept my mouth shut when they were considering canning his ass.

While in Germany, a lot of little incidents happened but there is one that seems to linger with me more than the others, it was also a classic. This guy from our Island was stationed near-by and was in the air force, he often went to a club that mostly blacks went to. A lot of the guys from our company went there also and they found out he was from Seaside, South Carolina. One of the men from our company asked him if he knew me and he instantly told them

"Sure I do, I used to f— his sisters."

When the conversation got back to our company and me, it was a test to see how loyal I was to the Negro race. At first I tried to ignore it, but it just seemed to drag on. Everyone involved wanted me to "show my colors," and no matter what I said, it would create a feeding frenzy. A very good friend of mine was there when he first said it and also the other nights that he kept bragging about it. Dorsey never told me he was doing all of his lying and bragging, but everyone else did. After about a week, it really began to piss me off. Dorsey kept telling me not to let it get next to me because everyone knew the guy was full of bull. He talked me out of going to the club and kicking the crap out of him. He kept saying to me,

"Man if you let that son-of-a-bitch get next to you it will only get you in trouble." I told some of the message boys,

"Ask him which one of my sisters did he go with, the one that was eight or the one that was ten when he left home?"

To give them a message to give to him proved to be the wrong thing to do. It just made them talk more. Finally this guy from Brooklyn started getting involved in it. Bloom was white but his color always matched the group that would spend their money on him while he ran his mouth. Bloom used more black street slang than any person I had known, but when he went out with the white guys it all seemed to disappear. About a month earlier, I was standing in a group of white guys while he was running his mouth a mile a minute and referred to a group of black guys as "Those nigger mother-f—ers." I left the group, and someone told him about me. I never mentioned the incident to any black person, but he didn't know I hadn't. He felt the need to do something that would get him back on their side. Bloom decided if he played his cards just right, he could get even with me and get back in with his black friends as well.

One Sunday morning Bloom got a couple of his black "friends" together and came up to me and asked, "A man, do you know a dude named James Hawkins from some little hick town in South Carolina?"

A bomb exploded inside of me when I heard the name and I knew what it was going to lead to. I tried to remain as calm as possible and said, "Yeah I know him, but I don't want to hear any of that bull-shit that you are about to bring up."

He put a smirk on his face and asked, "Hey man, why do you think you are too good for him to go with your sisters?"

The Brooklyn boy had an audience and kept it up because he needed the build-up before his black friends that morning. I told him "Maybe you should bring your mother and sisters over here for Hawkins, that way he wouldn't have to hallucinate about mine. Just think of all the money you could make, black guys just love to pay for white pussy."

The kid had to prove his alliance to his black friends that morning and he thought he had some help from them, but they laughed at what I said. He charged into me and I punched him in the pit of the stomach and he fell down. My next move was to go to the club and hope I would find Hawkins. I sat at the club until it closed and he never did show. He didn't show that night or any other night, I think he got totally out of the business of going to bars. Bloom's buddies told him I was looking for him. I have never seen him return to Seaside either. I have never figured why so many dark homeboys thought they must claim to have screwed your light skin sister.

I enrolled in some English and math courses that were given by the University of Maryland extension service and they kept me busy and helped time go by. I also took a course in photography, I learned touch-up and restoration of old photographs, which I still do today as a hobby. One of the most rewarding things about the course was I got to go on a lot of photo tours throughout Europe. We did a lot of tours on the Rhine River that were great.

I was asked to do some engine work on a 1950 Mercedes Diesel for a warrant officer who was in our company. The Mercedes was a dream car. When I tore the engine down I found that it had a cracked cylinder block and head. The warrant officer didn't want to wait until I found the parts for it and he bought a new Opal and gave me the Mercedes. I knew where there was an engine with a broken crankshaft. The German owner traded me the parts for some work on his tractor. I took Friday off and put the engine together with the help of three good buddies that wanted a ride to the soccer game in Metz, France. We had the car ready to go around noon on Saturday. I often think if I had brought it home, it would be worth a small fortune today, but hindsight is always twenty-twenty. I drove the Mercedes all over Germany and France.

It had a spot in the door that a liter beer bottle would fit perfectly into. We tried to make every October Fest in Germany and we always joked about it being able to bring us home. No matter how drunk we got, it would always find its way to the parking lot at the barracks.

In the summer of 1960 I had saved enough money from my pay and doing work on cars to take a leave home. I took a thirty-day leave and went to the Air Force Base at Frankfurt and waited around for a hop that would take me to the States. After a day of waiting, I decided that I had worked too hard for the money and I wanted to see my family. I went to the Eastern Airlines ticket counter and bought a round trip ticket to Charleston, and was out within the hour.

I got home and relaxed for a couple of days and went out and bought a car for Linda to have when I went back to Germany. With the car we started driving the Island and going to the drive-in theater as we had done before, and Stockton hadn't changed in the past year. Linda and I took my mother into town to look at some new furniture. We didn't want to go into the store so we sat in the car under a large oak tree on a ninety-five degree day. As we sat and caught up on our conversation for the past year, I spotted a soda machine across the street. We were digging in Linda's purse for some change when two white couples walked by and were staring in our direction; as usual we didn't pay them any attention.

In about five minutes a police car came and parked behind us. The cop remained in the car and when I pulled away from the curb, he followed. Linda and I looked at each other and I said to her, "Here we go again." We weren't afraid just disgusted. After following me for about two blocks he came along side and told me to follow him to the police station. I knew then what he wanted. I was home this time, not afraid, and had made up my mind to be a lot harder to deal with than I had been with the situation in

Louisiana. I started to ask him "What for?" but there was no sense in wasting my breath; I knew why, and told him,

"Go ahead, I'll be there."

I could tell he was uncomfortable or at least didn't know how to handle the situation. If he did, he would have come up to the car when I was at the furniture store. I drove to the station and waited for the cop to catch up with me, and told him,

"I know why I'm here, so let's go inside and get this shit over with."

He dropped his head and fell in behind me as I went up the steps in double time. When I got inside the station the chief was waiting for me at his office door. There was a secretary pecking away on a typewriter and stopped long enough to give me the world's dirtiest look. I gave her one that was worst and walked through the half swinging door to where the chief stood. He said in a slow southern accent,

"Come into my office, I want to talk to you about something."

I went in behind him and the cop who brought me there followed. The chief was cautious as he started questioning me, and for a while couldn't find the words to form his questions. I was very cool and not afraid of him and it threw him off guard. I kept my eyes glued into his and never blinked. He finally told me to have a seat, his chair being closer I sat in it. That seemed to get the cop riled up and he pointed to a straight chair and said, "Sit over here."

The chief nodded his approval and I stayed in his chair. Finally the questions slowly began to come.

"Where are you from boy?"

I very quickly told him, "Stockton"(still staring him down.)

"Who are the people in the car with you?"

"My mother and my wife"

"Is that your wife in the front seat?"

"Yes."

He fumbled around for a while and asked, "Where did ya'll get married?"

"Stockton."

I would not tell him I wasn't white, and he didn't know how to handle the situation. They now had to be careful or risk disturbance, but most of all they were no match for me because at the age of twenty-one, I felt I had a PH.D in racial complications. I had seen and experienced most of them and had been over most of the United States and a lot of Europe. I doubted he had ever been above the Mason-Dixon line or west of the Mississippi River. I also had grown up in Stockton and knew its policies and had been a victim of a lot of them.

He finally got around to asking me for some identification. I showed him my military ID card and it only had my picture on it. He tapped his pencil on his desk and tried to create a little humor.

"Being an army man, you must feel out of place among all of these airmen."

I never smiled or changed the expression on my face and he dropped his smile. The cop came over and whispered something to him and his eyes lit up. He said, "Let me see your South Carolina drivers license."

I lied to him and said, "I don't have one."

He raised his voice to try and intimidate me and asked, "Boy, do you know what the fine in this state is for not having a driver's license?"

I said, "Yep, twenty-five first offence and fifty second. I don't have a South Carolina driver's license but I do have a California driver's license, it's out in the car. If identification is what you are looking for, I can bring the whole damned town up here to vouch for me." I went on the offensive and told him, "I know what you want to know, and I also know why the rookie brought me here."

He told me to refer to the cop as a police officer.

I told him, "I have been questioned before, so let's get this crap over with, I don't know if you were a part of it or remember when the Stockton police sent me away when I was fifteen. I'll always reserve the right to come home."

I could tell from the expression on his face that he remembered me but didn't want to talk about it. His next question didn't surprise me when he asked,

"Why did you come back here?"

I was so disgusted that I held my hands up with a look of disgust on my face. I told him, "The woman in the car is my wife. We were married in Stockton and to set your mind at ease, I'M NOT WHITE! I grew up on Seaside from the age of eleven. If you want someone to explain me to you, I'll bring the whole Island up here. They all know me because I have been explained to them a lot of times."

Mother came into the outer office and overheard the conversation, and went into her Kaiser mode of not liking white people. She came into the office and let out a stream of curses that probably still echoes in the building. I waved my hand at mother and asked her to wait in the car. He was ready to get rid of me fast, but I took a few more minutes to say what I wanted to say.

"I will be here for another twenty-five days, and I'll be gone. I know all about people getting their cars run off the road by white people and the police being just as bad, or at least not doing anything about it."

I told him that I was going to the sheriff's department to get permission to carry a concealed weapon because I couldn't get protection from the police department. I again told him I was going to be here for the next twenty-five days only and I would be gone forever.

"Like it or not, people will have to get used to me being around." He than started the old speech about not picking on me, he said the people told him we were kissing. He also told me it was illegal for a white man and a colored woman to be riding in the front seat of the car.

I asked him, "Why in hell would I be kissing my wife on the street on a ninety-five degree day when we could go home, get into bed, and do anything that we wanted to. I saw the couple that called you, why didn't they say something to me if they didn't like it?"

He said it was his job to uphold the law and not theirs, and "After all, it's against the law."

He just had to keep putting, "It's against the law" into the conversation. The typewriter had picked up about three times its original speed it had when I first came into the office. The cop was still pacing back and forth, and his speed was increasing. They didn't believe that the chief would sit and listen to all that I was telling him. I really believed, deep down inside, they were surprised to learn how complicated segregation and the law could be as it pertained to me. I had kept it in too long and I told him everything I had ever wanted to tell anyone. Linda, Mother and a lot of people had seen the police take me up to his office and I knew he wasn't going to do a whole lot about it.

Probably the biggest motivation in me writing this book; is about two years later when I was living away from Seaside, someone wrote and told me the chief had been fired. He was caught in the back seat of his patrol car with a black woman. I often tell myself I must have given him the idea and had been the root of him getting fired. As he told me about five times that day, "It's against the law."

When I left the police station, I took Mother and Linda home and came back in to the sheriff's department and asked to see the sheriff. The deputy hesitated but saw the blood in my eyes and sent me in to see him. I had known the sheriff for a long time because he lived out on the island and was a good friend of my Uncle Bennie. Of course he didn't know me; I was just twelve years old when he last saw me. When I started telling him about what happened to me at the police station, I was speaking about two hundred words per minute and he didn't catch any of what I was saying.

He said, "Mister, would you please calm down and start from the beginning?"

I then realized he thought he was talking to a white person and what I was saying wasn't making any sense. I started over again by saying,

"I'm Bennie Kaiser's nephew."

Then it all began to make sense to him. He studied me for a few seconds and laid the pencil down,

"I'll be damned, I can see where it could become awfully confusing, but anyway, how can I help you?"

The sheriff leaned his chair back against the wall and relaxed. I pulled a chair from over by the door, sat down and managed to calm down and said,

"I want a permit to carry a concealed weapon."

His chair instantly came off the wall to an erect position and he said,

"Now wait a minute."

He was now about as angry as I was when I first came into the office.

"We can't allow everyone who has a gripe with the police department to go out and strap on a gun and take matters into their own hands."

He calmed down, half smiled, and said,

"You are being about as rational as your old grandfather William Kaiser would have been."

He must have seen the surprised look on my face when I realized that he knew my grandfather.

"That's right. I knew your granddaddy, I also know he was the world's biggest hard-ass just like you are being now, so just calm down and tell me what happened down at the police department."

I slowed my speech and told him what happened at the police station. I also told him about being put into the army at fifteen by the good old boys from Stockton and about the free escort service the Louisiana State Troopers provided us. I told him about other harassment I had experienced from police.

"I just don't want to get run off the road, clubbed over the head, or shot by the police while I'm here without at least a chance to fight back."

Of course that angered him again, and I backed off. I didn't want to piss him off, because he was at least listening to me and I respected him. After we had talked for a while, he told me he had grown up with the Kaiser family.

He told me the story about my grandfather being moved to the rear seats of the Salkehatchie Church. He also knew Jake Montgomery. I hated him for being able to see through my family and me as he did. For a long time I considered him trying to make me sound like a mongrel of some sort. Years later it turned out to be very good information and he was probably trying to get my self-esteem out of the gutter.

He told me, "Things are different in my county; people here don't do the things to Negroes that you are talking about."

I wanted to argue with him about it but I decided to quit while I was ahead. I then heard the statement I knew was coming sooner or later:

"You should stay in the army, or move up north if you get out."

Even though it angered me, again I remained very calm and said,

"I'm only going to be here for three weeks, and then I'll be gone forever. In the meantime, I want to feel safe while driving around with my family."

"You can do whatever you want as long as you don't break the law, and as far as the City Police are concerned, I assure you I'll straighten them out. If for any reason they question you again about something as foolish as this, you sue them, and I'll help you do it."

I went back to the Island and borrowed a pistol anyway, permit or not, as almost everyone carried one anyway. I somehow knew the sheriff knew that me being William Kaiser's grandson, I would carry one also. The next day when I came into town the police department almost controlled the traffic lights for me. They all waved very politely. The old sheriff had straightened them out as he said he would. I couldn't agree that Stockton was different than other towns; after all, he must have forgotten I grew in Stockton and had seen the rest of the country also. I must admit though, he certainly got the Stockton Police off my case for the next three weeks, and they made sure nobody else bothered us either.

As usual, my thirty-day leave went by too fast. It seemed as if it was little more than a long weekend pass and I had to go back to Germany. I only had eleven months left, and it didn't seem as impossible to do as it had been in the beginning. I was also in a good unit and was going to school.

I got back to the company in Germany and went out and hung a good drunk on. I wanted to rid myself of the thought of the police chief at Stockton and the stench of segregation. I had to resolve my renewed hatred of the white man and the thought of being away from my family. I woke up the next morning sick enough to die and made another great promise never to touch German beer again. I also made up my mind to get back into the swing of things and soldier like hell for the next eleven months. I enrolled in some mechanical technology courses and applied to another diesel engine school. I didn't think I would get it with less than a year to do. I convinced the captain I was going to re-enlist and he pushed it through for me.

No matter how hard I tried to occupy my mind to keep from thinking about being away from my family, there were times it drove me almost insane. It always seemed worse around Christmas time. I often blamed myself for taking the extra hitch in the army, I felt I should have done my regular hitch and gotten out to be with my family. I had to send most of my measly pay home for Linda and Vicki to survive on. I did KP for pay when other soldiers wanted to be off, and I stayed very busy for most of the time. I was very depressed at Christmas in 1960. I was going through one of the angry stages that I often got into. To me, Linda and Vicki were the only people who I cared anything about, and I was being kept away from them. I went to Chapel a couple of times but it seemed I always got a speech about duty and country. I wasn't too impressed about serving a country in which I had to ride the back of the bus or explain myself to every cop who was confused when I drove around with my family.

Even with the measly pay I got from the army, there was always something taken out for a cause I seldom considered important enough to contribute to. Even the four dollars a month for laundry services seemed as precious as gold. When I saw what had been taken out, my allotment to Linda, taxes, laundry and five dollars a month to an orphanage to which our company donated, my total pay for the month was fifty-eight dollars. The clerk told me I wasn't required to give to the orphanage but everyone else did, and he had already typed it in my pay record. To save him the task of typing it all over and me being the Company Scrooge, I agreed. At that time in my life, I felt charity began at home and I was even more convinced when I saw my next pay.

Chapter 19

SISTER MARIA AND THE ORPHANAGE

On Christmas Eve, the nuns from the orphanage put on a Christmas program for the company. I had not gone to the one the year before and I never knew what to expect. We were provided with a list of names of children from the orphanage, from which we each pulled a name to buy a gift for. In 1960, I drew the name of a nine-year-old girl from the box; her name was Heidi Bernbach. I took the slip of paper from the box and unfolded it and asked myself, "What in creation do I buy for a nine-year-old German girl?" I was flat broke and hadn't bought anything for Linda or Vicki. I also very much remembered the incident with the white police chief at Stockton a few months earlier. My thoughts were, "Why should I spend my money on some white German girl when I can't do anything for my own family back in the States?" To add to my anger, the German civilian population was snubbing some of the black troops. It was more pronounced at establishments where American white soldiers hung out. I also in some strange way, managed to blame Little Heidi for everything that happened to the Jews in World War Two.

In the weeks following the name drawing, I eased up on some of my hatred against the America Jim Crow system. At times I even looked forward to the Christmas program. I rebuilt a couple of engines, bought Linda the tape recorder that she wanted and sent some extra money home. I also went to the PX and bought a coat and a little set of dishes for Heidi. Just as easily as the depression left, it returned the day before the Christmas program. Every Christmas, I was reminded of the time we had leading up to my father's death in January 1947. Being in Germany, very lonely and away from home reminded me even more. When Daddy was alive, even in the leaner years, we always had some type of toys. When times were hard, and money was scarce daddy usually made toys for us, but the Christmas of 1947 we had absolutely nothing. We didn't even have our parents there with us. Mother was living in Savannah, and daddy was off on one of his many trips he took to see root doctors. Being seven years old and never having been told about Santa Claus (That's right young folk, we kept secrets longer back then.) I was sure he would come in spite of what the older sisters and brothers told us. After not being able to convince us and to spare us the disappointment on Christmas morning they told us the whole Santa Clause story that night. For a long time, Christmas became a very depressing time for me, and I almost hated it at times. During the year at the Seaside Schools, I had to be in a play or in some way expose myself to the parents of the other children while they pointed and asked questions, while I hated myself for looking different.

I got permission to drive my car to the orphanage for the Christmas program. I didn't want to ride the bus with the rest of the company nor did I want to take anybody with me. The orphanage was about eighty kilometers from the post. I let the bus and the others that drove their cars leave before me, I wanted to drive the countryside alone.

There were three things that went together well in Germany, Mercedes-Benz automobiles, Grundig radios, and great symphony orchestras. That combination would relax even me as I drove the German countryside. As the Mercedes rolled along the hills and around hairpin turns, and through towns with very narrow streets that dated back over a thousand years, I found peace within. It was Christmas Eve and the roads were empty of traffic. I saw only an occasional wagon, drawn by a huge draft horse or cow as the farmers made their way to the festivities that would be at home. It was early so I let the Mercedes take its time as it made its way over the hills. I had about two hours before dark, so I stopped at a small restaurant and ate. Someone was in another room practicing something from Brahms on the piano. When the pianist stopped playing and came into the room, I couldn't believe she was only about ten years old. When I realized Heidi would be about her age, I paid for my meal and left, looking forward to meeting her.

When I got into the town near the orphanage, I couldn't find it. The city was very old with narrow streets and tall stone buildings. I almost panicked from fear of not being able to find the orphanage and would miss the whole program. I drove for a couple of blocks until I saw this very German-dressed gentleman. I tried to find the words in my very elementary German to ask him for directions. He came over to the car and asked me in a perfect Brooklyn accent, "Where do ya wanna go kid?' With a very embarrassed look on my face I said, "The Orphanage." He laughed and said, "Go two blocks to Gau, dat's da main drag, hang a right and it will be a couple K's on your right."

When I got out of the car at the orphanage, the children were already singing Christmas carols. They sounded like the Vienna Boys Choir, and it was all in German. They were singing "Silent Night" in the language it was originally written in. The stone walls of the old buildings stirred my imagination to think that these same buildings could have been during the birth of Christ. The moon was full and when I looked up to the heavens I saw a very beautiful night with stars that sparkled like diamonds. Even though the temperature was down in the low teens, the beauty of the night gave me a warm feeling inside and took my mind back to my seeking days.

It was warm inside the building, and the children were on the stage singing their hearts out to us. To my right sat a lot of children who looked a lot younger than the ones who were singing. I tried to look the group over and guess which one would be Heidi. At their age and dressed in the school's uniform, they all looked almost alike, just boys and girls with a few blacks faces scattered in. The singing finally stopped when it was time for St. Nicholas to give out the presents. The man who was St. Nichols was a sergeant from our company, dressed as a Bishop. The sergeant was born in an orphanage in Germany and had been adopted by a military family of German descendants when he was five. He was perfect for the part. He was also in charge of the fund drive for the orphanage. As Sergeant Huber called their names, the children came forward and met their sponsor and they both walked up to meet St. Nick. Children were joining in from other rooms', which I hadn't seen, and it was a lot more than I had imagined. Finally Sgt. Huber called Heidi's name. At first no one came and the room grew quite, I stood up to see her as she came out, but again no one came. Sgt. Huber called the name again and finally I could see the crowd separating to let her through. Heidi was a black girl. At first I thought they had selected me for her or vise versa, but her name had been simply drawn from a box. The room got even quieter as she came down the isle. I met her in the front of the room and knelt down to be at her height and held out my arms for a hug. After the hug and kiss on the cheek, she stepped back and said,

"Hello, my name is Heidi, Welcome to our school."

I could tell she had practiced for the line in English because once she had to stop and start over again, but the second time, I couldn't have done better myself. I told her my name, took her hand and we got in line to meet St. Nick. He gave her the two gifts, and she led me into the dining area for coffee and warm ginger bread. Not all of the children sat with their sponsor. When I had been served and was looking around for a place to sit, I felt her tugging on my coat and pointing at a seat across the room. She was a very beautiful girl and I asked myself how could anyone leave her in an orphanage. I saw in her what my own daughter would look like in a few years. She was very talkative and took for granted I understood a lot more German than I did. She knew some English words and was eager to try them out on me, which made matters worse.

A couple of the nuns spoke excellent English and one finally got around to see how we were communicating. I asked her how many other black children were there. I instantly regretted asking the question about the girl's color because the Nun instantly took it as a negative question about her and for a while I changed the subject. I just didn't' feel comfortable with the nun thinking that I mentioned the girls color from a racist point of view. I sat and tried to think of an easy way to bring up the conversation again without angering her and causing her to take the little girl away.

I finally said, "I have a daughter at home who is two years old, and she also is *Schwarz* (black)."

At first, I didn't think that she believed me. She asked me, "Is your wife black?" I said yes, I am also."

I had to explain my complete genetic makeup to rid her of the notion that my mother was black and my father was a white plantation owner. Heidi was sitting between us and catching bits and pieces of what we were saying as we switched from English to German. From the expression on her face, we saw that Heidi wanted to know what we were talking about, especially, every time the word Schwarz came up. I was glad when the nun told her in German that I had a black daughter. Her eyes lit up and she became even more talkative.

Being reared as a Southern Baptist, or I should say as a black Southern Baptist, I had in the past had no contact with a Catholic nun. I had always pictured them as little old grouches of women who would constantly preach fire and brimstone to anyone who she could hem up long enough to listen. After our initial introduction and getting through the word "Schwarz" we became instant friends. She was very opened-minded and had a sense of humor that was unbelievable. In the month to come, Sister Maria would become a great source of strength for me. She looked to be in her late forties or early fifties and was one hundred percent energy. She also knew how to tap the reservoir of physical help available from the American GIs. She had a group of four men from our company who helped out on one weekend a month; she only wanted four at a time.

"You get too many of you Chicago gangsters around at one time and all you will do is play," she jokingly said to a group us one day. I volunteered for the weekend duty at the orphanage when one of the regulars rotated to the States. It became very interesting, but most of all it helped time go by. I got to know a lot of the children and they and the nuns improved my German considerably.

After Sister Marie got to know me, she had a thousand questions about the racial situation in the United States. Whenever something was printed in the German papers she often saved it to ask for my opinion. I could tell she freshened up on her United States geography after a long spat with me on Saturday afternoon about the different laws found in the North and South. We had a lot of painting to do and some of us would go almost every weekend. When I got there the next Saturday, as soon as I got out of the car, she said, "*Kommen zie mit,* you come with me, and started the North-South discussion again. She tried for a while to get me to explain the Mason-Dixon line to her. Even though she was fluent in English, I wasn't about to show my ignorance of American history while I tried to explain it all in part English and German. I knew it wouldn't come out right.

"You tell me I'm a South Carolina gangster and now you are asking me PH.D questions".

She put a stiff pompous expression on her face and said in a very British accent, "Elementary my child, elementary, you are only twenty-one years old and already you forget."

She told me all about the Mason-Dixon Line. The words she didn't know in English, she filled in with German. I still remember very little about the Mason-Dixon Line.

I had recently started going to diesel engine school, and the school was only about twenty minutes from the orphanage. We usually got out of class early on Friday. The orphanage had a lot of work to do and I was there on most Saturdays. Sister Maria soon found out I was a mechanic. At first she didn't trust me to work on the bus or the two vans that must have been World War One German surplus. I should have left her doubts alone. I got all three of them running on a Saturday, and after that, they all had to be like brand-new whenever they wanted to use them.

As my trips to the orphanage became more frequent, I saw that the friction between Heidi and the other children was about like it was in the United States. I had in the past wanted to ask the nun about it, but there were two things that she refused to discuss. WW II and why the other girls always wanted to fight Heidi. Whenever either subject was brought up she very quickly changed the subject. One Saturday morning we were out planting bulbs in the tulip beds when a fight broke out between Heidi and another girl. The nun went over in a rage and separated the fighting girls. When she got back to the flowerbed, she gave me a stern "I don't want to hear it look." At that stage in our relationship I felt she owed me one. She wanted to know everything about race relations in the United States and was so quick to criticize our shortcomings. There were times I felt I didn't want to spare her feelings, especially when it came to the race relationship between Heidi and the other girls at the school. This at least would give me a chance to tell her that Americans weren't the only ones who had problems accepting black people. In later visits to the school I got to know some of the other black children, and word had gotten around that I had a black daughter. I saw two other darker children that didn't appear to be Negro, one boy and one girl, they appeared to be from one of the middle east countries. They almost always isolated themselves from the other children.

I never had to bring up the subject of race relations with Sister Maria because she did it for me. When she got back to the flowerbed she said,

"That Heidi, the black one, she is always fighting. Someday we will have to send her to the school in Frankfurt where there are more black children."

This angered me because I had watched the fight developed this time as I had on other occasions. It was almost always this tall girl that came over and took whatever Heidi was playing or working with. It totally reminded me of my days in the Seaside school system. I thought, "As soon as Sister Maria cools off, I'm going to bring up the subject of "German race relations" with her." I would have to be very careful or I would get the tongue lashing of my life. She could be ruthless with words whenever she wanted to and the more excited she became, the more she spoke in German. In my mind I always accused her of cursing me whenever she changed to German, French, or sometimes Italian, in case I might understand in German.

It took me a long time to come up with a way to start the conversation with her that day. After we had lunch, we went outside and got ready to start planting bulbs again. She was generally a lot calmer as she worked, or at least she showed more control. Even as she worked I could tell when she was getting upset. There were times when she was painting, she would jam the brush into the bucket and then jam it onto the wall with paint flying in all directions. Whenever we were planting bulbs and she got upset, she often dug the hole too deep and had to put dirt back in. When she was calm, the holes always came out the right depth.

In about and hour, the argument between Heidi and another girl started again. Sister Maria decided to just let it run its course this time, but the holes for the bulbs kept getting deeper and deeper. She constantly looked between the girls and me to get my reaction, which was an absolute zero. I think she thought at my age I didn't understand the nature of children arguing, especially little German children who were being brought up in a religious setting. For the most part I found them to be like other children, German or American, black or white. I didn't want her to send the children somewhere else to work or play. I always kept a neutral expression on my face. If she had to discipline them, I always found something to take me away from the situation. When the disciplining was over, I came back. I knew all you had to do to get off the program, was to get on the wrong side of Sister Maria. I felt I got a lot more out of the program than I ever would be able to contribute. First, I got out of a lot of Saturday details from the army and second, it helped time go by. I always worked hard, so whenever she wanted someone to do something she usually asked me. A lot of the other guys from the company couldn't stand her, but I always enjoyed working with her. Her occasional tongue-lashings weren't anything that I hadn't experienced from my parents when I was growing up on the farm at Rice Patch; I also had a lot of respect for her.

As the afternoon progressed and Sister Maria got the holes the right depth on the first try, she became quite and settled down. I told her that Heidi reminded me of myself when I was at the Seaside School. She listened as I told her of my days at the Seaside School and of the constant fighting I was always involved in. The holes for the bulbs remained the right depth so I kept going until I had brought her up to the present in my life. She listened to me as if it was a confession I was making or just something I wanted to get off my mind. When I finished talking, all of the bulbs were in the ground and the children were putting away the tools and getting ready for the evening meal. Sister Maria and I remained outside among the huge flowerbeds and talked. It was getting dark, so we went inside and sat down in a quiet corner away from everyone. As we sat and I continued to talk, or confess, she reached across the table, put her hand on top of mine and held her finger up to her lips in a gesture for me to stop talking, and listen to her.

"Of course I have never been black and I can't tell you what it is like to live in America as a black person. I can't tell you even what it is like for Heidi to be here as a black German girl in an orphanage. My hair is blond and my eyes are blue, so it is quite evident that I am not black. I have also had trying times in my life and it has made me a better person for it. I was born here at the orphanage, and I will probably die here. I sat through all of my childhood waiting to be adopted and never was. I sat through "line ups" as you say in your police station, and every month or so, I was rejected. Finally when I was fifteen, I was too embarrassed to be among the smaller children, I told the mother I didn't want to be adopted, but I always did, I even dreamed how I wanted my parents to look. Every time I saw a little boy or girl leave the orphanage, I looked through the window and cried as they went home with their new parents. As I grew older and knew I would never be adopted and I would never know my real parents, I gained inner strength from it." The church has been my only family, it has given me life and I decided to give my life back to it. I could be in any of the universities in Germany, France, Italy or England, but my life is here. I have studied all over Europe, I have a Ph.D in History, but that is nothing when you are not happy. Being rejected by others is one thing, but don't ever do it to your-self. People who are rejected or persecuted by society usually become very strong. Don't worry about Heidi, she is a very good student and her art looks like the paintings in the galleries at Frankfurt. She plays the piano and the flute very well. If she ever started rejecting herself, she wouldn't be worth a single penny. Sure she fights, but all children fight. She is a natural fighter; she fights until her art is the very best it can be. She fights until her math and language is through." As we talked, Heidi was washing the last of the tools and putting them away. "She also fights until all of the bulbs are planted and the last tool is put away. Heidi is not the only child here who is a fighter; we must make all of them strong if they are to survive when they leave here. They will have no family to look to for help. You tell me how your father fought the system, but you see what he did to himself when he gave up the fight."

Sister Maria quoted scripture and told of men and women throughout history who had been persecuted and later became leaders of nations. Some had contributed to art, science, and religion or had done other great deeds.

After we had eaten supper and I had a small glass of wine, it was nearly ten o'clock. The day of digging in the flowerbeds was taking its toll on me and I was dog-tired. A couple of the nuns made a bed for me and I spent the night there. Even as tired as I was, I didn't go to sleep right away. As I lay there looking up at the dimly lit and very high ceiling, I tried to imagine what it would be like to spend the rest of my life there. I got out of bed, knelt beside it and gave thanks for my life with all of its small complications.

I got out of school a few weeks later and was assigned to a modification team that worked on NATO launch vehicles. It was excellent duty, but I was no longer able to get to the orphanage on weekends. During the week before I left Germany, I drove to the orphanage. Sister Maria was in Frankfurt for the week and I never got to see her again. For a long time, whenever I got depressed I often thought about the little sermon she gave me that night.

Chapter 20

MY MIGRATION NORTH

I left Germany in June 1961, and this time I knew for sure I wasn't going to re-enlist. I was only twenty-one years old and had put in six years. I felt a lot more secure in finding a job because I was more mature and had more education and experience.

If at times I sound anti-military, it is not intended; I wouldn't exchange the time I spent in the military for any other time in my life. Sure it was hectic, but I found it was a very good learning experience. I still have little sympathy for the person who can't keep his or her nose clean long enough to do a hitch without getting kicked out. Most of the people who were there in the 1950s and 60s were drafted away from their families and had very little to say as to what kind of jobs they were given. They served with dignity and were proud of the fact that they had served. And so am I.

I take issue with the idea that today's all-volunteer army is better. I doubt very seriously that there is anyone in the military who has ever served with a draftee. What does that statement say about the thousands of men and women who fought and died in previous wars? I served with a lot of enlisted people who had master's degrees. To me it is all about politics. Let rich and poor serve equally. The family members of the people who start wars should be the first to go.

I was discharged at Fort Hamilton in Brooklyn, New York. I knew some people from Seaside who were working for a truck rental company, and the company offered me a job. I told them I would go home to my family and would give a lot of serious thought to the offer. I still wasn't too impressed with the idea of living in New York City.

I got to Seaside Island on Saturday morning, and as usual, I just loved it. The slow pace of the Island was quite a contrast from what I had been through in the past three years. The Island had a way of holding you there, and you never wanted to leave. It was also home to Linda, and she didn't want to leave either. I decided once again to try and find a job around Stockton. I also had to buy another car, because the one that I bought when I was on leave turned out to be a lemon. I went out on Monday morning to look for a car and a job, but the job situation was still as it had been for black people in 1957. The only thing available was very poor service jobs that paid very little.

I saw a sheet on job listings with the state. I went to the state maintenance shop in hopes of getting hired there. The supervisor said he didn't need any mechanics but needed a person for the survey crew; he also told me I would have to take a small test in subtracting minutes and degrees. I took the elementary math test and scored one hundred. He gave me the forms to fill out for the job application and I started to fill it out. When I came to the race block I remembered I was in South Carolina again. I started to put white in the space, but I knew it would be just a matter of time before he found out and would find an excuse to fire me. But the guy seemed friendly enough, so maybe, just maybe, he would hire me anyway. I filled out the rest of the application and turned it into him. He looked it over while I was standing there, and I could see the expression on his face change from a positive attitude about me getting the job to an absolute no. He laid the form on his desk and asked,

"Where are you from?"

I told him "Seaside."

"Are you kin to them light-skinned colored people out there?" It pissed me off but hoping he would still hire me I told him I was, even though I wasn't related to the family that he referred to.

He told me "It will probably be at least two months before they hire anyone, and even then they might not hire anyone. You know how the government works, but if you want a job working on the roads we probably could work something out on that?"

I asked him what did it paid. "Twenty-five dollars a week, and we have a lot of benefits and paid holidays."

I told him I would decide later and walked out of the office. I heard the form being torn in half as I closed the door.

I tried a couple of other spots and filled out an application for civil service at all of the government installations in the area, in hopes of getting something at a later date. I went home and made preparations for going to New York. I called my sister Mary who was living there. She and her husband said I could spend a few weeks with them until I got a job and an apartment of my own. I, like thousands of other blacks had done in the past, left South Carolina on that rainy night to find work in New York. As I drove off the Island I turned the radio off and the only sounds I heard were the sounds of the flopping sound of the windshield wipers and the steady sound of the tires as I made my way on the wet pavement. It was a sad occasion for me, I was leaving my family behind again and I began to wonder if it was ever going to work out. Vicki was almost three years old and I had spent very little time with her as a father and we didn't want to have any more children until we were settled.

I drove all night and got to New York about two in the afternoon. My brother-in-law met me in Manhattan, and I followed him out to Queens. I was tired from the trip, and I spent some time getting caught up on what had been happening in my sister's life; we hadn't seen each other in the past three years. I went to sleep while we were still talking.

The next morning I was up early and went out to buy tools I would need if I got the job. I rested for the remainder of the day and early the next morning, I was on my way to Manhattan for the job interview.

I had driven in Seattle, San Francisco, Los Angeles, Rome, Paris, and Frankfurt but none of them compared to driving in New York City. I left Queens about seven-thirty and hit midtown Manhattan traffic about eight. Not knowing the main through-streets, I took it the hard way by feeling my way around. When the line of traffic got long I decided to take another street, not knowing that a hundred other people had the same idea. I later learned the only way to maintain your sanity in New York traffic was to turn the radio on and wait in line and blow your horn like everyone else to relieve the tension. The secret to New York driving was to always know where you wanted to go. If not, take public transportation preferably a cab because the subway system to a first timer can be just as confusing as the traffic on the street.

I got the job that morning and went to work right away. The pay was excellent compared to South Carolina but only fair by New York standards. I had a job, which meant everything to me because I was beginning to get a very insecure feeling, one that I had a lot of times before. I even had a job that I was enjoying doing.

I worked for a truck rental company and a lot of time was spent in a service truck. We had to check and repair trucks throughout New York City and northern New Jersey. My driving in other cities was a big help. I soon learned to drive like the rest of the New Yorkers and life became a lot more bearable when I had to go out with the service truck. One of my biggest problems was the "Stop Here On Red" sign. I saw them in other cities in later years, but they were probably a first in New York. A light that was blocks away served as traffic control for the blocks preceding it. The first week I was there, I must have run half of the traffic lights in Queens. Another one was the "No Commercial Traffic" sign. I had seen them in other cities, but I had never driven a commercial vehicle and they never meant anything to me. One morning, one of New York's finest brought it to my attention. I was barreling down Central Park West and met the police coming from the opposite direction. He waved for me to stop, and we had a divider. I pretended not to see him and with the divider, I told myself it would be a long time before he could get turned around and catch me. I sped up to get to the truck, and hoped he wouldn't catch me. I was trying to beat him at his own game, I got caught behind slow traffic and he caught me in less than five blocks. The police came up to the truck, looked at the tags, and asked for my driver's license. He started to write the ticket, but when he saw I had a South Carolina driver's license and was black he asked,

"Home boy, do you know what you were doing wrong?"

"I sure don't, unless I was speeding."

"No guess again."

"Run a red light?"

"No."

I held up my hands as in surrender and said,

"I give up."

They both started laughing and the black policeman asked me, "How long have you been in New York?" I told him a week. He laughed again and said,

"You mean you have been here for only a week and the boss allowed you to leave the block with his new truck?"

I laughed also and said, "Fools are born everyday, but tell me, what was I doing wrong?"

He put the pad away, and I relaxed. "This is a no commercial Traffic zone," he told me.

I again threw up my hands and said "School me, what in the hell is that suppose to mean?"

By now they both were in stitches and one said, "Home boy, you really are on the level and you really don't know what you were doing wrong."

I said, "Hope to die if I do."

I knew what he meant, but I'll sound as much of a hick as need be to keep from getting a ticket. I talked with him for about ten minutes and he told me he was from Charleston, South Carolina and he had relatives at Seaside. He said he was going to give a fellow Geechie boy a break and wished me luck with my new job, he promised if he caught me again he would write me up for both offenses.

I soon learned to take the subway to work because parking was hectic to say the least. The subway amazed me as to how it could move so fast, make so much noise and get across, or under town as quick as it did. It was efficient and crime wasn't like it is today on the subway. I pride myself in just knowing how to use the system. The one thing that was always noticeable on the train was a lot of people dressed like executives. A lot of the mechanics from our job wore suits to work, changed into greasy coveralls, worked all day, and changed back into a business suit to take the train home. I never wore a suit to work, but I also dressed well to take the train. I never did figure out why, but I am sure it was pride, Pride in my job and myself. No matter how much you may hear people complain about the city, don't you, as an outsider try to degrade it.

I was there for three weeks when I decided to get an apartment and bring Linda and Vicki there with me. My sister Mary and I went apartment hunting and found a place on Clermont Avenue in Brooklyn. The neighborhood looked good so I took it. It was as we had in San Francisco, a one-room small kitchen affair, but it was all we could afford at the time and it meant we could be together, and that would be worth any sacrifice we would have to make. I paid the deposit and the landlord gave me the keys. After work on Friday night, I left New York to get Linda and Vicki. They were all packed and ready to go when I got home, and Vicki was talking a mile a minute, she had a million broken questions about New York.

To avoid traveling in the heat of the day, I left home around seven o'clock on Sunday evening. We were having a good trip until around three o'clock in the morning when I stopped for gas in upper North Carolina. Linda and Vicki got out and started to the rest room, the attendant yelled out, "Wait until I get the key to the colored bathroom for you."

Vicki had already dashed into the only visible rest room and locked it from the inside. From the way she was rushing me to stop, I knew for sure a team of wild horses couldn't have pulled her out. The attendant didn't like it but went ahead and pumped the gas anyway, and when Vicki came out, Linda used the same "white" rest room. The attendant said,

"Damn it! I thought I told her to use the colored one."

He was through pumping the gas, and I told him I needed a quart of oil.

He said, "It's over there, and if you want it put in, you will have to do it yourself."

I had already gassed up and would have left the oil but I needed it and didn't want to stop again. I decided to swallow my pride and ignore him. I went over to the rack, got the oil and put it in as he stood there with his face screwed into the most disgusting look I had ever seen on any human being. When I finished putting the oil in, he noticed that some oil had spilled on the pavement at the pump. He came over, pointed it out and said,

"You spilled some oil on my pavement."

He was alone and talking that much bull at three in the morning. I decided it was time this kid was given a lesson in manners and public relations. I told him, "I don't see any."

He came marching over to the car with his little sparrow chest sticking out while I acted as scared as possible to get his ego up.

He said, "There, see it there."

I told him he better go and get a mop and a bucket of water and if he scrubbed like hell he should have it up by daylight.

"I'll bet if I go get my daddy he will make you get it up," and I lost it.

I grabbed him in the front of the shirt and slammed him into the post that held the sign over the pumps.

"Let me really give you something to go and tell that asshole you call daddy."

I let him down and slammed him again. Linda got out of the car and pulled me off of him, Vicki had watched the whole thing with a grin on her face. I let him go and drove off. I somehow felt bad about having done it, especially while Vicki was watching. He was probably only about sixteen years old. It seemed that everyone wanted to get into the harassment business. A couple of hours later, to break the ice and to calm me down, Linda told me,

"You should have asked him for some ice water."

When I got back to work I was put on the night shift with Sammie, or "Big Man." If anyone knew New York, Big Man did. Not only did he know how to get from one place to another in the fastest time possible; he also knew who "ran" what part of town and who to go to for a job in that part of town. He knew all of the bosses or owners of the major produce and trucking firms and all of the police department heads. One day I asked him, "If you know all of these people, why are you still working as a mechanic?"

"I don't have the education for them and they would only want me to do their dirty work and I would soon wind up in jail, or dead. Whenever someone needed someone to feed to the dogs I would be it."

Big Man had a grave distrust for the white man. When I was put on the night shift with him, he didn't like it at all and made no bones about letting me know it either. We had to go out on a service calls the first night I met him. I got into the right seat of the service truck and settled down for the ride into New Jersey. When he came out he said, "I am not going to chauffeur your ass around, so you drive."

It pissed me off, but I wasn't going to get into it with Big Man without having a damned good reason. He was very efficient but hardly said anything. He kept a bottle of T-Bird (Thunderbird wine) in his coat pocket, which he occasionally took a sip from but never enough to get drunk. He always said it kept him from getting a cold. I don't think he was called Big Man for his size but more for the fact that he knew everyone. When we went to the different companies to check their fleet of rented trucks, all of the bosses knew him and would invite him in for coffee. That was the only time we would have any conversation. When we got back to the truck and on the street, it was silence as usual, except for,

"Turn right, or, get into the other lane! Or, damn it, you just passed it!"

We often had to go into New Jersey, and I didn't know the area. When I asked him to drive, he looked at me with an evil look on his face and said, "White folks, how do you ever expect to learn Jersey if I drive for you? If I was to drive, you would probably be asleep as soon as we got through the tunnel." He smiled lightly for the first time that I had seen when just the two of us were together. "Further more, if I can ever get you to know where the hell you are going I can fall asleep as soon as we get through the tunnel." I never asked him to drive again.

One Saturday we both had to come in for a company meeting, and the meeting was to last for an hour. I brought Linda along and she stayed in the car or walked around the block with Vicki for the hour. When the meeting was over and we came outside, I went to the car with Linda and Vicki while Big Man was looking. That was the first time I had ever seen anything surprise him. I enjoyed watching him squirm around while he tried to figure me out.

When I left the car and we walked back to the shop together he asked, "Is that your old lady?"

I said, "Yes."

Big Man became his old self again and laughed out loud with me for the first time and said, "No wonder those crackers ran your ass from down south."

I had never found any reason to explain myself to him, he had never given me a break because he thought I was a southern white and was put on shift with him to keep him straight, or as he put it, "Keep a white eye on me."

After seeing my family, he began to loosen up, and after a couple more days we began to talk. He told me he was born in Alabama and had lived there until he was fifteen years old and got into some trouble. He would never tell me what or why and I never asked him. He was put into some sort of reform school where he had been constantly beaten. They made him stand in a corner, sometimes all night. This went on for about six months until in 1930 he escaped and walked fifty miles home, often at night and through the woods. He was finally able to sneak up to an uncle's house. The uncle drove him to Atlanta and put him on a train to New York. There he came to another uncle who found him a job in a sweatshop type factory and took all of his money when he got paid. He ended up on the streets for about two years, sleeping wherever he could. Big Man had sense enough to save his money and finally got a room at a boarding house after having had pneumonia. From that day on he decided never to be without a dollar in his pocket, depend on anyone else, get thrown in jail, or go back below the Mason Dixon line.

He took me home with him one night when we were working in his neighborhood in Queens. He had a fabulous home and family. I would have never suspected it, because He never talked about them, so I assumed that he had no family. I learned a lot from Big Man while we worked together. I often bought a bottle of scotch on pay nights to "keep the cold out" as he put it.

One night he asked me, "Why do you spend so much money on that stuff when you can get the same results from a half-pint of T-Bird and you can put a couple of dollars in your pocket to boot?" I bought a bottle of wine the next pay night.

He once said, "I don't want to sound like your damn father white folks but you should save every nickel you can, and get your ass out of this city while you are young enough to do it."

One night we were over in New Jersey in the railroad yards and we watched these two guys take this other guy behind some cars and we could hear the blows from a stone as it crushed his head in. I was getting ready to go over and try to help the poor guy. Big Man quickly grabbed me by the sleeve and yanked me back and said,

"If you just keep putting this wheel on they won't do the same to us." He said he knew them, not by name, but the family they were from and that they wouldn't bother us if we didn't interfere with them. I got back into the truck and wanted to throw up. He put all of the tools away and said, "If it will make you feel any better, we can stop at the pay phone and call the cops, but we won't give our names."

We drove all the way across town before he decided to call the cops. I'm certain this was to make sure they had gone when the cops got there. I stayed in the truck while he supposably called the cops. For a long time I wondered if he actually called the cops, I don't believe he did.

On the way to Manhattan, he told me, "Just tell yourself the mother probably told on someone and deserved to get his ass kicked, and forget about it. I started seeing shit like that when I was sixteen, and I'm sure that one we saw will not be your last."

I really hoped it would be my last. What Big Man told me, as rough and as rude as he said it, probably saved my ass one night.

We were sometimes split up and had to make the rounds alone and I would have to go to the darkest end of a pier or alley to get the mileage or check a truck. I would turn the flashlight on as soon as I got out of the truck and kept it on until I got the information I wanted. I put the light on, not to see anything, but to be seen, I didn't want to surprise anyone. I was on a pier one night and heard a big splash. I unconsciously turned the light in that direction and saw two men with their car trunks open. I knew they had thrown something into the water. I very quickly put the light on my work, but they had seen the light come their way. In about five seconds they were beside me with their light in my face. The one who was closer to me asked, "What are you doing here?" I said, "Checking trucks officers." They both had long hair, so I knew they weren't cops, but after a pause and some low mumbling between them, one said to me "Okay just making sure you aren't stealing anything." They put their lights on the decal and permit on the service truck, compared it to the rental truck and my uniform and ran back to their car and sped off. I still had five more trucks to check at that location, but they never got checked that night. As I headed back to the shop, my heart finally slowed down to around one hundred beats per minute. When I got inside, Big Man was sitting in the bosses' chair having a sip of T-bird. He offered me the bottle; I took it and emptied it. He laughed and said, "Damn, dog ass, you're getting as bad as I am with that stuff. I told you I was going to make a spook out of you!"

I told him what had happened at the pier, and he thought it was funny.

"No wonder you needed a drink," he reached into his coat pocket and produced another bottle. "Here, take another hit on this, you look like you need it, but this time don't empty the damn bottle. You should whistle or sing when you get out of the truck, slam the door real hard and throw some tools around.

Keep up the noise until you are sure everyone knows you are there. Always let them know you are coming and they won't do a damn thing to you, but most of all mind your own damn business."

I was looking over the employee's roster one night and it had a column for "type license." I looked at Big Man's name and the column had "none." Then I realized why I couldn't get him to drive. He knew how to drive and the company allowed him to drive, but he didn't have a driver's license. He also drove whenever he couldn't get out of it, which also explained why they always kept me on the shift with him, even after I learned my way around. I began to enjoy working with him so I didn't mind.

One night I asked him "Why don't you get a driver's license?"

He said, "I told them I can't pass the test, but the real reason is if I get a license and get stopped they will run me through their files and find out I ran away from prison in Alabama."

"You are talking about something that happened thirty years ago. They probably forgot about it six months after you left. They were probably glad to get rid of you, it was costing them too much to feed your big ass."

He had a social security card, but I could never talk him into getting a driver's license. I later thought he probably couldn't pass the test and never said anymore to him about it.

Big Man constantly teased me about my color; it was always "white folks" or "blondie." Once we were uptown on 125th Street and he really started getting on my nerves.

He told me, "Man, I could get rich with a mulatto like you up here. These gals would pay good money to get your yallah ass in bed!

I told him "Linda probably wouldn't go for the idea."

"Hell man, who would tell her? Man it feels good to have you chauffer my black ass around Harlem."

I told him, "The next time we come up here, I'm going to put Alabama plates on the truck and you will have to do the driving."

We went into the Empire Restaurant for dinner. When we got inside he said, "I'll bet you thought yours would be the only white face in here. Hell man, this is where all the Jews get their pork chops."

Sometimes I would think I could deal with him a lot better when he wasn't talking to me and thought I was "Mr. Charlie." Mr. Charlie was another name he called the white man who was in charge. When we got back into the truck and he had his sip of T-Bird, it was all work with him again.

My younger brother came to New York to work with us for a short time, but it didn't work out for him. It was comical when he told me about it a year later. He was sent to the southern tip of Manhattan to change a truck tire. It took him almost an hour to get down there. He got into the wrong lane and came to the Battery Tunnel where someone asked him for fifty cents. He turned around in Brooklyn and went back into the tunnel to Manhattan, only to get back in the wrong lane and back through the tunnel again. The shop was off Canal Street, and on his way back uptown he got into the wrong lane and wound up in the Holland tunnel. He often tells me New York has too many tunnels to suit him. He started out around ten o'clock in the morning and finally found his way back to the shop around four in the afternoon. He turned the truck in and caught the next bus home.

We had to check about 150 trucks for mileage, service time, and needed repairs. They all had to be checked between Friday noon and Saturday noon, and it was an all night project. We often found notes telling us what had to be done to the vehicle. If the truck needed serious repairs, we took it to the shop and brought a replacement. I had to drive a lot of tractor-trailer type trucks around New York City and northern New Jersey.

Once when I had only been there for about two month and still had my South Carolina driver's license, I was driving a truck out of Elizabeth, New Jersey and came upon a license checkpoint. The cop came over and asked me for my driver's license, registration and bill of laden, I told him I wasn't carrying anything and had no bill of laden. When I gave him my license, he looked at it and then at me and said, "Get out of the truck!" I got out and stood there expecting him to give me a ticket for not having a New York license. The truck was a rental and I was telling him any state license would do.

He told me, "This is not your damn driver's license."

Then I got the message. The cop was black, and for him to tell me that, really pissed me off, especially he being only a shade darker than me. I asked him, "Why the hell can't this be my damn license?"

"This is a negroes license."

I said to him, "No shit! I expected one of those Mr. Charlie types over there to ask me that, but I really didn't expect it from you! Don't you know that we come in a choice of colors? If you don't think its mine, arrest me and let me get to a phone and call the company and tell them to come and get their damned truck because some cop don't like the color of my damn driver's license!"

I was getting loud, and one of the white cops began to walk in our direction. I knew he didn't want them to know what we were talking about so I told him, "Either arrest me or let one of them handle it. He snapped at me, "Go ahead."

I made an appointment to get my New York license the next day. I didn't want to go through the harassment again. I had to keep my South Carolina license to prove I was black when I came into South Carolina with my family. You could get into a lot of trouble coming into South Carolina with New York plates on your car if it looked like your marriage was interracial. I remember on one of our many trips into South Carolina, this interracial couple (or what appeared to be) drove along with us from northern Maryland. We didn't know each other, but I suppose they thought we would have security in numbers. I had no problems relating to the situation. All went smooth until we got into South Carolina and the highway patrol pulled both of us over. The other guy was in front and the patrolman went to him first. He talked to the driver for a couple of minutes and told him to wait until he talked to me. We both knew what the charges would be, at least I did. He came to me and I showed him my South Carolina driver's license. The patrolman looked at the license and said, "Go ahead." I didn't consider it funny but I told Linda,

"That brother better get his wife a Negro's license or stay out of South Carolina."

I had never used any of my GI Bill for school, and when I went to the night shift it allowed me to enroll in school again. I took another diesel engine course. I got the pay from my job and the money to pay for school. Linda started working, and we were able to get a bigger apartment and buy a new car. We often went out to eat, traveled around the city, and visited family out on Long Island. In January 1962 Linda told me she was pregnant, and I hoped she would have a boy this time. Vicki often tells me I have never forgiven her for not being a boy.

When our second daughter, Joy, was born, Vicki was almost four years old. We brought Joy home, and Vicki had the usual bigger kid jealous spells. Linda and I noticed Vicki kept putting powder on her face at all times during the day. At first we took it as just little girl's play. In the coming weeks she became more and more withdrawn and never wanted to play with her new sister. One day we were all sitting around and Vicki was staring at Joy with a sourpuss look on her face. I asked her, "What's wrong Vicki?" She asked me, "Is she white?" At first we thought it was funny, and then I thought, "Some day I am going to have a long talk with that kid." I told her she was the same color when she was born and in a couple of years they would both be the same color. Vicki stopped putting powder on her face, started playing with Joy and all jealous spells left.

After a couple of years of living in the city, Vicki was five years old and a constant bundle of energy. We began considering moving back to South Carolina. Maybe things had changed, and we wanted to bring our children up in the country. We started saving all the money we could. Vicki constantly wanted to go to the park. I enjoyed it at first, but she always wanted to go when I had just come from work and being tired. I was father, big brother, sister and Mommy when Linda was at work during the day. Other kids managed fine in the park alone, but I could never allow myself to let her go alone. While in the park, I was also big brother and father to all the other kids there. I decided we needed to move out of Brooklyn. We looked into buying a house out on Long Island, but I decided I didn't want to make the investment of buying a house there. I also dreaded the thought of moving back to South Carolina. I loved the Island with a passion, but I would have to make a living there and I knew what would be involved.

All of my friends and relatives kept telling me I was a fool to even consider it, and they almost had me convinced. I had fought the system all of my life, and if anyone knew how to fight it I did. When everyone said we couldn't do it, they convinced me that I had to, even though it would be a decision I would have to live with for the rest of my life. I figured it must be done or they would have won when they asked me to leave in 1954, 1959, and 1960. I had learned one thing thus far in life; I never wanted to be a quitter, but most of all I wanted to be a thorn in the side of Stockton as they had been to me in my earlier years. It hadn't really gotten any better in other places we had lived. The working conditions in South Carolina would be next to unendurable after working in other areas. Each time we went back to the Island, we had to force ourselves to leave.

While at work one morning, I felt a sharp pain in the area where I had the hernia operation in San Francisco. I took the next day off and went to the doctor. He checked me over and found the rupture had returned (at least he thought it had.) He suggested I have the operation right away. I told him I would go to the VA hospital and have it done because it might be a return from the rupture I had before. The doctor told me the VA hospital there wasn't worth a damn and the reason I was having trouble with it again was because the government did it before. He finally talked me into letting him do it. I told him I could either use my Health Insurance or workman's Compensation. He said I should use my health insurance because workman's Compensation wouldn't pay enough to cover all of his and the hospital's charges.

I entered the hospital and was prepared for surgery the next morning. I was to have another hernia operation in the same spot as before. They gave me a spinal and I could over hear their conversation. This young doctor (or intern) asked, "So he didn't have a hernia?" One of the older doctors said, "I guess not." I thought to myself "So what the hell am I doing here?" When I got out of the hospital a week later, the hospital and doctor sent me a bill for the entire cost of the operation. They said the insurance company wouldn't pay for it. I called the insurance company and the clerk told me the surgery was written up as "exploratory surgery on a preexisting condition." I knew if I didn't pay them, they would have it taken out of my pay and I wouldn't have enough income to live on. I told myself, someone else beside this poor guy is going to have to pay for it. When I was well enough to travel, I took

Linda and the kids to South Carolina and came back to finish out the month on my job. When I told Big Man I was leaving, he said, "Those crackers will have your red ass back up here before the end of the month." My boss told me the job would be there as long as I wanted it.

Chapter 21

LEARNING TO SURVIVE IN THE SOUTH

When we came back to the Island in September 1963, I rented a house that was incomplete to store our furniture in. A white family lived between the main power line and us and would never allow the power company to run power across their property. They refused to let the power company cut some small trees, which really didn't amount to anything. I also learned they wanted to buy the property next to theirs, but they didn't know who owned it. I would have given up and rented another house but I had hopes of buying it at a later date. We stored our furniture in the house for six months without electricity while we constantly fought with the power company and the family next door. At one time, the power company told me they would put it under ground for three thousand dollars. In 1963 three thousand dollars was a lot of money; I could have bought a new car for less money. I decided to find out who owned the property next to the family who wouldn't give the power company permission to put the line across their property.

I went to the Court House and found that the owner lived in Savannah. I took his address and wrote him a letter explaining my situation to him. When I didn't hear from him in two weeks I decided to go to Savannah and try to find this mysterious person. I took my father-in-law with me in case I needed someone to vouch for me. I knew if he thought I was white, he would never trust me enough to give the power company permission to put the line across the property. I was determined to talk to him, even if I had to pitch a tent in his front yard. We got there about eight on a Saturday morning and knocked on the door but no one answered. I told my father-in-law, "I'll spend the whole weekend here until I see him." Around noon we went to get some lunch, and came back to set in for the afternoon. About thirty minutes later one of his neighbors came out and told us the owner's sister lived a few blocks away.

When we got to the sister's house, she and my father-in-law started talking. They both remembered each other from when they were both young children, and the ice was broken. I told her I was his son-in-law and we were there to talk to her brother about putting a power line across his property on Seaside Island. She told us the reason her brother never answered my letter was a lot of people had been after him for years trying to buy the property. The people at the courthouse had even transferred some of it to another deed and he now only had five acres left, and he wasn't going to talk to anyone about it anymore. She said, "It's been a constant battle to keep it."

I told her, "I didn't come here to try and buy the property, but I'm getting awful tired of not being able to live in the house."

She was very light-skinned, and I had no trouble making her realize that I wasn't white.

We soon had a long conversation going about the Island, and she asked me, "Would you buy the land if Willie would sell it?"

I told her I would if I could afford it. She told me she would see that I would be able to buy it at a price I could afford. She said her brother was sixty-seven and didn't need the headaches of paying taxes and owning land that far from Savannah.

I went back to the Island feeling I had accomplished a lot. I wasn't too optimistic about buying the land but I asked myself, "Why not hope?" The next week the power company came out and put the line across the property. Seeing the power line up, and me walking in the woods looking for property markers, the guys from next door came over to me and asked,

"Did you ever find out who owned that piece over there?"

"Not yet, but I'm working on it." I told him.

"I sure would like to know," he said.

About two months later, I came home from work and saw this older white man sitting in my living room. When Linda saw the inquisitive look on my face she quickly said, "This is Mr. Roberts from Savannah." I had just done the same thing people had been doing with me all of my life. After we both got over the fact we were both black, we laughed about it for a while and he told me a lot of experiences he had and I could relate to most of them. I also realized why his sister told me she would be sure no one got the property but me. After talking to him for about ten minutes, I knew he would let me have it. For once, I had found someone who belonged to the same club I did, and he was going to help me.

Mr. Roberts spent the night with us and was up at five the next morning. We sat around and drank coffee until it was time for the bank to open. I was there when it opened and withdrew the token price he charged me for it. We went to the Court House and did all of the documents to transfer the property to me. When it was all legally done, he took off to Savannah with his 1937 Chevrolet truck purring like a kitten. I appreciated what he had done for us and felt certain closeness to him for a long time. He died at the age of seventy-five. A few years later I drove by where he had lived and saw what was left of his old Chevy truck as it sat out in a field near the house rusting away.

I was quite upset with the family next door for not allowing me to put the power line across their property. When the purchase of the property was complete and I had the deed to it, I took a walk in the woods near their house. Only this time I made sure he saw me. As I expected, he came over to me and asked,

"Did you ever find who owned it?"

I told him, "Yes, I own it now."

His eyes almost popped out, but he quickly recovered his composure and said, "I sure would like to buy that corner over there, it would square mine up. If you ever want to sell that little piece I would sure like to buy it."

I told him, "I bought it for the same reason you wanted it, to keep you from beside me, and I expect you to clean up all the trash you dumped there." They sold the house about two months later. I was learning to survive in the South.

When I first came home from New York, I didn't try to find a job right away. I had a month's disability pay coming from my workman compensation. I also needed to get in shape after the operation, but most of all I had decided to try and come up with a "hustle" instead of trying to enter the famous Stockton job market. Self-employment would provide me with more money if I could find the right thing. I considered a lot of things, but none seemed to be what I wanted to do or would provide enough income. I even thought about going back to New York to work for a couple of months, but the idea didn't sound very promising. My experience with working in Stockton sounded even less promising than going back to my old job in New York. I would come home on one weekend a month as a lot of other people from the Island did.

I am often asked today, "Why did you go to New York to work? I would never live in that stinking place." The white person didn't have to leave home to find a job unless he had more ambition than to work in the state for a "position" for less pay than people in other parts of the country. Most blacks that left South Carolina to go north to work did it out of necessity, not because we wanted to leave home. Often the difference in the pay was enough to live a good life in New York, pay rent there, and buy a home in the South. You had to be ambitious to do it, but most of the people who went north were very ambitious. A lot of skilled and hard working people left the South, which left the idea of the southern black being uneducated and unskilled. I have often seen a person living in the South who seemed to be the most worthless person to hire, but I have seen the same person leave the south and go north to work where he or she was respected as an employee, and become a very productive person.

My brother Ron was working for a company that was developing one of the old plantations for "Private Use Only." This was in 1963 and the South was gearing up for integration. A lot of private schools, resorts, and clubs were being built. Construction work was plentiful but it didn't pay anything. Ron kept asking me to come and work on the job with him because his machine was always breaking down. He often had to repair it himself or wait until someone came from Charleston or Savannah. He had to take the time off while the machine was down. The company needed a diesel mechanic but I wouldn't rush right over and ask for the job. I knew equipment mechanics were scarce in the area and I could probably get the job whenever I wanted it. They hired another mechanic in the meantime. When he didn't last more than a few weeks, I decided to go in and apply for the job. The secretary told me I would have to wait until the boss from Columbia came down. He was the person who did all of the hiring, except for laborers. I told myself at least they weren't considering it a labor position. I wanted the job because on my trip to the plantation I saw they had dozers, dirt pans, draglines and some heavy diesel water transfer pumps. I saw it as a chance to do what I had wanted to do since I got out of the army. Finally I was given a telephone number in Columbia to call. After about three days of trying, I finally got through to the person that I needed to talk to. He asked me where had I been working before, I told him New York. The conversation turned to ice, but I knew enough about the southern gentleman to know if you were from New York, you were union and most likely communist. I tried to change my speech manner to sound as local as possible and told him, "I only worked there for a few months." I also told him I was Ron's brother. He told me he would have someone get in touch with me in a few days.

Two days later the foreman from the job came out to talk with me. He brought Ron along to show him where I lived. He seemed like a level headed, down to earth and hard working person who I could communicate with. He put it all on the line and said,

"I only work for the company and I don't necessarily agree with their policies, but this is what it is." He hesitated for a moment and said, "We are building a private resort and no state or federal funds were going to be used in the construction of the plantation. A gate will he put up to screen the people who come on the plantation, and between you and me, they don't want any outsiders to come down here and cause trouble for them."

I told him, "I don't have any trouble with the rules, whatever turns them on, as long as they pay me."

He said it would be good if I could start the next day, because everything was broken down. The foreman had worked with enough people to at least respect them. He and I always got along good.

Pay was lousy for what they expected me to do. There must have been at least ten salesmen, and they all wanted to be my boss. Even the secretaries in the office were all bosses. In fact, anyone white was automatically in charge. They always kept the workers confused as to whom they were supposed to take orders from. When I came to work the first morning, I found three large truck engines scattered across the shop floor. They were all mixed together in a pile of sand and grease as if no one was supposed to put them back together. I took one look at the mess and started to go home, but I looked around and saw some of the operators with a smile on their faces. One said to the other,

"I wonder how long it will be before we run another one off."

I looked at the mass of engine parts and found there were enough parts in the mess for me to probably come up with three running engines. The foreman had earlier told me the operator with all of the excess mouth had taken all three of the trucks apart as a way to get even with the other mechanic. They all needed work, but he shouldn't have taken them apart while the poor guy was off for the week. When he came back in on Monday morning, he took one look at the mess, packed his tools and went home. I can't say I blamed him.

I finally made up my mind to stay, but just long enough to put the mess together for the poor guy who had just left, and to show those two assess it was possible. They both were from the Island, and I knew them both to be a pain in the neck. The foreman asked me if I wanted a helper. They both came forward and said, "I'll help." I chose a man who appeared as if he would listen but didn't know a pair of pliers from a screwdriver. The next day we cleaned the parts and started putting the three engines together. They were all surprised when they found out I owned Micrometers, Torque wrenches, and fuel injection equipment and were even more surprised when they found I knew how to use it all. Each day I would bring another puller or some strange tool I would need to get the work done. We worked straight through the weekends on straight time pay. I stayed cool in spite of the salesmen that constantly came by for me to "Check the oil, put some air in that tire, or, you can't leave until you change the oil in my jeep."

I know there is no such thing as an irreplaceable person but my strategy was to make myself as irreplaceable as possible and try to bargain for more pay. I needed the job and I was sure the job needed me. I would have to change a lot of their policies if it was going to work for either of us.

One of the first things that would have to be changed was; I was not allowed to go into the office to use the phone when I needed to order parts. In New York I was in charge of the four o'clock to midnight shift. My job included renting trucks, ordering parts and scheduling repairs, all with the help of the simple telephone. At the plantation, I wasn't allowed to use the phone in the office.

One of the property salesmen or the foreman would always tell me "Give me a list of what you want and I'll go to the office and order it for you."

This got to be awfully time consuming because if any questions were asked, and they didn't have the answers, they would have to find me and ask,

"What does this mean?"

I would tell them only what they asked for, and back to the phone they would go, only to come back a few minutes later for more information. After a while it got to the point where they would get arrogant and tell me I didn't know what I was talking about. They wanted some sort of description written out for what I wanted. One day I needed a hydraulic hose and a control valve, the hose had special ends on it that would only fit that machine because it had been modified. I wrote the description, "Due to the fact this machine has been modified to use only NP (national pipe thread) or SAE hose, I find it necessary to convert it all back to the standard manufactures hose (Euclid.) I'll need all the hose that supply the valve that dump the pan, including all hoses to the upper control valve. It appears to have been changed to the General Hydro system. This conversion will eliminate the problem of having to use hoses with your fittings on one end and NP on the other." I gave the note to the foreman, and he took it to the office and laughed all the way there.

A little later the salesman came out to me and said the people didn't know what I wanted. I told him to take their phone number and the person's name he had talked to and I would go home to my phone and call him. He told me that wasn't necessary, as he would have the company people from Charleston come out and take a look at it. The man was a total idiot. I went to work on something else and forgot about the whole thing until about three days later; I saw the distributor's service truck parked near the machine. I went over to watch he and the salesman work out the problem. The mechanic from the distributor went up on the machine, looked at what had been done and said to me,

"This thing has been changed, do you know whose control valve this is?" I said, "It looks like General Hydro." He looked at it for a couple of seconds and said,

"Looks like all you need here is a piece of hose and the Euclid control valve." I said, "Yep, that should do it. I'll need the Euclid fitting on both ends of the hose." The salesman stuck his chest out as if he had just solved the world's financial problems. The whole thing had gone right over his head. He was real proud of that distributor mechanic for showing me up. I told myself I would have to try again. A month later, the transfer case cracked on the same machine. The salesman came charging out in his jeep and asked,

"What's it going to take to get this thing going this time!"

I was busy trying to see what damage had been done to the machine, and I said off the top of my head, "Probably a transfer case." He got back into his jeep and went bouncing off to the office. The foreman and I looked at each other and we both smiled. Tommie, the foreman, asked me,

"I wonder what will he come up with this time?" I said, "Only the Lord knows."

I went ahead and took the machine apart, welded the case, went to Savannah for bearings and had the machine going in a couple of days. About a week later the boss came down from Columbia and made a beeline to me with fire in his eyes and asked, "What did you order that cost forty-six hundred dollars?" I hesitated for a second to control my desire to laugh and said, "Nothing that I know of."

Tommy got scared, jumped into his truck and took off to get out of the line of fire. The salesman was standing near enough to hear the conversation. He knew the conversation would get around to him shortly, so he came over to defend himself and put all of the blame on me.

"You told me you needed a transfer case for the pan,"

I told him, "You assumed I needed it and you went and ordered it, so don't stand here and try to lie your way out of it."

That was a no-no for me to tell him in that manner, especially in the presence of the boss. Telling him off was what I had been waiting to do since the incident with the hydraulic hose. I just couldn't pass up the chance.

I really didn't care if they fired me or not, but the salesman had a good salary and a good "position" to lose, so he surely couldn't risk arguing with me. At this stage I knew they needed me but would fire me in a heartbeat for "Talking back" to the salesman. I backed off and told the boss I knew most of the people at the distributor and I felt sure I could get them to take it back for a ten percent handling fee.

"Let's go up to the office and you can call them and see what we can do about this thing."

On the way to the office I told him "Things like this can easily be avoided if I'm allowed to order my own parts, and it's keeping me from getting my work done." I suggested they set up a purchase order system for theirs and my protection. I was allowed to use the phone after that. I was still discussed over the fact I had to go through all of the headaches for a simple thing as using the telephone. Even after the conversation with the boss about using the phone, I had to go into the office. When I got inside, one of the office crew would always ask in a paternalistic manner, "What do you want?" My answer was always the same: "Need to order some parts." Do you have a number we can call the people for you? Write down what you want and someone will call them in a minute, which usually turned out to be an hour.

One day I was at the office when a new (very cute) secretary was there who didn't know me. She was talking at a disgusting pace that I thought would never end. I could tell from her expression she was very impressed with my looks. I had on only a T-shirt from the waist up and had a great tan and build. Her eyes were also green. She came very close to my face and said in a voice that was just above a whisper,

"I just love a man with green eyes."

In the back of my mind I heard a little voice saying, "*Go awaaay, little girl.*" I asked myself,

"I wonder how many things I can make her say to embarrass the rest of the office crew."

The gate at the entrance to the plantation was being put up. I asked her, "What are they doing at the entrance?"

"Putting up the gate," she told me.

"What kind of gate?" I felt the office go quiet. Even the typewriters in the back offices stopped.

"You know, a gate so we can say who can come here and who can't."

"I played dumb. What do you mean?" Now it was really quiet.

"You know, to keep the niggers out. We don't want them over here, we could never sell any property if they were allowed to come."

I was looking through the telephone directory as I talked to her, but I could see from the corner of my eye all kind of signs were being given to shut her up. I was having fun and took one last stab.

"Why don't they want them over here?"

Before she answered, I picked up the phone and started dialing. Someone in the back called her and she went smiling to the back.

I came back in about ten minutes, I figured by now they had gotten her straight. She was supposed to have gotten some information for me and I was supposed to ask for it. They told me she was busy in the back and they would ask her if she had gotten the information. Before anyone had a chance to stop me, I walked to the back office, and to her desk. I carried a normal conversation with her but she couldn't look me in the face. All of the friendliness she had earlier was gone. I walked back through the front office about to burst with laughter, and it showed on my face. It was about a month later before she realized I wasn't angry with her, and she renewed her pursuit of me. At first she would find me and ask me to fill a Jeep with gas or check the air pressure in tires. Later she started coming when there was no one else around, usually when everyone had gone home. She often had a piece of candy or cake for me. She was quite a morsel but I was very happily married. I knew what the gate was for; I had heard it a hundred times from people who didn't know me. Almost everyone talked about it in his or her spare time, but now, they knew that I knew.

One day the foreman hired a guy who had just gotten a dishonorable discharge from the Marine Corps. He was automatically put in charge of labor, and of course labor meant blacks. He told some of the older guys they would have to call him "mister." A few of them said, "Yas sah," and called him mister from then on. Most of the younger group refused to ever call him mister. He told this one guy if he would call him mister he would see that he got a raise. The guy told him, "Man, if you could get a raise for me, you would have one for yourself." He yelled it out so the whole crew could hear it.

Most foremen would do anything, even for less pay than a lot of blacks if he was "put in charge." The rule was to put "Manager" or "Foreman" on his shirt in bold print and he would work all week for peanuts. Often he was uneducated, without any skill, and a natural hard-ass, which was his only asset. The new labor foreman found I was paid more than he was, and it bothered him. One day he finally got around to asking me about it. He asked me in the only manner he knew,

"Why do they pay you so much, you don't do anything?" They pay you more than they do me.

I answered in the same manner he asked me. "They need me but they don't need you. They can find a little dumb-ass foreman anywhere, but they had to import me from New York." He always said he couldn't stand people from New York.

He told me, "If you keep talking like that, I'll have you looking for another job."

"I can find one easy enough, but what if you got fired? You have a DD from the Marine Corps, no skills and only a tenth grade education. Now you tell me who do you think is more employable?"

He got flying mad and promised to have me fired before the week was over and headed to the office. He was the next on my list to teach that "foremen" weren't God. He started the next week wanting to become a dragline operator. I suppose I had awakened the need for a skill in him.

Every time one of the operators got off the machine he would get on it and screw up the control cables. He considered himself above asking one of the black operators to teach him. Every time he used the machine, he tangled the cables and came to me and said, "Straighten out that machine." I did it the first two times for the sake of the operator. When he came to me the third time I told him,

"That's your screw-up, and the operator is about to get a piece of your little white ass."

He changed it himself, but the next noon hour he was back on it again. This time the operator had taken the safety off, and he put the boom over the cab and did about a thousand dollars worth of damage to the machine. The boss came out and started raising hell with the operator. I got into the discussion and told him the labor foreman had done it, and in the past week, he had destroyed over five hundred dollars worth of cable. The next week he was gone. I didn't feel big about what I had done, but it was getting to the point where it was going to be him or me. I knew all of their ways and could use it against them, but I also felt I was becoming one of them. The new labor foreman had finally got to me and I was able to push harder than he could.

When I first came home from New York, I made a lot of stills for the local moon shiners. At a hundred dollars each it was worth it to stay up all night, finish the still, and be ready for work the next morning. I started keeping a sheet of copper in one of my spare bedrooms so I could have one ready the next morning, in case the sheriff's department broke one up. I sat up many nights to get a still out for someone who had to have it for the next days run. One night I was building one for an older man who had been in the business for more than twenty-five years. He was down on his luck, someone had stolen his still and most of his stash of moonshine and it had left him flat broke. He told me that he probably wouldn't be able to pay me until he got back in the woods and made a run.

"What I need is someone to back me," he told me.

"What do you mean, back you?"

"Someone to let me have enough money to get started for a part of the business."

He kept talking as I welded on the copper pot. He told me he had made a living from making moonshine whiskey for most of his life but never made enough to get into the big time. It had always been a struggle for him even though he knew as much or more about making whiskey than anyone else on the Island.

"I use to make it for all of those crackers that use to come over here. They had us make it while they took it all away and gave us five dollars a gallon for it."

Knowing what a gallon was selling for in the upper counties, they were getting over on him like fat rats. As I listened to him I decided he needed a break, and out of pity, or the desire to make money, I agreed to go into business with him. He became very excited when I told him I would be his partner.

What started out as a very depressing day for him was now, at three o'clock in the morning, turning out to be a very good day. The pace of the conversation picked up about twice its original speed as we both started planning for what was to become a new hustle for me. At first I didn't know anything about making whiskey but it didn't take me long to learn. I bought all of the rye, sugar, and all other supplies that we always seemed to need. Bob, the older man, did all of the cooking; I hauled it and sold it to retail buyers in small lots at first. Hauling the whiskey got too risky, and the profits were too slow in coming. I contacted a person in North Carolina who would take all we could supply and he told me how we could ship it out on his tractor-trailer trucks. At first I was afraid to do business with him. I went to North Carolina and checked with some of the people that knew him and they all assured me that it would be safe to do business with him.

A driver would come and pick it up from any spot we chose, but I never told him in advance where it was going to be. I would always meet him and take him to the pick-up point. After a few weeks I learned the driver was safe to do business with and I always had him come to the same spot. We were in the big time but I constantly had problems with Bob getting drunk while he was at the still. I soon figured out he was so saturated from all of his years of constantly drinking that he only had to smell a glass and he would become absolutely useless for the rest of the day, or when he finally decided to sober up. I had to learn to cook so I could-pinch hit when Bob was on one of his binges. It got to be fun, but I was always afraid in the woods at night; every time a bush would shake or a rat would run, I would swear it was the law and almost panic.

Bob wanted to keep me out of the woods as much as possible, which kept him sober more often. Staying out of the woods was no big problem for me. Bob always said he wanted me to stay home and out of trouble in case he got caught and I would be available to get him out of jail. I remember a very dark night when both of us were in the woods around three in the morning. As we changed the water from the cooling barrel, we threw it under a large tree that a storm had partially blown over. We were both tired and finally fell asleep. Pouring water under the leaning tree had softened the ground under it and it fell down. The noise it made sounded like a lightning bolt hitting only a few feet away. We both woke up running and never stopped until we were out of the woods. Bob's fear of jails was almost as great as my fear of being in the woods at night. One of the local merchants would supply and deliver the sugar we used. The money from my job would pay the bills, but we wanted to save extra money to build a house. Linda was pregnant again and couldn't work even if she could have found a job. I had to keep the extra hustle going to make ends meet.

Making moonshine can he almost comical at times. I saw moonshine stills a lot of times when I was a young boy at Rice Patch and Seaside. The tales from both places were about the same. Once some of us boys were out rabbit hunting at Seaside when we came upon a still and some of the older boys knew what it was. We took the top off the barrels of mash, found a quart jar, dipped it full and started passing it around. After about thirty minutes of passing the jar we were all flat on our behinds. We had a large freshly plowed field to cross to get to the main road. We walked about half way and had to crawl the other half. Most of the people at Seaside who are my age can tell some strange tales about coming upon a still in the woods and leaving it barely able to walk. We continued to go to the one we found for a couple of weeks until one day the owner caught us as we were leaving. We had just started to cross the plowed field when he spotted us. I saw him before he saw me and hid behind a little clump of bushes. He caught a couple of the other boys and took his belt off and tore their behinds up. I stayed behind the brush until someone discovered that I was missing. I saw them pointing at the bushes where I was hiding and I knew they were making plans to catch me for the old guy to use his belt on. They had walked back to the woods and had a good distance to get to where I was hiding. Before they started to move, I ran toward the road. With the distance they had to close on me, I knew they couldn't catch me, and I beat them to the road. The running and the mash made me throw up about three times. The man later told me he could have followed me from the vomit trail I left.

To make moonshine, scrap iron, bush, or what ever you will hear it called is quite simple. You start with about a hundred pounds of corn or rye, put it in a barrel, add about twenty gallons of water (some people will use more or less), let it swell and begin to sour. Then add about fifty or sixty pounds of sugar and wait for it to ferment. Experience will tell you when it's ready to run. You can use the grain over for about two or three times, but the yield starts dropping off after about the second time of using it. When it's ready, strain and pour it into the pot, put the condenser on it, and from the condenser, attach about ten feet of copper tubing. Coil the tubing down inside a barrel and run it out the lower part of the barrel. Make a watertight seal around the tubing, fill the barrel with cold water, and you are ready to make moonshine. At first you have to cook it slowly or it will boil over into the condenser (puke) and ruin what could be a beautiful run and become awfully expensive. When we got it coming out of the coil, it was a beautiful sight and all we had to do was keep the fire going, change the water when it got hot, and change the jugs when they got full. We usually ran about five barrels at a time, and it would yield about thirty-five to forty gallons that would wholesale for around eight dollars a gallon. The sugar cost around six dollars for each barrel, so the profit was very good. We ran about every three days during the summer. I bought a 1954 Chevy to haul it in.

The merchant who we bought sugar from was making a good profit on it with the inflated prices that he charged us. He was never satisfied and always wanted a part of our business as well, but he didn't want to take any of the risk. He was white, and Bob didn't want to trust him at all, but I didn't want to get caught hauling three hundred pounds of sugar either. Hauling large amounts of sugar was just as much against the law as hauling 'shine, so I decided to trust him, and it proved to he a mistake. He got to know most of our operation and even got an occasional gallon of whiskey from us for his friends. He knew where we picked it up from, but he didn't know where the still was located. One evening I made the pick-up that Bob had run earlier that day. As soon as I pulled away from the spot a highway patrolman pulled in behind me, and when I got on the main road, he stopped me. He had a state and a federal officer in the car.

"What do you have in the trunk of the car?" He asked

"Watermelons." I told him

Watermelons were the only thing I could think of that would make the Chevy set down in the back as it was. He looked in the back seat, where I had it loaded also. "Watermelons in jugs?" He asked

I knew he had me so I said, "Not the whole melon, just the juice."

He laughed and said, "Yeah sure, I'll bet it has already soured too."

He took me into town but didn't lock me up. I filled out the required papers and went home. They took the car and the load of whiskey. The fine was three hundred dollars (less than one day's run).

Law enforcement claimed that they spent years and millions to break up the moonshine trade. One reason for the moonshine was they only allowed a very few state stores to be opened in the area. When they allowed more state stores to open, you had to look awfully hard to find a still on the Island. The fine was only three hundred dollars for the first offense, and the profits were unbelievable. Sometimes it could be the only source of income for years. I have traveled over most of the United States, and almost always where you have a dry county or state, you will find moonshine whiskey.

At first I didn't believe we had been set up, but Bob insisted, "The sugar man is the lousy bastard that set you up."

To show Bob he was wrong, I decided to set the sugar man up and see if he had squealed to the law. I went by his store and sat around for a while. I told him I had a big run to haul but I didn't want to use my new car because I didn't want it taken. I asked him if I could use his old pickup.

I said to him "Nobody would ever suspect me in an old truck."

"It's not running, but if you wait for about an hour I can probably get it running for you." He replied.

I really didn't need to use any of his vehicles but wanted to see if he sat me up, as Bob believed he had.

I told him, "I have to meet a tractor trailer rig from North Carolina which will be here at eight o'clock and it's seven now, I suppose I'll have to use my new car."

As I was getting into the car to leave, I told him, "If you see any patrols over here, let me know so I can send the truck back."

I headed to the intersection where I told him the pickup would take place and got there right at eight o'clock. As I crossed the intersection the whole area turned blue from the lights of law enforcement cars. Now I knew who sat me up. I knew the patrolman and told him,

"I don't have anything. I was just trying to find out who sat me up."

"I just stopped you to check your driver's license," He said.

We had gotten to know each other, and we could talk. After all, he could have locked me up before and didn't, so I felt I owed him one. After all of the others had gone, we sat on our cars and talked.

"Look, I know what you are thinking, but for your sake don't do anything to get yourself in trouble. You made good money running 'shine, so let it drop at that."

I took his advice. He acknowledged the sugar merchant was the one who sat me up the first time. We both knew that if anything were to happen to the bastard I would be the first person everyone would come looking for. I found myself hoping nothing would happen to him.

The only thing that really got next to me about the whole ordeal of me getting caught for hauling moonshine happened when I was at work about two weeks later. One of the company officers came out to me and told me he wanted to see me in the office. I finished what I was doing and went in to see him. I noticed he had a look on his face that he wanted to make me think was a frown, and it was supposed to intimidate me. He pretended to shuffle papers around on his desk to look as important as possible and to make me wonder as long as possible why he had called me in. He finally looked up from doing absolutely nothing and cleared his throat to make it sound as authoritarian as possible.

"Look, we have a policy here, we don't like to hire people who have been in trouble with the law or keep people who get in trouble."

For the life of me I couldn't figure out what he was trying to tell me and I asked, "So?"

"I understand that you were caught hauling moonshine whiskey a few weeks ago?" I said, "Yes, I was, but why are you telling me this?"

He began to turn red from the tone of my voice and said, "Well, like I said, we don't like people working for us that have been in trouble."

I got a little hotter and asked, "What do you mean, trouble?"

The bastard was actually trying to use the incident to play with me.

"If you get into anything else, we will have to let you go,"

He actually seemed to enjoy toying with me, and it pissed me off as never before.

"You got to be shittin' me. This whole thing came up because I asked you for a raise last week. Why the hell do you think I was able to work for the measly wages you people are paying me? I made moonshine, that's why. We both made out in the deal, you tell me who you will find to replace me for the salary that you are paying me. If you have in mind to fire me, do it now, or give me the raise or I am quitting anyway."

"I'll have to let you know in a couple of days."

I started to press it, but I knew what the outcome would be. The next week the raise was in my pay as I suspected it would be. He was just trying to get even with me for asking for the raise and the time I had made the new secretary tell me the purpose of the gate. I went back and was talking to the foreman about what happened in the office. He was scared as usual and said,

"You know he can get you fired."

"If everyone on the job can fire me, I didn't have much of a job anyway." I told him

They finally fired the foreman from the job when he came in drunk, and the boss was there. I tried to get him to go back home for the day but he insisted on staying. I finally got him to lie in the cab of a pickup, and he went to sleep. As soon as he went to sleep, the boss needed to use the truck. He opened the door and the foreman almost fell out of the vehicle. The boss cursed him for some of the worst things I had ever heard another human being called. The foreman stood there at what looked like a staggering position of attention as if he felt the boss was entitled to call him such names. After standing as long as his drunken state would physically allow, he wandered over to a soda crate where he tried to sit upon it. Nothing was working for him that day because the crate fell down and he gave up and lay down beside the crate. He either passed out or pretended to while the boss continued to curse him.

I came back to check on him in a couple of hours, and he was just coming around. He was ready to go back to work, but they had truly fired him this time. His ride wasn't to come until five, so I told him I would take him home. As we went out the gate the boss was standing there and told me to put him off at the gate and, "Let him find his own damned way home." I insisted that I would take him home. I hated to see him leave, because he was about the only level headed person there. I also didn't know what his replacement would be like. That would determine whether I would stay there or have to find another job.

I often thought about going back to New York when the pressure got almost unbearable, but we had already built a home on the Island and we didn't want to leave. If we went back to New York, my pay would more than double, which would offset the cost of living away from home. If I had never lived anywhere else, the pressure wouldn't have been so great. I had lived and worked with a lot of different people, and to come back home and have people try to reduce me to the lowest form possible would drive me mad at times. It seemed every white person on any job had a first name of "mister." As far as a black person was concerned, even the whites who were considered to be in a "lower financial state" (poor whites) called most of the others mister, mister Bill, mister Bob, Mister Sam and they got awfully upset when I refused to do it.

One of the worst ways to antagonize them would be to use intelligence in communicating. Everyone would try to belittle you. I often thought "I took all of those English courses for nothing." I was on the phone one day and asked the operator for the phone number for Philip's Diesel. The operator asked me if it was a person's name, or was it an establishment. I told her it was an establishment. When I got off the phone everyone at the office made such a big issue out of such a small thing.

"Why establishment? Why not just a garage, or a mechanic's shop?"

Of course, they were all trying, without much success, to speak with the Gullah accent to suggest I should do the same thing.

The job had gotten to be just a cover for my moonshine hustle anyway. I walked out of the office without giving them the benefit of an argument. Another disgusting situation would be for me to come up with an intelligent way to get a job done. When it was all implemented, it was always someone else's idea. The person who usually got the credit was the simplest person around. Even when everyone involved knew it was your project. The foreman or the person with "Manager" written on the front of his shirt was always given credit for it. After all, he was the one who "supervised" you while you planned it all out, took a lot of pride in it, and worked your ass off to get it all put together, only to have some "Boss" come around and say, "Look what a great job Tom got his boys to do." While Tom stood with a big shit eating grin on his face and lapped up all of the brownie points that were so important to him. Actually, "Good ol Tom" couldn't find his ass with both hands, and was a nuisance to you throughout the whole project. The one good thing about Tom was if he watched you for ten years he would never be able to comprehend what I had been doing throughout the project. If at any time he got to be too much of a pain for me I could always screw something up or delay the whole thing. He usually tried to get along with me.

The system demanded that you always make "Good ol Tom" feel important. You could always use him to get what you needed. Pressure could come from both directions on him, and I never let up as long as he wanted to be an ass, but the day he came down to earth, we became friends. Just before he was fired from the job, it had gotten to the point where I became his supervisor without him even knowing it. With laying all of the water and sewer systems, along came blueprints, which he didn't know anything about, and his keeping the job depended on me. He had always treated me with respect, and I always did the same for him because I was afraid of who would replace him. I often thought we were each other's prisoners. After about the third time we went to the supply house in town together, he stayed outside in the truck and told me,

"You go ahead, I'll stay outside and sleep."

What really bothered Tom was whenever we went inside, this one jerk behind the counter would always bring up something about "Those niggers in Alabama and Mississippi." When he started telling "nigger jokes," everyone would join in. It never really bothered me because I had heard everyone of them at least twice, but it sure as hell put foreman Tom in a bad spot. I am sure if he didn't laugh at them they would have branded him as a "Nigger lover," and if he laughed at them, I would give him hell when we got back in the truck. The guy behind the counter who always put all of his shortcomings on all the black people of Alabama and Mississippi, knew me, and did a lot of it to try and aggravate me, or at least to remind me "who I am" His biggest problem was I often made a diagram and took it inside with me and used it to order supplies.

"You don't need that thing, just tell me what the hell you want and I'll get it for you," he often told me.

One morning I gave a drawing to Tom to take in to him while I went next door to get coffee. He and Tom were to get everything we would need for the days work. He came out to the truck and asked,

"What's this bull-shit you got on this paper?" You better come inside and let me know what the hell you want."(I didn't think he could read very well.)

I must admit there were times when I wanted to tell him a piece of my mind, but that was what he wanted me to do and give him the opportunity to spill all his hatred and prejudices on me. I figured results would be greater if he kept it inside or at least told it to other whites. That situation seems to never end. Often a white person who has known me for years would start telling me "Nigger jokes" as if I am suppose to appreciate them. It's often done as a joke, but more often it's done as a method to keep reminding me "who I am." It's usually done whenever a conversation is in my corner or they think I'm getting too much attention.

Someone will start by saying,

"Let me tell you about this old nigger that lives down the road from me."

Usually only the whites will be embarrassed about it and would rather the person shut up. Ron has often told me if he really wanted to find out something in a crowd of strange white people who don't know him, all he had to do was walk in their midst and start telling ethnic jokes and the crowd will automatically become his.

He said that he often took bets within on how long it would take for the crowd to start telling him what he wanted to know. He always stayed up on the strategy of the whites and often found it humorous.

Our third daughter was born in 1966. When I took Linda to the county hospital at six in the morning, her pains had just started. I said a prayer of thanks to the little life she was carrying inside for allowing me to sleep through the night. You must remember, in 1966 the whole country was going through a complete revolution on integration, government programs, equal opportunity, quotas, and government funding. People who ran institutions that were getting federal funds were under a lot of pressure to get all of the paper work done and do everything right, or have it all cut off or delayed. After a very short wait, most of the staff nurses came to Linda's bedside to help her. We were totally surprised by the excellent treatment she was getting.

Our last daughter was born in Brooklyn and Vicki was born in a naval hospital. Linda had never been to the county hospital before and had been somewhat reluctant to go there. She almost talked me into taking her to Savannah, but I finally convinced her to go to the local hospital after I told her I would stay at her bedside as long as they would allow. The treatment was unbelievable. All through labor she had two nurses helping her and I was allowed to stay in the room with her. They even brought me a chair to sit in. I know by today's standards this sounds minute, but it would have been unheard of in the sixties for what appeared to be an interracial relationship to get that much attention. They gave Linda a sedative to help her relax. The two nurses sat and counted every second between the labor pains. Linda told me she was glad she had come to the local hospital instead of going all the way to Savannah. We were both very appreciative of the excellent treatment, and I began to think the South was finally beginning to come around.

Everything was done almost too perfect. Linda had a cousin in the hospital at the same time, and she wasn't getting any treatment at all, just the same old system, and she was complaining about not getting any attention.

On the third morning, a black nurse from the Island was working. She came in to visit Linda and as they were talking, I came into the room. She knew me, but she didn't know that I was Linda's husband. She started laughing to the point where I thought that she was going to fall out of the chair. She finally gathered her composure and said,

"So you are the couple all the uproar is about." She told us, the morning we came into the hospital, the staff called a meeting about that "Integrated" couple in room 215.

"They are here to try our integration policies, and we don't want to get mixed up with all of this red tape, so we want everything done just right. Whatever she wants, give it to her."

The nurse also told us the staff had picked the nurses who would attend Linda. "Nothing but the best," the nurse jokingly said. I would have given them an A-plus on their compliance policies. The nurse made one mistake when she asked them,

"You mean Linda's husband? He isn't white?"

After she told Linda she had corrected them, she walked out of the room. As she was leaving, Linda said to me in a perfect Gullah accent, "fass affie."

The secretary in the office almost blew it all as she was typing the birth certificate. We wanted to get everything done before we left and would wait until everything was completed. She stopped in the middle of the form and never got started again. I finally asked her what was holding her up. She said she needed some more information and it would be a while before the doctor came down. After a long wait, Linda went out to the car to wait for me and to let the other kids see their new sister. I finally asked the secretary,

"What information do you need?" At the same time I walked behind her desk to look at the form, but she put her hands over it and said,

"I'll have to get it from the doctor."

"Try me, I should be able to help, after all, only so much information is put on the birth certificate."

She moved her hand and I saw she had stopped at the famous race block. I used as much tact as possible and asked her,

"Is that what you need to know?"

To cover up her ignorance of the matter she became angry, turned red and asked, "How the hell should I know?"

"She is 'Negro' and for your information sweetheart, if she is one-eighth, she is it." I didn't get angry with her, as a matter of fact I sympathized with her up to the point where she got angry. She made record time in finishing the certificate. We left the hospital, and they returned to normal. The following year our son was born (we decided to give the rascal one more chance). The treatment at the hospital was standard this time, but we took it in stride and Linda was home in two days. She and her nurse friend still laugh about the meeting of the minds that was held when our daughter was born at the local hospital. She once told Linda,

"Girl, it's a good thing your old man went with you, if not, they never would have given your baby to you."

I have been in on long strategy sessions on school integration laws, and "How we must deal with the problem" on more than one occasion. It gets to be fun when one person in the crowd will know the others, but not me, and won't shut up. Someone will constantly try and get me to leave, but try as he or she might, I won't leave and the person won't shut up. I won't leave because I feel that "I just gotta hear this" after all has been said, I'll go to the bathroom for a few minutes. When I return, one person would have told the others about me. Everyone will often find a quick excuse to leave, and think, "All of the bull I just put out, and one "Of them" heard the whole thing."

If I had to work or be with someone for a while, I often found myself wanting the person to know right away for the sake of getting a good relationship started. I didn't want it to come up later and lose a very good customer over some small thing he or she might have said weeks ago. It probably went right over my head when they said it. This is one of my biggest problems today in working with the public. I accept jokes as human nature. We all tell them, but where it hurts most is when I lose that person as a customer, or worse, fail to gain their friendship and they become my enemy. I find a lot of people were forewarned before they came to me for service. I was never offended by it because the people came to me for my services and not for my race or color. People don't always disassociate themselves from me after a negative racial conversation either. I worked as a volunteer with a youth group in my spare time and had my two younger children in the program. Once I came in to give one of the other chaperones a break and when I came into the room I asked him,

"How's it going?"

He instantly told me, "If I had my way I would send all of these nigger boys home."

I asked him what kind of problems was he having. He couldn't come up with anything that made sense. I decided to drop it and see if it was prejudice or just talk. We were still talking when my son came up thirty minutes later and said, "Hi, Dad." The guy saw my son's nametag, looked down, shuffled his feet, turned very red, and didn't really know what to say.

I broke the ice by saying "This is my son Harold." He said, "Hi, Harold," and the conversation went back to normal and it never came up again. He has never openly apologized for the incident, but he has shown in a hundred different ways it really bothered him. Later I found that he was the most helpful person with young people of any color that I had ever worked with. Like I have done on more than one occasion, he put his foot in his mouth and I didn't think an apology was necessary. I am sure he wanted to bite the foot off.

Stereotyping is no different when it comes from blacks or whites. I often get into detailed discussions with people, mostly blacks. As a rule, we will usually be in agreement on most racial or political matters. Often a person that doesn't know me will join the conversation and he or she will start giving me the old "white" treatment. I can see it right away and have build up a system that will surprise the person, but most often drive them raving mad. I know very well where she or he is coming from in their conversation. Often the person refuses to see me as a black person and get the idea that I could never understand what he or she is trying to get across. The best way is to converse with the person as if you are black but let him continue to think you are white. Take him on one on one, on a subject that you are more familiar with than he is and be on the same side but be a different color. When he calls you a "motha," call him one in return, with the same accent. Every so often be a little negative with him, just enough to get even with him for trying to keep you "white." I use the term "white" and "black" here only as a state of mind and not as an indication of a person's race or color. I probably get more rejections from blacks than I do from whites because I am assumed to be white by both groups. I will be readily accepted by white groups on looks but will also be rejected by blacks for the same reason.

Once I was at an outdoor cookout and had done most of the planning and cooking for the event. I was having quite a conversation with a couple of middle-aged ladies who had been over the hill for a couple of years but weren't quite ready to admit it. They had come down from New York for the event and were having a good time on scotch and water. I was pouring drinks for them and one of them asked me if I wanted to play whist with them. I am sure it was to see if I was as liberal as I pretended to be or was it just a front to get accepted by the group. I accepted the invitation to join their card game, and instantly beat the hell out of them at what was suppose to be "their" game. They had to take one more shot at "finding me out." The one that looked more available whispered something to one of the others. I wasn't as high as I let on to be and overheard her say to the other woman, "See if he will drink out of your glass, that way we will know if he is for real or not." She held her glass out to me and said, "My drink tastes funny, how about tasting it and see if there is something wrong with it." I told her, "If it tastes funny, I sure as hell don't want to taste it." They all began to shake their heads as to say, "I knew he was like the rest of them." I gave them time to let the idea of me being a bigot soak in. I took the other ladies' drink and downed it in one big gulp, and said,

"I don't find a damn thing wrong with that one. If it tastes strange, I would pour it out."

Shortly after, Linda came up and sat on my lap, I introduced her as my wife and a new set of rules were formed.

"Now why in hell would she want to marry a white guy?" was the new question in everyone's mind.

We continued a great game of whist until near midnight and they finally got around to asking someone to "explain" me to them. We had a good laugh about the whole thing when I told them I knew what they were up to the whole time.

I do a lot of work on some of the other Islands. I know most of the people there and have an excellent relationship with them. A friend of mine will help me play the trick, whenever he is not ragging me himself. A lot of the older people that left the Island in the earlier years have come back to retire after working in the northern cities for most of their lives. A lot of people still see the

South as it was when they left years ago and for a white person from the South to socialize with blacks still seems strange to a lot of people. Many times it is an excuse to tell a white person what he wanted to get off his chest for years, especially now that he is retired and the person is no longer considered a threat. The white man is the reason he had to go elsewhere for work in the first place. I have often taken a tongue lashing for the deeds of the southern whites and have also been through the segregated south as a black person. I'll assure you, both can be hard to take at times.

Even though I often have to take the verbal abuse meant for the white man, it doesn't bother me as much as it use to. First, I understand where the black man is coming from when he says the things he does. Secondly, I have learned to find humor in the way that it is applied to me. I have built up a system to offset the agony I might experience from being used as the scapegoat. I was often very greasy from working long hours in the bilges of boats. I wore bib overalls, and I used to chew tobacco. To the average person I sometimes appear to be a, "hick" or "red neck." When I came out for a break and joined the group of blacks for conversation. There will often be someone in the crowd that doesn't know me. The person would often dislike white people and don't want me around. He might have wanted to discuss the numbers game or anything the white man is not supposed to hear and take back to the wrong people. I know all about the numbers game, about the conversation on dreaming numbers, even though I don't believe in it. I know all about Harlem's 125th street and who used to do it there and I could also carry a hot conversation with the women standing around. The guy will usually develop a deep dislike for me and try to make me "white." I'll be white and play his little silly game. The hotter he gets the more I play the game with him.

One of the funnier incidents that come to mind is, once the minister and the chairman deacon from a church on the Island stopped by a group of us standing in front of my shop. The minister asked for directions to Sarah Adams' house. No one knew whom he was talking about. Just before they started to drive off, it came to me that Sarah Adams was Linda's aunt. Everyone referred to her as, "auntie." I told one of the other guys,

"I know who she is, he is looking for Auntie."

The deacon just couldn't pass up the chance to put this white man in his place. He must have been saving it for years. He got out of the car and stood up so all present could see and hear him, and said, "So, she is your aunt also?"

"No deacon Harvey, she is not, she is only my aunt-in-law. I'm married to her niece."

At that time the minister recognized me and gave thumbs up with both hands and laughed. I am sure it took Deak a long time to figure it out. Now, for all of you non-southerners, the term "aunt" or "uncle" was often put on older blacks' names when the white person wanted to show some amount of respect for them but didn't want to say "Mister." or "Mrs." and most blacks, including myself, don't like it and will often try for a come-back. I sort of hated to do it to Deak, but like him, I also couldn't pass up the chance.

I constantly applied for civil service jobs but have never had any luck. I have never figured out the proper method to gain federal employment. I have heard all sorts of things you have to have or be, to work for Uncle Sam, but nothing ever worked for me. I have been told I didn't fill the application out right. You have to know someone. You have to hold your mouth just right during the interview. You must have done the job in the armed service to qualify for it, and it must be on your discharge. You must be a ten-point veteran. You must be a five-point veteran. You must be a World War II Veteran. You must be a Korean War veteran. You must be a Vietnam veteran. My hat is off to anyone who has landed a Civil Service job.

I started applying for any civil service job, mostly labor jobs that kept coming open, just to get my foot in the door to advance to what I really wanted. Everyone said that was the best way to get started. I was brought in for an interview for a janitor job at an administration building. The interviewer (an air force first lieutenant) looked at my application and instantly told me I was over qualified. I didn't disagree with him, but I tried to plead my case. I told him I just wanted to get into federal employment and work my way up. He also agreed that was probably the way to do it. We discussed the pros and cons of the whole thing and I began to feel I had a chance at it until he told me,

"What we are really looking for is a colored boy, that's what we had before."

The government had the race word removed from the application at that time. Without a long explanation I told him I didn't care what kind of job it was or who had it before, I just wanted it now. I was very tactful about how I said it but he insisted it had to be a "colored boy." For me to tell him I was black at this stage surely wouldn't have gotten me the job. He told me if I were selected he would let me know within a week. Somehow I knew I wasn't going to be hired.

Sometime later I went to an air force hospital for another labor job. I was met by a gravel voiced senior master sergeant to be interviewed. We sat down and talked idly for a few minutes to break the ice. He then started asking me questions about my application. Again I began to feel positive about getting the job until he leaned forward on his desk, looked in all directions and said,

"I would like to hire you, but I can't."

"Why not?" I asked him

He leaned over a little farther in my direction and lowered his voice and said,

"Because all we have is nigger supervisors, and I don't think you would like working under them."

Somehow I knew that was what he was leading up to, and when he said it, I wasn't surprised, just disappointed. I knew to tell him I wasn't white would only put him on guard, and he surely wouldn't hire me. I again tried to plead my case, and told him

"I don't have any objection to working for black supervisors, I just want a job."

That seemed to anger him, but he told me I would be given the same consideration as everyone else. I decided to hope and not make an issue out of the interview. I knew the supervisor he was referring to and if he saw my application, maybe I would have a chance. I hoped but had no luck.

The next job I really wanted was as an equipment mechanic. The notice stated: "To be considered, applicant must have diesel engine experience." The job was in Charleston, and I was more optimistic about this one than I had been with the labor jobs. At least they couldn't say I was over qualified or it was considered a "colored" job. On the day of the interview, I left Stockton early to make sure I would be on time. When I got there, I found that they were going to hire two mechanics. I became more optimistic while talking to the other people there. I was the only one with diesel engine experience. I felt real good when I was called in for the interview. I went into the office and I tried to look and sit as professional as possible.

Some of my experience was gained in New York, even though he had never been there, he hated New York with a passion. The whole first five minutes of the interview was on how he hated New York. I tried to maintain and told him,

"Yeah, that's why I live here now, I didn't like it there either."

I tried to put on my best southern accent but he never slowed down. Finally he got to the spot on the application that said I had once belonged to a union. Having worked in New York was bad enough, but having worked union in that God-forsaken place was just more than he could tolerate. He finally asked me,

"Are you one of these jokers that like to work seven hours and get paid for eight?"

He didn't have to tell me I wasn't the person he had in mind to hire. I lost it, and asked him,

"What kind of dumb-ass question are you asking anyway? What have New York and unions got to do with what we are here for? The job application said forty-hour workweek, and that's what we should base our conversation on."

He turned very red and had the nerve to try to justify his asking me the ridiculous question.

"Some of these questions might sound a little ridiculous to you, but we have to get a background on how you think, to see if you will work out here." I really couldn't believe him and said,

"The FBI is doing enough of that crap without you getting involved in it also. You should stick to what you are being paid to do."

He remained disgustingly calm, and I realized he had accomplished what he set out to do, piss me off.

"That's all, your application will be considered and you will be notified of our decision,"

He was enjoying rubbing it in. I told him to take the application and wipe his ass with it as I left the office, and he still had the smile on his face. I asked myself "Why not?" I wasn't going to get the job anyway.

I very often hear whites in the South getting very angry and do a lot of complaining about all of the northern people coming down south and buying all of the choice property. It's not the "Yankees" that are screwing them, they did it to themselves, and the state of South Carolina contributed to it with its right to work laws. The same people who complained about the northern unions and their decent labor laws that forced companies to hired blacks as well as whites on the same job with equal pay, has now come back to haunt some southern retirees. With all of the prejudices, they cut their noses off to spite their faces. They still don't get it, I still hear about "Those Yankees and their unions are buying up the property that we can't afford."

On the way home from Charleston, I decided I had enough. As I drove along, in my mind I started to compose a letter to Washington. When I got home I put it on paper. My complaint was about how the interview had been conducted. It didn't matter in the least how much experience or how qualified or unqualified you were. The person doing the interview had the prerogative to hire or not hire you and the good old boy system would always prevail. I wrote about all of the interviews I had at all of the other installations and I thought they all had been conducted unfairly. In about a week, I got a letter from the Civil Service Commissioner from Washington and Atlanta the same day. The letter said I was claiming racial prejudices. At no point had I said race was the issue, but I didn't complain; at least I had gotten an answer.

In about three days, a black air force master sergeant came out to me and told me he was sent out to investigate my accusations of racial prejudices in the air force. We talked about the issues I had complained about, and he raved on about how unfair the whole system was and promised he would get it all changed. He went back to the base and opened up all of the civil service records and found a lot of things that shouldn't have been there. Most of all, beside every black person's name he found someone had penciled in "neg." He told me the lieutenant had been transferred and the air force master sergeant had been sent overseas and couldn't be reached. (About a month later I saw the master sergeant in town.) I knew better, but that was what he told me and I also knew it would be my word against theirs. I didn't claim racial prejudice because there was always the chance I would be accused of using my unique situation to get hired, or at least make trouble for someone. I also considered the fact someone would use me as an idea for reverse discrimination. I also thought about who would be on my side in a hearing. All I wanted was a job, not to create a new set of rules.

The master sergeant seemed to be on my side and I believed him. He told me he was going to send a copy of all of the things that he found wrong to the Civil Service Commissioner and I would receive a copy also. He even sat down with me and helped me compose a letter on the incident at Charleston but stayed away from anything about the other two installations, the ones that *he* represented. He said he would take care of that when he got Washington off their backs. I was gullible enough to believe everything he told me. It took me a long time to figure out why, mostly because he promised he would make sure I got a job with the air force. He was black, and I trusted him, which was my biggest mistake. In the years that followed, I got to know him and realized the only thing black about him was his face. I am sure he was hand picked by the air force for the job of silencing me. He once told me Dr. King was communist.

When I got a letter from Atlanta, it contained a copy of a regulation that had a paragraph circled in red ink. The paragraph read in essence, a member of a minority group shouldn't be passed over if his or her qualifications were higher than a non-minority. Mine were, so I thought, "Just maybe" and submitted the form for a hearing on those grounds.

In a few days, I received a letter stating my time for appealing the complaint had expired, but if I would come to their office at Charleston, they would review my case and see if an extension was warranted. They gave me a date and time to be there. On the

Monday morning they sat up to review my case, I had to wait for at least two hours past the time I had been scheduled. When the guy finally had his lunch he came in. He must have practiced a long time on the line that he used as his defense.

"How was I supposed to know he was a member of a minority group," were the only words that he wanted to discuss, and of course he denied any of the contents of our discussion during the interview. I found out the two people who were hired that day were his cousins and were from the same small town as the interviewer. Both cousins had worked in the same sawmill. I finally told myself that Charleston was probably too far to go to work anyway.

I went back to work with a different attitude after the civil service hearing. I felt, had I pressed harder I probably could have forced them into giving me the job. I also knew as soon as my temporary status was over, I would have to go through the same fight again. I gave it all up after deciding that with the hassle I was getting and the thought of moving to Charleston it wouldn't be worth it. There were too many uncertain factors involved.

The job at the plantation was getting to be more than I could stand. With the class distinction system getting worse with each passing day, I began to feel I would soon lose my marbles if I continued to work there.

The company started getting help from Georgia. They were all white, and all were made instant foremen. They all wanted to become equipment mechanics.

The man who brought them up there came over to me one day and asked, "Why do you only want to use colored help? I could bring you a helper from down home that would do anything that you wanted, just tell him what you want and just leave him alone."

I told him, "The helper that I have is doing fine, and he wouldn't want to become my supervisor as soon as he learned what a screwdriver looked like."

He just couldn't figure out why I would take sides with a black person, he stayed away from me after that.

I finally decided that it was time for me to leave when one morning the labor foreman came in and said that he had been promoted to superintendent. I knew with "superintendent" written on his shirt I would never be able to work with him. He had everyone gather around while he had a table brought over for him to stand on while he gave us the good news. With the help of a couple of his newly found lieutenants, he stood up on the table and cleared his throat about three times, and took his voice down to the pit of his diaphragm.

He said "I was promoted to superintendent this morning, so from now on all of you will be under my control, anyone caught going direct to the office will be fired, and that means everybody."

As he put the emphasis on "everybody," he looked at me. About halfway through his speech I started putting my tools in my truck in preparation to leave. We had been having problems before, so I didn't want to stay around and have to fight with him. When he came down from the table, he came over to me and said,

"I want to see you every morning to plan your days work."

In a very calm way I told him I wouldn't be around anymore. He asked, "Mind if I ask why?"

I told him I couldn't work under conditions like that. We both remained calm as he told me,

"I am just trying to make your job easier. I'll order all of the parts for you so you won't have to waste all of that time going to the office to do it yourself. Let me know at the end of the day what you need, and I'll order it for you."

That office was one hell of a sacred place. I told him I had tried that system before and it just didn't work. I also had another job offer that I either had to take or turn down, and this morning I decided I had better take it. He asked me to stay around for two weeks to help him get started and to find someone else. I promised that I would, but I put all my tools into my truck and left that afternoon.

They often called me back for the next two years to do work for them, and I always went back to do it. This time I would set the hourly rate and I didn't have a boss to deal with. I also was allowed to use the phone that they had gotten smart enough to install in the shop. I often laugh to myself when I am driving along or just sitting idle and think how sacred the phone and office was. I'll bet when I was able to use it, they must have thrown it away when I walked out. We shouldn't even begin to talk about the use of toilet facilities. Only the office had bathrooms, and there was no way that the black workers would be allowed to use one of theirs. As the rules were relaxed on segregation, it was always said to be out of order. That "white" toilet must have had a lot of problems. For spite, I often went in and used it. It looked like any other crapper to me. I always wanted someone to say something to me about it but they only got angry and held their peace. The southern crapper is a book all by itself. Porta-Johns came on the scene about twenty years late. I now realize why it's often called the throne.

While working at the plantation I built a workshop at home. Not only was I working at the plantation, I had also built quite a business at home. I worked eight hours at the plantation and came home and worked another three to five hours. I also worked most weekends at home. After a while my income at home was a lot more than it was at the plantation. One transmission overhaul job paid more than my week's salary. I always had a fear of becoming unemployed until some point in my life I realized that self-employment was the only way I was going to make a decent living in South Carolina. I had totally given up the idea of going back to New York to work. I cut my work day down to ten hours a day, and on two nights a week I took a small business course. I am not sure how much I learned from the course or if it was worth the time I put into it, but it at least gave me the desire to remain self-employed. Working at home also gave me a chance to be near the children for most of the time. They pitched in and helped until they got in my way. I often sent them running back to the house only to have to call them back an hour later to hold something in place while I welded it, help me with the jack or start a car.

My two older daughters insist that I tried to make boys out of them. I probably used them about a dozen times, but of course it seemed like a continuous thing to them. They always got sparks on them as they held a piece of metal in place as I tacked it. Vicki said she still remembers me trying to convince her that she wasn't going to get shocked or burned. Vicki once worked at a shipyard in Virginia. To get into the shipyard and to get to the job she wanted, she had to go through their apprentice program. She was given a choice of machinist, electrician or welding, as an apprentice course. She told me she never even considered the welding course. Even though it had been a lot of years and she had been through four years of college, she still wasn't about to hold a piece of metal while someone welded it. When she was home a few years ago she asked me to teach her to weld, we never did get around to doing it. I figured she only wanted me to hold a piece of metal while she tacked it. The two older girls still like the smell of diesel fuel and gasoline. They said it reminds them of their days of "Working in the shop with me." I spent a lot of time with the children in the late 1960s. Linda went to the local tech school for two years for cosmetology and I became mommy and daddy for the duration of the course. The mommy years for me were the most challenging.

When Linda got out of school in 1971, we built a shop for her and we both became self-employed. We worked hard and saved money for our children's education. I was still doing the twelve to fifteen hour days in the nineteen seventies and we began to see it pay off. Linda and I got along great and saved as much as we could. A lot of the long hours were because of my fears of having to go back to the employment office. When I left there in 1957 I promised that I would never return.

In the early and mid 1970's the shrimping industry in South Carolina had reached a high point. I began to get a lot of diesel engine work from the marine industry. The shrimp boats kept me away from the shop a lot, but it paid a lot more than working on cars and trucks. I never really liked to work on cars. I wont complain about working on cars because it provided a good living for a long time. It was almost as good as the moonshine business. I was right at home on the diesel engine, but I had to learn a lot of other things about boats. I finally learned that the pointed end was called the bow and the square end was called the stern. I still have to think when I try to remember which side is port and which is starboard. It took me almost two years to learn where the lazarette was located.

Shrimpers as a whole are very independent, and the industry has its own lingo, especially radio procedure. When you get the local dialect going, along with the captains from the Outer Banks of North Carolina, you need the shrimper's dictionary to figure out what's going on. After a couple of years, I learned the language but I also learned a lot more. I soon learned about propellers, marine gears, automatic pilots, and most things that it took to make the boat a productive tool. I had a chance to use my mechanical technology training and enjoyed doing it.

The shrimping industry has been very rewarding to me, not only financially but educationally as well. Each boat captain usually has his own way of doing certain things in a particular manner and usually has a good reason for doing it his way. I respected all of their individual ideas and soon came up with a lot of knowledge that became helpful, not only to me, but also to a lot of other people. I have repaired boats along the Atlantic coast from the Outer Banks of North Carolina to Key West Florida. I knew shrimpers in most of the towns along the southeast coast and some on the Gulf. One of the major problems with working out of a small town like Seaside is that I had to drive at least fifty miles to get most major parts for boats. I had to go and get them or have them shipped in, which often became expensive in terms of downtime. At one time it seemed that I was spending more time on the road for parts than I was actually working.

Chapter 22

FLYING WITH LESTER

In 1972 someone suggested I needed an airplane to make the trips to Charleston, Atlanta and Jacksonville. I gave it some though because it had been something I wanted to do for some time. I gave it some serious thought, and the next day I went to Ritter and enrolled in a flight program.

I drove the fifty miles to ground school every Wednesday night and took flying lessons on weekends. In the beginning I kept asking myself, "Are you sure you want to do this?" I had never been afraid of too many things but every time we practiced stalls I told myself when I got back on the ground that would be my last lesson. I had a very good instructor and he soon settled me down and after my initial phobia I became anxious to get back in the plane. Jerry was the type of instructor who never let up on you. There was never a moment of relaxation in the airplane with him. It was all business from the time we got into the plane until we had done the flight and landed. After we took a short break, he took me into the conference room and raked me over the coals again on what I had done wrong. He also complimented me on the good points. I soon got over my fear of the plane, worked really hard, and soloed in less than ten hours. In 1985, when my son soloed, Jerry was his instructor.

Even though I had soloed the airplane, I was still afraid. One day Jerry left some solo work for me to do. I took off with the Cessna 150 and felt good about being free of the instructor. The humidly was down in the mid 30s and the sky was clear as far as the eyes could see. I did a few trips around the pattern and decided to take advantage of Jerry not being there and enjoy it. I went out into the training area and did a few shallow turns and decided I should get back to the airport and do the touch-and-go's that I was suppose to be doing. When I reduced power to set up for the landing, the thought of having to land frightened me. I told myself, "Get a hold of yourself fellow, you have done it a lot of times before," but I couldn't talk myself into it. When I reduced power and the plane began to descend, I almost panicked. I added power and went back up. The idea of me being alone in the airplane had just struck me. Jerry had always been there, even when I was flying solo he was always there on the radio if I needed him. He had never left my imagination even during the first solo. I, like I have heard a lot of other pilots say, could hear him during the whole trip.

"Get the nose down, you're going through your altitude, watch your heading, you forgot to make the landing checks."

This time my imagination couldn't pick him up because I knew he wasn't there. I had never felt so alone in my life. I pushed the throttle in and went back out to the training area, but I knew I had to land. I soon came back to the pattern, sat up for a long final and greased it on. I had enough flying for the day. I taxied up to the tank to refuel and tie it down.

When I got to the pump and started pumping gas, an older experienced pilot came up to me and asked,

"Why are you coming back so soon? Did something scare you?"

I thought to myself, "now how in hell did he know."

I swallowed my pride and told him what happened. He told me he had the same problem on his first flight away from the airport. He got lost and promised if he ever got back, he would never get into an airplane again. He told me he spent about three months of finding excuses not to get back into the plane, until one day he took off and did stalls all afternoon and has never been afraid anymore. Finally in a stern voice he told me,

"The best thing for you to is get back into that thing and fly it until you can see it in your sleep. Jerry is not going to be with you every time you get into trouble."

I didn't want to be a quitter, and I knew he was right. I taxied back on the runway, lined up on the centerline and shoved the throttle home. I climbed out to three thousand feet and went back out to the training area.

I worked on accelerated stalls most of the afternoon. The accelerated stall was the maneuver that frightened me more during pre-solo. I did about ten left and ten to the right and they were all perfect. I allowed the plane to slip slightly out of control to feel what it was like to recover. The Cessna rolled back to straight and level each time I released the backpressure on the yoke. I almost laughed at myself for being afraid of it earlier. I had transferred the confidence from Jerry to myself, and I was no longer afraid of the plane. I went through the private pilots' course in about two months. I took the written test, passed it, and received my certificate.

If you were eligible for VA (Veteran Administration) funding, the VA would pay ninety percent of your commercial pilot's license if you could show a job potential. I enrolled in the commercial pilots course a week after I got my private certificate and flew as often as I could. I needed to get as much time in as possible before my VA funding ran out. I had a private license and could rent an airplane to make the Wednesday night trips to ground school. Two other students from Stockton were going also, and we shared the cost of the rental plane.

While doing the commercial pilot's course I often got a different instructor. The one instructor that I never wanted to get, I finally got one morning. Lester Long was the world's biggest bigot, redneck, and Klan member all combined into one. I would have given him a perfect ten on being the world's biggest ass. I had made up my mind not to let him get under my skin. Lester found out a week earlier that I was something less than "Lilly-white" when some of my cousins came by the airport to visit me. I could tell from the expression on his face he was upset when he found I was black. I started to refuse to fly with him but after giving it some thought, I asked myself, "Why not give old Lester a try." I knew if I refused to fly with him I would have to explain why to everyone and I knew what their argument would be. The theory is you should be able to fly with anyone, because it could always be worst in the clouds or bad weather. I also knew why Lester wanted to fly with me. I knew I could handle the airplane, but it and an ass like Lester at one time could become more than I wanted. As we took off on a Saturday morning he looked at me and gave me the old "I got you now" look and said, "Go ahead and climb to three thousand, I want to see how much you know, Bo."

The weather was calm, and I put the Cessna through its paces as if it was a part of my body. Lester sat and didn't say anything until finally I blew a stall. He yelled, "Who taught you to do them like that, Bo?"

I didn't answer him so he grabbed the yoke and did some almost as good as mine. "Now, that's how I want them done!"

He didn't say too much the first day. He sat there and waited until I did all of the maneuvers and then yelled that they all had been wrong. I always managed to remain calm, which really angered him. I tuned him out when I first cranked the engine. Lester was impressed by how well I could handle the airplane even thought he constantly tried to screw me up, and that also angered him. I checked my progress report and it was the worst I had ever seen. I don't feel that Lester would have seen me as a threat if I didn't fly the airplane as well as I did, didn't speak proper English, and said "yasa" and "nosa" to him. Lester had never seen a super one of us, especially one that had the same color that he did. He put a lot of effort into trying to make me into what he thought a black man should be. It always amused me as to how predictable and how much of a trick he could be. I often unloaded on rednecks and white people, but I kept my cool while I did it and it pissed him off even more. One morning Linda and our children dropped me off at the airport while they went to visit my cousins at Rice Patch. When Lester saw them, a snarl appeared on his face and his red hair and face became the color of a beet. Later that morning when everyone gathered around for coffee, Lester said

"I wouldn't fuck a nigger woman if they were the last ones on earth."

I smiled at him and said, "You can drop the fantasy Lester, because it takes a good man with the proper tool to screw a black woman, so that leaves you out." Everyone except Lester thought it was funny.

Lester scheduled to fly with me the next day. Again I started to refuse to fly with him but he was the only person available. He failed to get next to me the day before so he tried a new technique. He started telling me "nigger jokes." We were climbing out at about eight hundred feet when he said,

"Let me have it for awhile Bo, I want to go out here in the country and scare the hell out of some of these niggers who I sell insurance to."

We came down to about fifty or a hundred feet from this black man who was washing a Cadillac. Lester made two passes on the man and he never even looked up. He raved on about "dem niggers and dem damn Cadillacs." After the man didn't look on the second pass it really pissed him off. His face turned very red and I could see the sweat beads forming on his forehead.

He said, "God-dammit, I'll show the black son-of- a-bitch this time!" He came around for another pass and almost put the wheels on the roof of the house. While looking back, he pulled the nose of the plane straight up. The stall warning screamed at us and the air speed fell off the indicator. I was in the left seat and knew that was a dangerous altitude to stall the airplane. I yelled, "I got it" and shoved the throttle to full power and eased the yoke forward.

Lester looked over at me and yelled, "I am in charge of this God-damn airplane, and don't you ever put your hands on it unless I tell you to!"

I told him, "That's a damn lie because I'm paying rent on it while you want to play your little silly games!"

As I headed to the airport he tried to calm down and asked me if I wanted to go up higher and do some high altitude work.

I told him, "Hell no, we are going to put this mother on the ground so you can get your ass out of it. The only thing that we are going to practice today is taxi work, like to the gas pump and to the tie down spot!"

He tried to convince me that I had gotten afraid over nothing, and if I wanted him to pay for that little flight time I was arguing about, he would. I could tell he was building a case for Jerry to hear but I considered the whole thing between the two of us, and considered it over with. I never even brought it up when we got to the office. When I came outside he was telling all of his redneck buddies about it and they were lapping it up like dogs. Finally one of them came over to me and started telling me I should be able to handle Lester if I was going to get a commercial license. The guy meant well but he didn't have any idea in hell what had taken place in the plane between Lester and me. I walked to my car and drove off while he was still talking.

I have talked to other black people who learned to fly in the South in the fifties and sixties and a lot of us have about the same story. After a while you get the feeling that you are supposed to be able to handle the instructor calling you a nigger or anything that he tries to belittle you with and like it. It just doesn't work like that; we are way too intelligent and we pay a lot of hard-earned money for flight instructions. It's supposed to be part of the disciplinary procedure. The excuse used is, if you can't cope with the abuse he dishes out you won't be disciplined enough to keep from flying the plane into the ground and killing yourself. Flight under instrument conditions can be very hectic, and I am not trying to take it lightly; however, trying to keep you from learning is not a part of what it takes to do it. Try telling some white person his mother sucks, and see how long the relationship will last while he is under the instrument-training hood. Even Jerry thought I was being "a little sensitive."

"After all, Lester was a very good instructor."

That got to me more than anything else. All of the people I rode with on Wednesday nights just couldn't understand why I had trouble getting along with Lester. I am sure they all wanted me to say he was prejudice so they could defend him and say it was my fault for being too sensitive.

I remember once when a middle-aged black man came to the airport and was doing preflight on a high-performance, turboprop twin-engine airplane. All of the regular airport crew was there that afternoon. They stood amazed as the gentleman very calmly did the preflight on the aircraft. The brother remained cool, and seemed to enjoy the quietness that had come over the crowd. When he had flown out of sight, an older man finally said,

"You mean that nigger can really fly that airplane?"

Finally someone in the crowd said, "Yep, sure can, he even got a license."

Lester was standing near and couldn't let me off without taking a hit on me.

"Damn few of them have a license, and damn few will get a commercial license." I broke the conversation up when I told him,

"Yep, they even give rednecks flight instructors certificates, but they are still dumb ass rednecks," Lester never put his name down to fly with me after that afternoon. I suppose he just figured it wasn't worth the trouble. I had always given him a rash of crap every time he started his nigger jokes. I knew a lot more jokes that offended him than he did that offended me, and he finally gave up. He finally told me I was the blackest white man that he had ever seen. I later learned the black man who flew the turboprop aircraft was a retired air force fighter pilot that flew the F-86 in Korea.

Just before my check ride with the FAA, someone came into the lounge and said he was going out to the training area to practice spin recoveries. I asked him, "Why spin recoveries?" He said that was the most horrifying thing that he could think of to get in shape for his check ride. I had never done solo spin recoveries so I had to think about what I would do to get in shape for any strict examiner that I might get from the FAA. I gave it a few minutes and thought,

"Hell, I know what I can do, I'll go fly with Lester."

He was shocked when he saw I had scheduled with him. I even believed he thought I had buried the hatchet. He even smiled with me when he came out to the airplane. Even though I had well over two hundred hours of supervised flight training, Lester always sat and watched me go through the preflight, just as he would have a pre-solo student. He had always given me a rash of crap during the simple preflight. As we were walking to the plane, he said,

"Let's just forget the preflight check this time." I had already done it, and we got into the airplane.

In the beginning of the flight course, Lester actually thought I was afraid of him. Mostly because I put up with most of the crap he gave me. I just wanted to get as much flight time in as possible. To change schools would have meant I would have to do a lot of paper work and would lose a lot of valuable VA funding, so I decided to stick it out. I now had all of the required flight time, so why not take a spin with old Lester. I chose the airplane we would fly. I chose a new Cherokee with variable pitch prop and retractable gear, one that he had never flown before. We took off and climbed to five thousand feet to do maneuvers. He wanted me to practice slow flight and wanted it done at ninety miles per-hour. Every time the airspeed came down to around one hundred miles per hour, the landing gear would drop out and the aircraft would stall. After the third time of trying it he said,

"Bo, you ain't doing something right, let me hold it." He took off his cowboy hat and mirrored sunglasses and said, "Gimme dat hood. I'll show you how to do it."

I knew what was wrong after the second time but I wasn't going to tell him. The landing gear would drop out automatically when the plane was put into the landing configuration. This was a safety feature in case you forgot to put the gear down. It also had an override on the feature.

We had a chart and my sweater covering the override and he couldn't see it. Lester put the hood on, pulled back on the yoke, and around 105 miles per hour the gear fell out again. He recovered and eased the yoke back again. This time I eased my hand under the chart and held the override and the airspeed sat right on ninety miles per hour. He was just beginning to brag when I released the override, the gear came down and the plane went into a stall. He tried it a couple more times, but I never held the override, and each time it stalled. Lester broke out the book and started reading while I practice without the hood. Once when he was glued to the book I eased my hand down and held the override. The plane sat right on ninety miles per hour. I held it there for a few seconds and eased the nose forward to recover.

Again he said, "Let me see that thing Bo."

He pulled the hood down and started the maneuver. I held the override and it came back to ninety. He eased the nose forward and made a normal recovery. He just had to try one more. This time I allowed him to go to ninety before I released the override.

"There must be something wrong with this thing. Let's take it back to the airport before the mechanic goes home."

After we landed he found the spot in the book about the safety feature. He instantly knew what was wrong but he also remembered the system had failed to work a couple of times. He reported it to the mechanic as being faulty. I told the mechanic what I had done and assured him the override was in perfect shape. He swore not to tell Lester until after I took my check ride, and we had a good laugh about it. I don't think the mechanic ever did tell Lester, but for once he never had time to give me hell while we flew. I took my check ride the next day and one of the very first questions I was asked was about the automatic landing gear feature. I had to explain how the override system worked, I smiled as I went through the explanation. I also passed my check ride that day.

I bought a Cessna 172 in 1974. I did use it a few times for business purposes but most of all it became a fun machine for the family. For five years I was a Civil Air Patrol Squadron Commander and have tried to introduce a lot of young people to aviation. It has been very rewarding to me whenever I give a young boy or girl their very first airplane ride and looked at their faces as they are given a chance to take the yoke and control the plane on their own. I have found that far too many young people from our Island believed it would be certain death to get into an airplane. Out of all the young people I have taken up, I don't recall even one who didn't want to fly over and over again. I always tried to make sure it was a pleasant experience for them, and after my encounter with Lester Long, I made sure a lot of them were black.

Chapter 23

THE CADET PROGRAM

Out of necessity I became self-employed about the time that racial strife climaxed in the mid 1960s and early 1970's. I became a workaholic and worked, lived, and socialized all within the small world of the Island, and I put most of the past behind me. My work kept me busy enough that I seldom concerned myself with the news of the outside world. For the most part I centered my life on family activities. We flew, went to Disney World and played in the creeks and rivers around the Island. I had almost forgotten about terms like affirmative action, quotas, segregation and integration. The black man and the white man became customers, and people that I respected. The people who paid their bill were good and the ones who didn't were bad.

Our children became active in band, sports, scouting, and most of the school activities. A lot of nights I sat at the school and waited for the activity bus that was suppose to be there at eight but seldom got there until midnight. Harold and Lisa, My son and youngest daughter, brought home some literature on Civil Air Patrol (CAP). Being an aviator and wanting my children to learn about aviation, I signed the permission slip for them to join. I took them, along with a vanload of other children, to Charleston Air Force Base and bought complete air force uniforms for Lisa and Harold. I usually took them to the meetings and stayed at the squadron building until the meeting was over. The unit was new and short on adult help. Being a pilot, having my own airplane and a van for transportation, they asked me to join. I was never an organization person and I had my own airplane, and really didn't want to devote the time to it. I had already invested over two hundred dollars in the program and they would have a fit if I didn't allow them to continue. I finally told myself if my children were to become a part of it I would have to be there also. I would make sure they didn't get brainwashed.

Civil Air Patrol is one of America's great organizations, especially for young people who are interested in aviation. I don't want to take away from other great aviation programs for young people, I happened to be a CAP member at that time. I wasn't familiar with other organizations, and we had a CAP unit in our hometown. As whole, CAP is a great organization, but when the rank and file enters into the equation, sometimes racism raises it ugly head against affirmation action and civil rights. CAP has a lot of functions, but I was primarily interested in the cadet program. I have never been one to slay dragons, not very competitive or had a very high ego when dealing with other people. I have always tried to do the very best at whatever I undertake. I won't get into the total functions of CAP because it would take too much space. I will explain very briefly how the Cadet program operates, or at least how it did in the 1970's as well as my memory serves me now. Civil Air Patrol (CAP) is an Air force auxiliary. It has an air force officer and an NCO (non commissioned officer) assigned to each state as a liaison between the state and the air force. The State (or wing) runs the program with supervision from the air force. CAP has a national headquarters at Maxwell AFB, Alabama. It is divided into eight regions and fifty-two wings. (One Wing in each state. D.C., and Puerto Rico). South Carolina is in the Middle East region, which includes, Delaware, Maryland, West Virginia, the District of Columbia, Virginia, and North Carolina. Each Wing is divided into squadrons; I worked at the squadron level.

For a cadet to become a member, he or she must be at least thirteen years old or twelve and out of the sixth grade. To join as a cadet they must be under eighteen, however, if they join before their eighteenth birthday they can remain in the program until they become twenty-one. In any given squadron you could have cadets from the age of twelve to twenty. The squadron has a chain of command that the cadet must follow. It has a rank structure as the Air Force, from Basic Airman to Cadet Colonel. CAP has a lot of benefits for the cadets as he or she moves up the ladder, which includes the national Air Cadet Exchange Program, flight scholarships, ranger school, the Air Force Prep school, and others that are too numerous to mention. A lot of the Air Force Academy cadets are former CAP cadets.

My favorite activity in CAP became the cadet program and the cadet competition. They were my favorites, but at times they brought out the worst in those who were involved. The competition consists of a timed mile run, volleyball, in-rank inspection, standard drill, innovative drill, aerospace quiz bowl, and aerospace written test. Each squadron was required to have sixteen cadets for a standard team, twelve team members, three alternates and a team commander. All team members participated in all events except the drill competition. If your squadron didn't have the required sixteen cadets, you were penalized. National headquarters issued a set of regulations that covered all of the events. The squadron was graded on overall points and some events had a higher point value than others.

In early summer of 1979 we started practicing for cadet competition that would be held in August. The senior cadets worked their heads off to get everyone polished like a well-oiled machine in drill. The cadets had quiz questions coming out of their ears. The cadet commander practiced everyone until they got their run time down to where they would meet air force standards. My son being only twelve, ate, drank, and slept CAP. As a moral booster, I took all of them up for plane rides. After the rides we came back inside the building and polished some more. Every thread and ravel was clipped from their uniform. Shoes were shined until you could see your face in them. Haircuts were checked on boys; the girls had to meet air force grooming standards. Nametags, insignias, and patches were measured to make sure they were on just right. Everyone had to participate in all of the events, so we had to get the girls mile run time down to air force requirements. The girls had to compete with the boys on the volleyball team; some of the staff wanted to exclude some of the girls from the competition. I told the slower cadets that I would work with them to get their time down in the mile run. Lisa was an excellent runner, and she worked with us. No matter how hard we tried, there were always some cadets of both sexes who just couldn't make the team, but we carried them anyway.

On the Saturday morning of the competition, the team loaded in my van and headed for Bane AFB. Everyone was taking extra care to keep his or her uniform wrinkle free. Robert, the drill team commander, had settled down to a "It's now or never attitude." He always seemed steadier when he was under pressure. He later flew helicopters for the army. Even as we drove to Bane, the cadets practiced their aerospace and current event questions. We stopped as a rest stop and as soon as everyone made a potty call they formed to practice the innovated drill. While they practiced, motorists watched and applauded as they did their fancy movements. A lot of the motorists asked questions as to how they could get their children involved. We handed out leaflets and explained the program to them.

When we got to Bane, most of the cadets were so full of CAP that it was coming out of their ears. As the other teams unloaded from their busses and vans, we only saw one other team that had the required sixteen people. Our older cadets knew most of the other older cadets from throughout the state. They looked the other teams over and saw very little competition and declared themselves instant winners, but they would be in for the shock of their lives. We were totally in the dark as to who the judges would be, or how the competition would be scored. As all the teams and judges formed for the event, we saw about half of the judges were from Bane and the other half was from the local squadron. The chief judge was a senior master sergeant from Bane, and his children were in the local squadron (a slight conflict of interest). The competition was a two-day event, and on both days Sgt. Appleton walked around with a chip on his shoulder. Whenever he was approached about an event that was very obviously judged unfair, he threatened to have your team disqualified.

I knew top military NCOs considered themselves above Jesus, but even God would have to drive for this guy while he sat in the back seat and gave orders. I tolerated a lot of the unfairness because I was totally new at the game and wasn't familiar with the regulations. About half way through the first day I was totally disgusted with the whole thing. I had never, and I never will, use children as pawns to satisfy my personal ego as Sgt. Appleton did. I hope his children are now doing better than they did at the competition. At the end of the first day, I decided we weren't going to win, not from lack of talent but because of the judges. I also decided I would become part of the cadet program. My children wanted to be involved and I saw the program as a great learning experience. CAP is not designed to make combat troops out of young boys and girls, but a lot of people on ego trips would try and make them combat ready. I saw it for it's educational value and a part of molding young people into accepting responsibilities. They could quit anytime they wanted to and regulations forbid any hazing. I realized that any regulation is only as good as it's enforcer. I decided to remain active in the program to see that mine and other children never got brainwashed into becoming storm troopers. My only desire for the cadet was when he or she became old enough to join the military, they would know whether they wanted to join or not. If they did join, they would have a good idea of what was expected of them. This philosophy wasn't shared by a lot of the senior staff, especially when it came to their own children. Of course for their child to become a leader, they had to find someone for their little boy or girl to harass.

Even though we had the best mile time, the right numbers, and a victory at volleyball, we came in dead last. The local Bane team was given first place with a team of seven people. At the beginning of the trip back home, our team was really depressed. They had worked too hard to be demoralized as they were. Young people have a way of getting over things a lot quicker if left alone by adults. About an hour into the trip back home, we stopped to eat. As they sat and ate, they dwelled only on the good points of the pass two days. Robert was going away to college and wouldn't be there next year; and they planned on who would replace him as the team commander. As I sat and watched them devour pounds of burgers and fries, I asked myself "why dwell on the negative." I would have to become totally familiar with the program and make sure it never happened again. I would chalk it up as a negative experience, one that I would put behind me as soon as possible.

The new squadron commander at Stockton was a military retiree and his son was also part of the Stockton squadron. He was a Vietnam veteran and had decided the air force regulations were a pile of garbage. He believed anything that we taught the cadets wasn't any good if it couldn't someday be used in combat. He hated liberals, the NAACP, Yankees, and Air Force personnel. He knew enough about the quotas and funding to have two blacks in the squadron. When Lisa and Harold came into the unit, they brought the number of black cadets up to four. I never really had any problem getting along with him; he had strange ways that I ignored a lot. I took over as Deputy Commander. To a large degree, I began to keep the program moving according to regulations. After studying the regulations, one will get the understanding that the cadet regulations are designed to protect the cadet from hazing, oral and physical abuse, and especially life threatening situations.

When we got back to Stockton, I dropped the cadets off at the point where their parents picked them up. The ones who lived on my way home, I dropped them off at home. As soon as I got into the house, the commander called me. When I picked up the phone, the first thing I heard was,

"What in hell are those playing soldier S.O.B.s trying to do up there?"

I hesitated, held my breath, and counted to ten. I gave him a very limited briefing on what happened over the weekend and sat and listened as he cursed himself into a tantrum. He tried a couple of times to make it my fault for not protecting the children from "those crooked mother f——." I was tired from the trip and had about all I cared to take from the great military minds in one day. We had words about it, and the friction began to build from that phone call in the middle of the night. I finally asked him why if he was interested, hadn't he gone to the competition, and I hung the phone up.

I started that night as I would a hundred times to quit, but Lisa asked me not to. Most of the children didn't want their parents to get involved with them, but most of the time mine wanted me there. The other cadets didn't want me to quit either. I provided transportation for them, and I was the only pilot in the squadron who owned an airplane. For a long time I was the only active pilot in the squadron, so I also taught the aerospace education course.

After my children joined, they began to recruit their friends, and the black faces increased. A lot of the adults (senior staff) didn't know I was black, and I began to get a lot of negative conservation about getting "too many niggers;" as always, I ignored it. One incident I remembered very well. This woman came in with her son; he couldn't find his behind with both hands and a mirror. She and the boy's stepfather wanted him to be put in charge of everything: "The boy just had to have some leadership training." The mother was very good with the tons of paper work that had to be done. I tried to handle the situation with kid gloves and hoped it would go away. Her son couldn't or wouldn't pass any of the tests that were required to advance, but he just had to be put in charge of something. I also knew if her son didn't advance soon, she would quit. She hated Lisa with a passion, mainly because she had advanced to sergeant and was her son's squad leader. One day when we were out in the field, she told me

"I just can't stand that little nigger gal who is the second squad leader." Finally, after a couple of weeks she learned I had two children in the squadron. The cadets were all outside and I couldn't show her which two were mine. As she proceeded to guess, she gave me every little white boy and girl that came in. When a couple of black kids came in, she laughed and said, "I know that none of them can be yours." I thought to myself, "You'd be surprised." When they were all seated and filling out permission slips, Lisa came over to where we were seated. When the woman saw her she put a smirk on her face and continued to talk. Like a well-mannered little girl, Lisa stood patiently until the woman finally stopped talking. She handed me her permission slip and said,

"Here Daddy, you might as well sign mine now so I can turn it in tonight."

I thought the woman would swallow her tongue, all the times she had called Lisa a "nigger gal" or "bitch" was now coming back to haunt her.

In spite of all of her negative habits, she was very good at keeping the records straight, something I was never good at. She never came back after that night, even though I told some of the others to ask her to come back. She told them she had said something that probably hurt my feelings, and she couldn't face me anymore. If I said it didn't piss me off for someone to call my fourteen-year-old daughter a nigger bitch I would be telling a lie, but I wasn't seeking revenge. I had heard it a million times before, and good administrative people were hard to come by.

The squadron commander never got over not winning the cadet competition. He became obsessed with getting even with everyone who was involved, including me. He constantly wrote letters to commanders, congressmen, and senators and tried to get the state funds cut off. When everyone ignored him, he cursed himself into a tantrum. He constantly asked for hearings that took a lot of precious time and made a lot of enemies for our unit. He wanted all of the cadets to quit as a protest to show support for him. A couple of parents who thought he was a sort of hero, kept their kids at home. We now had a lot of moral support from the parents who lived on the Island, and I decided to continue. After almost a year of bickering and letter writing, the CO was finally relieved. He was relieved for "going over the head of his superiors." I thought, and hoped he would quit, but he didn't. The wing commander called me at home and told me I would be the new squadron commander. Even though he had seen me at commander's call, he never knew I was black. I quickly realized that it wouldn't have made any difference.

All of his mail to headquarters had to go through me. That put me between him and his enemies, which multiplied my problems. Headquarters wouldn't recognize his mail unless it had my signature on it. I soon found a stack of letters in my box from him, even one protesting me being the squadron commander; I signed it and sent it to headquarters. The rest of his hate mail I sent back to him. Out of frustration, I once said I was going to resign, in a couple of seconds I heard a typewriter clicking away over in a corner. In a few minutes, one of the people who said we were getting "too many niggers" shoved my typed written resignation in front of me to sign. He would be the next in line to become the squadron commander and the squadron would have become all white the next day. I looked out across the room and saw all of the black and white smiling faces and picked up the form and tore it in half. He never came back after that night. He had recently dropped the word "nigger" when referring to the black cadets in favor of, "That bunch from the island." I decided that night I would be there for a while, I just couldn't figure out why they wanted to get rid of me so bad. I also decided I would make our unit which included male, female, black and white cadets the best in the state. I would simply take it away from them by out performing them, and if it wound up as a "black thing," so be it.

I planned a lot of overnight camping trips for the squadron. I often had to ask some of the other parents to help with transportation. I was totally shocked when some of them told me they didn't want to take black children. They said they were afraid of getting sued if anything happened. For most of the time I had taken their children without even asking for gas money, but we often traveled in segregated vehicles.

CAP cadets are required to have orientation flights. On his or her first flight, the cadet will take the controls and get hands on experience, which to me is one of the great things about the program. I was in charge of orientation flights once and I formed all the cadets in a line and had them stay in place until the pilots came to get them. I left a cadet in charge and went to do other things. About two hours later, one of the black females from our unit came and told me some of the pilots were skipping over the black cadets. When the planes came down for other cadets, I put the girl from Stockton in front of the line and stood back and waited. The pilot went to the middle of the line and took three white male cadets. I came over and told the next pilot to take cadets from the front of the line I was relieved when she took the first three cadets and left. The black female cadet, Karen, was sixteen years old, very intelligent, and very outspoken whenever she thought she was being discriminated against. With the pilot's attitude I'm sure she wouldn't have gotten much out of the flight anyway. A couple of the pilots used the excuse, they "didn't want 'them' puking in the plane." (I always thought puke was puke.) I reported the incident to the Air Force Liaison Officer, and the practice was stopped. We talked about it later over a couple of Jack Daniels. We both decided the last person we would need on our case would be Karen's air force father, and we got it straight in a hurry. Each incident made me more determined to stay with the program. To a lot of children, especially those from the Island, that would be the only chance they would have to compete if they ever wanted to get into air force or navy flight schools.

I learned a lot more from the young minds of the cadets than they learned from me. A lot of them were from the local air force base and were whiz kids in aviation. A lot of their fathers were pilots or connected with aviation in some way. Often while teaching the aviation course, I had to get a group discussion going to get me off the hook, especially in the outer space chapters. In the beginning I had to study a lot harder then they did. On bivouac, they could come up with some very unique ways to cook. Not being a bad chef myself, I often made large pots of chili, or chicken and rice dishes. There were also the old standbys, hotdogs roasted on the end of a stick, somehow tasted better when roasted in the woods.

After a few bivouacs with other units I decided to take the Stockton unit alone, unless I knew the person who was in charge of the other unit. As I said earlier, some people have to play war games. They allow their cadets to carry all sorts of knives. I remember once I saw a group of boys who had rifles with them. A few weeks later, one of them got hit in his butt with twenty-two-caliber birdshot.

I have a lot of fond memories of, "Life on bivouac," with a group of cadets. Trying to get them to be quiet and go to sleep so they would be able to get up at five the next morning. Trying to convince the girls they had to dig and use latrines like the boys did. Trying to convince boys and girls that mosquitoes and gnats had to eat also, and they preferred them at attention while they ate. You can't take burgers and fries on overnight trips in the month of June. An aerospace book is a lot more entertaining than a portable radio. It is a lot more fun washing airplanes than it is flying in them. Trying to convince the boys it was okay for the girls to bend the rules, "just a little bit," on the regulations for hair. Trying to convince a fifteen-year-old girl that eye shadow and the air force uniform just didn't go together. Trying to convince Lisa and the other girls from the Island that my correct title was not "Major Daddy." Convincing them a tent is a lot more comfortable than my warm pop up travel trailer, especially when it is wet and cold outside. My old army days as a cadre often helped me get the point across.

To choose the drill team commander for the next year became quite a challenge. Most of the white parents assumed I would choose the commander. They all assumed I would choose the cadet whose father kept insisting his son be put into a "leadership position," even though he contributed very little to the overall team. Eric spent most of his time trying to impress his dad and me on how great a leader he would make by screaming at everyone else.

We had a very bright black cadet who would be excellent for the drill team commander. Carl had passed all of the tests at the minimum time to become the next warrant officer. He was excellent with all of the drills. He came to every meeting and was helpful to all of the other cadets, black and white alike; everyone liked him except Eric and his father. To give equal incentive to both boys, at the next meeting I announced the next cadet to reach the warrant officers grade would become the drill team commander. Both cadets needed another month in grade before they could take the test. Eric had been in the unit for almost two years, and in the past had put very little time in trying to past the tests. I got the feeling neither he nor his dad thought it was necessary, and up to that point he had been put in charge of everything. I wanted to give everyone an equal chance, boy, girl, black or white.

When I made the announcement, Eric, his dad and most of the white adults turned red in the face, and I saw the disapproving look on their faces. They just couldn't believe that I would give both boys equal chances and possibly put a black cadet in charge. Eric and his Marine Corp dad also didn't believe the other white adults would allow me to get away with it.

A month later Carl took the test and passed it. When I pinned the insignia on him, I announced he would be the next drill team commander. Eric and his dad got up and left the room with dad screaming that I would never get away with it. At the next meeting, we were down to only six white cadets and all the others being black. The whites that left had the audacity to believe we couldn't put together a competitive team with a team that included that many black cadets. The ones who left had never reckoned with a person as determined as I was. I inherited my father's determined and vindictive ways and wouldn't let them deter me. When most of the other cadets left, it put a strain on the ones who remained. One man's ego had taken away a lot of talent. Sergeant Kennedy tried to get permission to start another unit to compete against us but it wasn't allowed. He even got desperate enough to call me at home and tell me if I would take the drill team commander's position from Carl and give it to any one of the "other" cadets he would bring all the white cadets back. He told me we could never win with that "Colored boy" because the white cadets would never work with him. With that statement, he finally succeeded in pissing me off and I had to show the other side of me. I felt it was time to break the good news to him.

I told him, "The problem is, you don't want to work with black staff or cadets. As a black man I resent the idea that your dumb ass consider yourself superior to even the lowest black cadet in the unit so please take your brain washed SS troopers and stay the hell out my way."

I had often wondered whether he knew I was black, I didn't think he did from the language that he often used, and that night he got the message. At first the "black" word went right over his head, and when it sank in, his tune of voice changed. I always thought he believed I was "Some liberal Yankee." When he tried to apologize for the things he said in the past, I hung the phone up. I hated to see all of the other cadets' leave because they had a lot of knowledge they could share. When they left it didn't deter me, it would only make my job harder and me more determined.

In August we started practicing with a seventy-five percent black team. At the time most of the other units were all white but it didn't seem to bother most people. We got very good support from the Air Force and the state of South Carolina. I'm sure they were glad to see some black faces in the program. It was just a lot of individuals who were in certain positions that were determined not to let a unit with black faces win the events. The white adults and cadets who stayed with the unit were penalized along with the black cadets. They knew the reason for it and nothing was ever said about it and they continued to give one hundred percent of their support. The unit had purged it self of the nonconformist and we set in to build a great team, and I became more determined. The air force LO was able to get a lot of new uniforms for us, which was a tremendous help to the cadets that had outgrown theirs and couldn't afford to buy new ones.

When the wing cadet commander, who just happened to be from Bane, watched us perform one day, he saw the skills that we had perfected and the racial composition of our squadron; I could see the disappointed look on his face. His most pronounced disapprovals would be when he would see something that he considered to be "black." He constantly got angry when a black cadet made a mistake and became even angrier when I wouldn't reprimand the cadet. When a white cadet made a mistake, he quickly turned his head in another direction and nothing was said. Everyone had in mind the team they wanted to win, again, the Bane team. The Bane team was one hundred percent white and wouldn't be able to match the Stockton team. This year they had the required numbers but not the talent. I was determined that I would never let them get away with what they did the previous year. I studied the regulations until I could almost recite the whole book without looking at it. The LO remembered what happened the year before, but it wasn't his job to run the wings program, and his hands were tied, but he gave us all the support he was allowed to, and more. The cadet commander went back to Columbia and pressed the panic button. He felt that he had to come up with a way to keep us from representing South Carolina at the regional level. The first mistake he made was to form a composite squadron from all of the other units, and yes, they all looked alike. He didn't ask for anyone from our unit. I don't think we had anyone that was blond or tall enough to fit into his group. When our group first saw them they became determined to put a good whipping on them and send them home with their tails between their legs. Their biggest problem was they were never given enough practice time. The composite team was from all over the state. They were provided transportation to Columbia on weekends. The practice usually turned into a weekend of mass confusion. Trying to out do our unit created an injustice to the other group and eventually they would tell us it did, and they were upset about it.

That year the LO brought in air force reserve officers for the judges. The colonel and I were on the same page without even talking to each other. Even among the reserve officers we had a couple that the colonel called aside to have a long talk with. The two gave me a very dirty look but kept everything on the level after that.

We won the state championship that year and would go to Beckley, West Virginia to compete at region level. We had a retired marine sergeant major in our unit who was Alabama old school, but to this day was one of the fairest people I have ever worked with. Sergeant Smith always went along with me and was always there to keep me straight whenever I was about to blow a fuse. Without Smith, I could have never made the squadron what it was. He did all of the paper work for the unit.

Sergeant Smith and I took the bus to Beckley W VA and I did all of the driving while he kept peace among the teenagers in the back. At my age I had no problem doing all of the driving. In the past I had driven the bus to the Marshal Space Center at Huntsville Alabama, to the Smithsonian in Washington, DC, and Fort Lee Virginia, to mention just some of the trips we made. I was squadron commander, pilot, and bus driver among other things, and for most of the time I enjoyed every minute of it.

Our retention rate from the Island in the past three years had been very good. When we got to Beckley, we had a well-seasoned and very physical group. They all knew what it would take to win. From that group, a couple of the male cadets would go to the Canadian Football League. Harold was now a senior in high school and was as hard as nails. Even though a couple of the female cadets were slower in volleyball or the mile run, they were whiz kids in the quiz bowl and the written exam, which was a big help for our points.

When the competition started, our first event would be to play Delaware in volleyball. As in our team, they had a mixture of male and female cadets (all white). I quickly saw the Air Force Reserve master sergeant referee had a serious dislike for our black cadets. The only thing he was there for was to referee the game, but as soon as he saw our group he started yelling at them. The LO and I looked at each other with a look of disgust on our faces. He hadn't broken any rules, so I had no choice but to go along with him. As the game proceeded, every time one of the Stockton Cadets scored, he would blow the whistle and take it away from them. After a while it seemed every time our cadets moved a foot, he blew the whistle. Once when we were leading, he went two points back and said, "Back there you touched the net." Finally everyone else began to see what he was doing. Now that we were representing the State of South Carolina everyone began to take notice. Allen, the wing cadet commander, was jumping up and down and screaming his head off. At one point, after one of his tantrums he came over and asked me,

"Why do you think he is doing that, do you think it is racial prejudice?" In my raging state of mind I screamed at him,

"You give me your damn version of what the hell you think it is!"

With all of the cheating by the referee going on, our cadets got angry and started getting vicious with the ball. A couple of our star high-school football players started spiking the ball with the precision and speed of a bullet. That night my son Harold gave me the thrill of my life. If he never accomplished anything else in life, that incident would have been enough. Harold was six feet tall and weighed around one hundred and eighty pounds. He just happened to be one of the cadets the Delaware team wanted to set up and spike a ball into. Near the end of the game they finally got him set up. Delaware's best and most vocal player reached up and with his entire might drove the ball at Harold. The ball traveled only about thirty inches. Harold went up at the same time he did and smashed the ball into the guy's face with the force of a mule's kick and it knocked the Delaware cadet sprawling on the floor. The whole gym went into a roar.

After all of the cheating from the referee, no one would replace him until after that game. We lost by one point, and it demoralized a lot of our people. They stopped the playing until another referee was bought in the next day. This time they brought in an Air Force reservist who was a coach at the University of Maryland, and the game was strictly by the book. A lot of senior active duty Air Force officers came over and sat with the Stockton team. They complemented our cadets on a great game because everyone saw what happened and were disappointed by the results.

I thought they got rid of the first referee but we would meet him again in the mile run as one of the timekeepers. During practice at Stockton we did a lot of running over a high-rise bridge, in case we would have to run in the hills of West Virginia. At region we only used our fastest team members. The mile run course ran around an area with a lot of long buildings. Everyone from South Carolina kept time and cheered our people on. There were about five of us standing together when the referee asked if there was a shorter way to get to the finish line. I pointed to a door that would take him through the building. Before he left he looked at the group and said

"Thanks, I sure as hell don't want to follow that bunch of coons all the way around!"

I ignored the remark. When he gave our mile time he had added one minute. All of us had a minute less than he gave, and everyone said,

"Something is wrong," but no one would question the outcome. I finally told the group,

"I'm not surprised," and asked if anyone heard what he said when he was asking for directions to get around the building. All the men had a surprised look on their faces when I told them what he said; it had gone right over their heads. One of the reserve captain's put a smirk on his face and asked me,

"Now don't tell me you are going to protest this thing like you did that volleyball game, are you?" I told him,

"No I'm not, I expect shit like that from people like that, but it would be great if someone else saw fit to do it, after all, it's a state team now." Everyone dispersed and it died right there.

When all of the events were scored, we found in spite of all the unfairness we received we came in at a very respectable second place. That was great but the best yet (or worst) was, on the way into the lounge, Allen, the state cadet commander, came up to me, not to congratulate me but to have the audacity to tell me

"That group of yours do pretty good in the physical stuff, but they need a lot of training in the book stuff."

That night I just had to show the other side of me. The LO was standing near, and Allen being an active duty air force officer, I tried to find a respectable way to put it, but didn't find any. I was tired, angry as hell, and just wanted a place to unwind. I got right in his face and yelled over the noise of the crowd,

"You take your best Nazi-looking group from throughout the state which you consider your best, and I take a team that include four little fat black girls and beat the hell out of them, now you tell me who the hell needs to improve!"

The LO had a smile on his face and put his hand on my shoulder and said, "Hey, its Jack time."

When we were seated and I had unwound I started to apologize to the colonel for saying what I said, he held his hand up and said, "Don't worry about it, Allen deserves everything you told him and more."

I know I will get a lot of flack from a lot of people for what they might see as my not "standing up" for the cadets. My only purpose there was to introduce them to aviation, discipline and working with a group, among a lot of other things. Nothing would have been gained by my protesting every time someone used the N word or give us a raw deal. I always taught my children and a lot of other cadets, the only way that we can win, is to do our very best to out-perform anyone who might try and keep us down.

Chapter 24

PLEASE BE CAREFUL DOCTOR

Early one Sunday morning in 1976 I was having severe stomach pain that wouldn't go away, and Linda drove me to the VA hospital in Charleston. When I got to the emergency room they did tests and found I would have to have an appendectomy. I was assigned to this very young female doctor. When she saw Linda with me she instantly got angry. When she was asking all of the medical questions, and I was straining to answer them, she would never take an answer from Linda. Linda saw I was in a lot of pain and she knew all of my medical history. The doctor wouldn't accept any information that she gave her. It didn't really upset her because she knew what the problem was and had grown to expect it. She usually got more resentment from white females than any other group and it usually humored her. I kept telling myself,

"This little lady is going to be cutting on me in a few minutes and I don't really like her attitude."

About half way through the questions, she told Linda she would have to leave the room. As soon as Linda closed the door behind her, she asked me,

"How long have you known her?" I told her, "I had been married to her for almost twenty years."

"Are all of her children yours?" (No one had mentioned children yet) I told her we had four.

She asked "four with her?" (Pointing toward Linda.) I knew what her problem was and would have played with her, but my stomach was hurting too much.

She finally asked me, "Why did you marry her?"

I soon realized I didn't want her as my doctor. I didn't want her to be written up or have to explain to everyone why, I simply didn't want her in the room with me while I was asleep.

This might seem strange to some people, but I didn't think she deserved the consequences that could have occurred if I had made an issue out of it. It also would have pissed off a lot of other doctors who would be cutting on me. Linda and I weren't offended by it because we had gotten to the point where we almost expected it. This was turning out to be a strange case. As an intern, I knew she wouldn't be the person to do the surgery on me alone. The thought of her being in the room with me while I was asleep was more than I cared to think about. She might decide to put me in a position where our fun would be cut off forever. I thought she was sort of cute and was flattered that she was upset about me being married to Linda, but I didn't want this to gets ridiculous, especially when I was asleep. I learned early in life, to report something like that usually brought out the worst in everyone I had to deal with; they would somehow make it my fault.

I finally decided to come clean with her. I told her I wasn't white. At first she didn't want to believe me, but after a few minutes it began to soak in and I could see the relief on her face. She finished examining me but didn't call Linda back in. She said she wanted to watch my blood pressure for a while before surgery and I had to remain quiet. She never left the room nor did she stop talking to me. Finally she asked me,

"Do you want another doctor?"

"Do you think that I need one?"

She said, "No," but she had a thousand questions about my life and told me she hoped I wasn't offended by anything she had asked me. I lied and said I wasn't offended. I told her I preferred direct questions and assured her that hers were very direct. I now had her calmed down, and she told me if she had offended me I had the right to ask for another doctor. I told her,

"Just get this pain out of my stomach, and I think we will get along fine." I had to explain to her why the state of South Carolina said that I was Negro.

Somehow my explanation didn't make sense, even to me. I finally told her the name of some good books on the subject and about South Carolina's constitutional convention, where the state of South Carolina had a field day with the Negroes in South Carolina. During the constitutional convention of 1895 the laws to disenfranchise the Negro of all of the freedoms and liberties gained during the civil war and reconstruction were created. Also the laws on who would be classified as Negro or White were created. As we were ending our conversation, two male residents came in and started giving her hell.

"Why don't you have him prepped? "Do this one and the one in number 21 and 26, you know we don't have any help on Sunday, so you have to do them."

I could tell the males were giving her all of the crappy jobs but I am sure she never knew the meaning of the word "discrimination."

This used to be a classic: the question usually came from a white female when I was with my children and Linda wasn't there. I was often asked, "Did you adopt them?" My thoughts would always be the same, "No lady, I really screwed that black woman."

Another doctor came and put something in the IV and the next thing I knew I was back in the room. I thought, "Maybe they decided not to do it," but when I felt my side, I found the bandage and realized it was over with. I also felt a little farther down and assured myself that no cutting had been done below the belt. I looked up and the female doctor was staring at me, as she had been when I went to sleep. I asked her if Linda was still there or had she gone home.

"I don't know, I haven't seen her."

Linda came in a couple minutes later and Dr. Adams was still there. She told Linda, "You can come in but you can't stay very long."

(I never realized I was in such serious condition.) Linda had only been in the room for about three minutes when the doctor said she had to leave while she checked my bandages. She kept giving Linda a pile of crap. The male interns gave it to her, and the vicious circle continued.

The doctor spent a lot of time in my room that week. She sometimes came in to do her studying. I wondered if it was to be on guard to keep Linda out. Each time she came in she had a new set of questions. She never wanted to leave when Linda came in until one day Linda came in and gave me a big kiss and made a couple of little sexy remarks. She immediately left the room. Linda laughed and said,

"I'll bet that got rid of her. Maybe now she can accept the fact that we have probably been to bed together after twenty years of marriage and four kids."

As I got to know Dr. Adams that week, I realized she had never considered a black person an equal by any means. I can't relate to anyone being born that way, she had to have been taught. When she found that I was black but looked like her father, brother or uncle, she just couldn't relate to it. I really believed she found something wrong with the way she had been taught. She tried very hard to make me agree with her that I was white. Once she said I reminded her of a "Triangular peg." "You don't fit in a round or square hole." It took me the rest of the afternoon to figure that one out. If I were to admit to her that I could be white, it would have blown my whole history lesson.

Chapter 25

RENEWAL OF A LASTING FRIENDSHIP

When Newell Philbrick and I parted company at Fort Lewis, Washington in 1957, we agreed to keep in touch. I would be out of the army when he returned to the post. We had been out that night but we didn't do the usual drinking and partying. We both had a beer and sipped on it for about thirty minutes until it got warm and flat and we finally threw it away. We both were in deep thought, he about the trip to the bomb testing range in Nevada. He never really knew what to expect. The training they had gone through in preparation for the stay at the range had only confused him and made him wonder even more about what would happened to him.

I sat in deep concentration as I tried to figure out my life, and what I would do with it for its duration, all within a twenty-minute span. I had less than a couple of weeks left to do in the army and I still hadn't decided where I would go or what I would do when I got there. I would be nineteen years old in a few days and thought I had to do it all in one day.

Philbrick left with the company the next morning for Nevada, and after a few days I went over to the discharge center. That was the last time we saw each other for the next twenty years. I eventually went back to my black world in South Carolina and he went back to Montana and the ranch he had grown up on. His society was totally without black people. I often thought about Philbrick, he was probably my first real friend and he never knew if I was white, black or green and it had never come up in our conversations. I often asked myself would we have been as close if he had known I was black

In 1976, Linda and I were working ten to-twelve-hour days and were getting very tired. Our hard work was beginning to pay off. She now had her own beauty shop and I was still self-employed and we were able to buy the new van that we both wanted for so long. One night we both dragged ourselves into the house and decided it was time we took a long vacation. By the end of the week we were very excited about going somewhere, but we hadn't decided where we would go. On Saturday we had a big cookout and made plans. We would take the van, rent a trailer, and go camping. The children had all been to scout camp and they just loved the outdoors. I wanted to do something big as a celebration for us finally getting to the point in life where we could feel some independence. As I stood there burning hamburgers and having had too many sips from my glass of scotch, I told them,

"We'll do it up right, we'll go to Yellowstone."

They didn't believe me at first but I finally convinced them and we started making plans.

I knew we would be traveling within thirty miles of the Philbrick ranch, and I knew I wanted to visit him. I came in from the shop one night and was feeling very excited about our up coming vacation and decided to try and get in touch with Philbrick. It was something I felt I had to do, and for a long time I never really knew why. All day I knew I had to do it that night because I was becoming totally obsessed with the thought of it. I mentioned it to Linda and she asked me not to, because if Philbrick didn't accept me as a black person, it would depress me and it could ruin our vacation. The thought of it depressing me never concerned me. Now that I had a family, very few things made me feel insecure anymore.

That night after Linda and the children went to bed, I made an information call to Forsyth, Montana and got Philbrick's phone number. I hesitated for about an hour and kept telling myself, "You are digging up the past, and it will destroy you mentally." I also kept remembering what Linda told me about it ruining our vacation. I told myself I really didn't know him, his neighbors, or the feelings of the people of Montana on racial matters. A lot can happen to a person in twenty years. Maybe he had joined some neo-Nazi group. After all, the country had gone through a lot of changes racially in the past twenty years. Maybe he was like Lester Long. Linda and I both knew how unpredictable people could be when it came to racial matters, and especially when it dealt with what was considered "mixing of the races." I finally dialed the number around eleven o'clock that night and a woman answered. I asked her if she was Mrs. Philbrick, and she said she was. I quickly ran all of his girlfriends through my mind, and she didn't sound like any of them. I told her who I was, and the first thing she asked me was, "Are you from South Carolina?" I told her I was. She told me Philbrick had been wondering for twenty years what had happened to me. He wasn't home but she told me he would be calling me back in about an hour.

When Newell called me an hour later, we talked for almost an hour and found we had a lot to talk about and we were still very close. I finally told him we were planning to come to Montana on vacation and would probably stop by to see him. He said he would send me some maps and directions on how to get to the ranch. Jokingly, I told him if it were in the same place it was before, I would need all of the directions I could get. He said, "They paved a short piece of the road since 1956, but other than that, it looks as it did before." When I hung up the phone, I went into the room and woke Linda up and told her about our conversation.

"Did you tell him about your black wife?"

"No. I'll save it until we get there. I'll call him and tell him to have all of the neighbors there to greet us."

The next two weeks seemed to drag along, and I thought vacation time would never come. Finally on the first Saturday in

August, we picked up the rented pop up trailer and headed out West. We drove all day Saturday while stopping only for gas. The kids were having a great time and the trip was more exciting than we had expected. We stopped in southern Indiana and made sandwiches for everyone. We drove all night, and until about three o'clock Sunday when we came to Badlands National Park in South Dakota. When I went to the camp office to register, I bought a six-pack of Olympia Beer; I hadn't seen Olympia beer sense I left the west coast twenty years earlier. After a couple of "Olies" I relaxed. The park in South Dakota was strange country for the children who had grown up on the low land coast of South Carolina. Every hill and rock fascinated them. Linda cooked dinner, and the kids ate like they were starved. They washed the dishes and went back out into the park to find another fascinating rock. For a while I considered not going by the ranch in Montana. I didn't want to spoil a good vacation. That night Linda had seen what a good time the children were having at the campsite, and told me,

"When we get to Miles City, if we can find a secure campsite, the children and me will stay there while you go out to the ranch and come back"

After giving it a lot of thought, I finally agreed.

We got to Miles City around three o'clock on Monday afternoon. I wasn't very tired because Linda and Vicki had done most of the driving. We set the trailer up and I talked to the owner of the KOA (Kamprounds of America) and told him I would be gone for a couple of hours, and he assured me they would be fine. The kids found other kids to play with and were lining up to bat in a softball game they helped organize. I found the map that Philbrick sent me, I looked it over and decided to make a quick trip out to the ranch and get back before dark.

Montana wasn't enforcing a speed limit so I shoved the accelerator down and leveled off about eighty miles per hour.

When I came to the Rosebud Creek Road I recognized the area right away. I even remembered some of the hills and turns we made twenty years earlier. Unlike a lot of other areas, Mother Nature had left the Rosebud Creek Road alone. It hadn't been disturbed in the name of progress.

Not having the trailer connected to the van, I began to enjoy the freedom of the open spaces. I took some of the curves too fast and the van almost skidded out of control on the gravel road. I began to play with the vehicle on the curves as we did in 1956. The thrill of it brought back a lot of memories, and I knew he would be the same person I knew in 1956. Nobody could change that much. I came to the ranch on one of the very few straight stretches on the road and had to brake hard to keep from skidding past. I decided to salvage the turn and held the brake and skidded into the driveway with a cloud of dust that engulfed the whole vehicle. Philbrick was out near the workshop and I recognized him right away. He, like myself, had put on a few pounds.

He introduced me to a man who was working on some equipment, and we had a good laugh on how I came into the driveway. As we began to move away from the noise of a tractor running in the shop, we were talking a mile a minute. He was constantly asking me, "Where is your family?" I decided to get it over with right away.

"I need to have a long talk with you." I told him

I almost felt like I was playing a practical joke on him as I had often done before. Now that the ice was broken between us, I knew he would be surprised.

At first I didn't try to tell him I was black, because I knew it would have taken the rest of the afternoon to get him to believe me. I just told him I was married to a black woman. It never changed the expression on his face, except to grin and say,

"That must be fun in South Carolina."

"Yep, shore is." I replied

I told him Linda was reluctant to come out, and she had stayed in Miles City and told me to come out alone. He said if it would make Linda feel more relaxed he would take his wife and children out to meet them in Miles City and invite them over. I told him that wouldn't be necessary. We went inside and broke the news to his wife. I almost laughed when he was trying to tell her. He never knew what to call me; I think he finally settled for "colored." As it was with Philbrick, it never changed the expression on her face, and I felt one hundred percent welcome. We got started talking in four fourth time and I almost forgot about Linda and the children back in Miles City. I rushed off alone to get them.

Linda had cooked when I got back and the ballgame had begun to sour, now that some ten to twenty children had joined in to play with the one ball and bat. With the number that had now gathered to become part of the game, they never could figure out whose time it was to bat. I called the kids in and we quickly ate, put the trailer back together, and headed out to the ranch. The children were still trying to figure out whose turn it was to bat when we turned onto the Rosebud Creek Road. We had a wonderful time at the ranch for the next three days. The Philbricks had three girls who were our girls' age. They worked cattle with horses like the old western cowboys. Our children rode horses for the first time and were totally fascinated by the Philbrick girls and the horses. Philbrick also taught my son to drive the jeep. We did go to Yellowstone, but the stay at the Philbrick ranch was the most exciting part of the trip. The children still talk about it today. Philbrick and I are still very good friends, and we communicate and visit each other on a regular basis.

Made in the
USA
Columbia, SC